Terrorism and the International Business Environment

To David, Chantal and Caroline

Terrorism and the International Business Environment

The Security–Business Nexus

Edited by

Gabriele G.S. Suder

Professor in International Business, CERAM Sophia Antipolis European School of Management, France

Edward Elgar
Cheltenham, UK • Northampton, MA, USA

Published by
Edward Elgar Publishing Limited
Glensanda House
Montpellier Parade
Cheltenham
Glos GL50 1UA
UK

Edward Elgar Publishing, Inc.
136 West Street
Suite 202
Northampton
Massachusetts 01060
USA

A catalogue record for this book
is available from the British Library

Library of Congress Cataloguing in Publication Data
Terrorism and the international business environment: the security–business
    nexus / edited by Gabriele G.S. Suder.
        p. cm.
    1. International business enterprises. 2. Risk management. 3. Terrorism—
Prevention. I. Title: Security–business nexus. II. Suder, Gabriele G.S.

    HD62.4.T466 2004
    658.4'73—dc22

                                                                    2004040440

ISBN 1 84376 801 1

Printed and bound in Great Britain by MPG Books Ltd, Bodmin, Cornwall

Contents

PART III   BUSINESS OPERATION STUDIES

PART IV   IMPLICATIONS OF CRISIS IN A SYNERGETIC WORLD

Figures and tables

FIGURES

TABLES

Graphs and maps

GRAPHS

MAPS

Contributors

Yusaf H. Akbar is Associate Professor of International Business at Southern New Hampshire University, USA.

Michel Henri Bouchet is Head of CERAM Global Finance Chair and Managing Director DEFI/Developing Finance, France.

Michael R. Czinkota is a Professor at Georgetown University School of Business, Washington, DC, USA, and adviser to the US Congress.

Frédéric Dimanche is a Professor of Marketing and Tourism Management at CERAM Sophia Antipolis, France.

Stefano Gori is Assistant Professor at the University of La Tuscia and Head of the Economic Research Unit of Poste Italiane, Italy.

Till Guldimann is Vice Chairman of SunGard Data Systems Inc., CA, USA.

Kai Hirschmann is Terrorism Researcher, Federal College for Security Studies, Bonn, Germany.

Robert A. Isaak is the Henry George Professor of International Management at Pace University in New York, USA.

Gary A. Knight is a Professor of Marketing at College of Business at Florida State University, USA.

Peter W. Liesch is a Professor in International Business at University of Queensland, Australia.

John McIntyre is Executive Director and Professor of the Georgia Tech DuPree College of Management Tech Center for International Business Education and Research (CIBER), Atlanta, Georgia, USA.

Gabriele G.S. Suder is a Professor in International Business and Geopolitics at CERAM Sophia Antipolis, France.

Eric Ford Travis is a Research Fellow of the Georgia Tech Center for International Business Education and Research (CIBER), Atlanta, GA, USA.

David H. Weir is a Professor at CERAM Sophia Antipolis, France, and at Lancaster University, and Chairman of Forever-Broadcasting, Newcastle, UK.

Georg Witschel is Federal Government Commissioner for Combating International Terrorism, German Foreign Office, Berlin, Germany.

Preface

This volume examines the impact of modern global terrorism on the international environment that results in the significant evolution of geopolitical risk, in risk and disaster management. The challenges at the corporate and industry sector level are well recognized in international business literature, which discerns asymmetries and symmetries in the analysis of these themes. While each industrial sector, each business structure and each geographic region on the globe has to cope with interdependencies and risk management specific to itself, contributors to this book recognize the urgency of tackling the international implications of a global terrorism that business has to deal with today.

Authors give much attention to problems identified particularly in Europe and the United States, but also refer to other regional and global impact centres. Analyses and forecasts will have been made that encourage more active international cooperation in risk and disaster management, for closer convergence in the face of international terrorism and its impact on the international business environment. This environment will need an adequate response to a difficult world and business reality, marked by complexity on a large scale.

Acknowledgements

The editor would like to express thanks for the particular support by her parents, Ingrid and Rudolf Schmid, as well as for the patience and never-ending comprehension and goodwill of David, Chantal and Caroline during the entire project – I hope they estimate that it was worth it.

The project for this book crystallized since September 11, 2001, and gradually took shape, until it was possible to launch it at CERAM Sophia Antipolis, France. It has evolved into a collective undertaking in a critical effort to succeed a cross-border and cross-disciplinary exercise. As editor, I was helped by a dynamic and very competent group of contributors. We are grateful to the many colleagues and institutions whose participation and advice in our research and discussions was very welcome.

I wish to thank SunGard Data Systems Inc. for their permission to include 'Business studies: the evolution of contingency planning: from disaster recovery to operational resilience' by Till Guldimann, Chapter 11 in this volume.

At Edward Elgar Publishing Ltd, I benefited in particular from the professionalism of Francine O'Sullivan and Luke Adams, who were of great help, and the confidence of Edward Elgar. Thank you.

1. Introduction

Gabriele G.S. Suder

The past century, the last of a millennium, saw many changes in geopolitical and economic structures that were established by the desire and need to open up or isolate human groupings, whether in the shape of nations, states, regions or economic zones. Geopolitics, economics and trade have therefore followed one another in the establishment, functioning and restructure of the international business environment.

The two world wars and the Cold War behind us, the main drivers of globalization were technological advance and geopolitical change made over the last hundred years. The last two decades of the century saw an intensifying of trade patterns with the end of the Cold War, of the Soviet empire, and of the bipolar superpower equilibrium between the Soviet Union and the United States. At the same time as the international business environment changes, international trade alters. For instance 80 per cent of international trade is now conducted by foreign direct investment, rather than the cross-border movement of goods and services (Rugman, 2000). The hegemonic strengthening of the one remaining superpower appeared certain, and international business developments have been structured around this superpower, in zones of power politics, economic integration and globalization. In matters of security, micro-conflicts, wars of intervention and multilateral negotiations have been the main focus of the international community during this time.

On September 11, 2001, the world held its breath and saw the unthinkable, terrifying, revolting truth of the new millennium: terrorism has globalized, too. Threat is intangible, and the untouchable is touchable. A common morality does not exist, and globalization presents two sides; it can be abused, and it also allows for an international integration of threat and fanaticism. On that day the world watched the World Trade Center tumbling down, the Pentagon hit and another terrorist flight crashing before reaching its target.

Reactions in the business environment revealed the extent of the trauma caused by this event to people and structures. We all remained silent in shock for the first hours, if not days, until the realization sunk in that the world had changed yet again: diplomatically, geopolitically, economically and in many other fields. In home and politics, in business schools and corporations, topics have come to the fore that deal with security and insecurity, risk and risk diversion, and uncertainty. We analyse risk, uncertainty and disaster and examine the international business environment. September 11 brought a new reality: traditional political and financial risk assessment theory alone is insufficient in the analysis of the international business environment. International terrorism is an entity. It needs to be taken into consideration on its own behalf; and this being so, then risk management today must include the study of international terrorism and its impact on financial, macro- and possibly micro-economic decisions for firms, investment decisions and the way international business views its world. Sector impact is studied in a selection of fields in which this impact is now discernible.

The initiative for editing this book was born from my conviction that the economics and corporate sectors need guidelines developed from research and case studies that analyse those adjustments made necessary through international terrorism as known since September 11. The implicit theme of this collective work is to examine why and how terrorism matters to international business. The pre-09/11 era of contemporary (economic) history has given birth to a transitivity of (1) globalization, (2) increased systemic vulnerability and complexity, and (3) the transition of terrorism. As of now, we believe that academic teaching and learning, politico-economic research and corporate policy need to take into account the risk of terrorism on a wide scale. The formulated call is for diplomacy as well as for business to incorporate the knowledge of international threat, security and disaster and their management that may reveal important competitive advantage and opportunities in the long run.

This book examines and analyses the legacies of September 11, 2001, and the various forces shaping the business sector that evolved from the traumatic impact of the events to international business and commerce. Each analysis places international terrorism into a different perspective, and concludes by arguing that it is at the root of major changes in the analysis of the international business environment if disaster recovery is to evolve into operational resilience. Adding the analysis of historical forces, we argue that September 11, 2001, and the effects of this new terrorism, can be considered as a rupture in the global political economy, different from previous disasters that shaped the world economy. Complexity, uncertainty and synergy have evolved into key issues since 2001.

In terms of risk and disaster management, however, September 11 was a predictable if not predicted event: not so much in its organization but by globalization, and in its traumatic impact on mankind and international relations. It has made visible what was already there: terrorism has to be considered as a major continuous challenge to the international business environment. We now need sufficient research and analysis to obtain a systematic theory on the security–business nexus.

The assessment of each contribution, and their argument as an entity, does not neglect the reality that September 11, 2001 was a traumatic event for the entire world, but in particular for the USA (Kagan, 2003). This reality in itself explains the diversity of analyses and assumptions made to date in academic literature. It is generally recognized in the literature's depth and profound implications. The aim of this book is to contribute to the discussion of risk management as an assessment of the implications that the events have for the business environment in which international business evolves. We do not attempt to make a political judgement.

Profound alterations are identified in this volume. Assumptions are developed about the future of what international business textbooks will generally call 'external forces' to the international business environment. September 11 was followed by the as yet unfinished war against terrorism. The reader will find a diversity of thought and opinion regarding these related issues in this book. It is important to show (and not undermine) this diversity of opinion, which does not hinder the achievement of relevant reflection and analysis, but rather enriches them. This is the basis of democratic and multi-opinion work.

While September 11 was the launch of major developments in the geopolitical and geo-economic environment for business, the war on Iraq has become a turning point in the post-Second World War arena: for the first time, what was known as 'the West' has divided. European countries had mainly been in agreement with the US, the liberator of the continent 50 years ago in international politics. Europe had become dependent in economics, and unable to compete in the military field; this has been a situation comparable to some extent to the case of Eastern and Central European countries today, freed from the chains of the Cold War. Some European countries decided to find a voice that pronounced its difference in history and politics (Hutton, 2002), and aims to evolve into another, different force that opts for a multipolarization of world politics; the belief that peaceful conflict prevention is a prevention of terrorism in the long run prevails in this argumentation. Others remain in close special relation to the US. The scenario that Europe finds itself in, reflects the essential asymmetries in globalization (Brewer et al., 2002) that may well be the cause for transatlantic tensions.

Asymmetries have a vital impact on the international business environment. The relationship between risk, security and geopolitical thinking has been paramount for trade since the earliest forms of exchange of goods. Pluralism and democracy have encountered unilateralism, hegemony and dictatorship over centuries. Today's society and business world have undergone interdependencies on a global scale, a scale larger than ever, through globalization and the establishment of routines and patterns of trade and geopolitical thinking that are altered profoundly through the horrors of international terrorism. This sheer scale of risk, threat, uncertainty and complexity has posed problems to citizens, to producers and consumers, to regulators and decision-makers on a governmental and non-governmental level, and for economic agents worldwide. A shift of preference in decision-making and in the distribution of profit according to risk has been acknowledged in the analyses of this book, in response to the deep suspicion of capitalism and geopolitical hegemony that may exist through globalization. The reaction and consequences examined in international trade and investment shed light on the crucial realities of the post- September 11 era: the trade-off between security and business has undergone profound changes. The resulting long-term implications to business are instability, complexity and uncertainty on a scale never known before.

Terrorist attacks have an important impact on the international business environment, that yet appears underexamined due to the complexity of the task. This is an attempt to establish a basis for future research and the construction of models that will help to find the necessary normative approaches. The first part of this book deals primarily with a view on trends in international terrorism, threat, the evolving geopolitical and geoeconomic patterns in the pre- and post-September 11 era, and the question of why this matters to the international business environment. In Part I we demonstrate the diversity of levels on which the impact of terrorism can be conceptualized. Part II focuses on the forces in the trade and investment environment that alter our understanding of finance, country risk assessment, the e-divide and investment flows, that are crucial to economic and corporate activity. We look at direct as well as indirect effects. Part III presents case studies of selected business sectors. They analyse the various implications that post-09/11 terrorism creates, on what Czinkota, Knight and Liesch will call the micro level of analysis. These business studies are chosen from different sectors for a wide understanding of the issues that prevail, and were selected due to the discernibility and diversity of impact analysis. They are written by academia and corporate authors, and are linked to the broader analyses made in Part II. Part IV concludes with a look into disaster management and international security in the long run.

The studies will hopefully arouse widespread discussion and enhance awareness about the security–business nexus that has gained ground, moving forward the debate on terrorism and the international business environment and their place in risk management.

REFERENCES

Brewer, T., A.A. Brenton and G. Boyd (eds) (2002), *Globalizing Europe*, Cheltenham, UK and Northampton, US: Edward Elgar Publishing.

Hutton, Will (2002), *The World We're In*, London: Albacus.

Kagan, Robert (2003), *Paradise and Power*, London: Atlantic Books.

Rugman, Alan (2000), *The End of Globalisation*, London: Random House.

PART I

The geopolitical and geo-economic environment

2. The legacy of September 11

Georg Witschel[1]

INTRODUCTION

Terrorism did not begin on September 11, 2001. Both Europe and the United States, as well as other continents, have a long and sad history of terrorist attacks. The IRA in Northern Ireland, the ETA in Spain, the Brigate Rosse in Italy, the '17 November' in Greece and the Rote Armee Fraktion in Germany are just a few examples of terrorist groups in Europe since 1950. Regarding the United States, we remember the terrible bombing in Oklahoma City in 1994 and even if we limit our brief historical survey geographically to New York's financial district we find that not even the 1993 truck bombing of the World Trade Center was the first terrorist event there: as far back as 16 September 1920, unknown perpetrators exploded a horse cart filled with explosives in the south of Manhattan, killing 40 and wounding many more.

Yet we have to realize that September 11 has changed the world. Not that everything has changed, to the contrary: as UN Secretary-General Kofi Annan has pointed out, none of the issues that faced us on 10 September 2001 has become less urgent.[2] But there is certainly a new quality to an old problem, which we have to face after that fatal date in September 2001. Terrorism has grown to an unprecedented extent and quality. In other words, September 11 has become a symbol and metaphor for the new threats looming on the horizon.[3] Even without the use of weapons of mass destruction (and there is no doubt among experts that Osama bin Laden would have used such weapons if he had them) more than 3000 people were killed in less than two hours; people from more than 60 countries, killed without distinction and without mercy.

Since then a number of smaller, but still very murderous attacks have been committed by al-Qaida, persons or groups related to or supported by al-Qaida, or so-called non-aligned *mujahedeen*. They include the attack on a synagogue in Djerba, Tunisia, killing mainly German and French tourists, the attack on a French oil tanker off the Yemen shore, the bombing of a bus carrying French submarine engineers in Karachi, Pakistan, the blowing up of a discotheque in Bali, the hostage-taking in a theatre in

Moscow and the double attack on Israeli tourists in a Mombasa, Kenya hotel and on board an Arkia flight leaving Mombasa airport. (The latter using surface-to-air missiles and missing the plane with over 260 passengers by only a few metres.)

Despite some differences and variations with regard to the perpetrators, their motives, political aims and *modus operandi*, all of the aforementioned attacks have something in common. They are all terrorism – premeditated, politically motivated violence perpetrated against non-combatant targets by subnational groups or clandestine agents.[4] But beyond that, they share a number of common features and seem to indicate some trends which have to be analysed carefully in order to find appropriate counter strategies. All of these common denominators are interrelated and most of them of a rather recent nature:

1. the increasing dominance of religiously motivated terrorism;
2. the globalization of terrorism;
3. modern business-like leadership structures;
4. asymmetric warfare, using the victim mostly as part of a communication strategy; and
5. the inseparablity of internal and external security.

2.1   RECENT DEVELOPMENTS IN INTERNATIONAL TERRORISM: INCREASING DOMINANCE OF RELIGIOUSLY MOTIVATED TERRORISM

More and more, religiously motivated terrorism has superseded other forms or rather motivations of terrorism. Compared with the 1980s and even the 1990s, so-called ideological terrorism which aimed at the revolutionary change of social structures, as well as so-called ethno-national terrorism, striving for the liberation of a certain territory, seem to have been relegated somewhat to the backstage. Religiously motivated terrorism is certainly not limited to Islam, it seems also to make headway in Judaism, Christianity and non-monotheistic religions like Hinduism. However, at least for the time being, only terrorism motivated by Islamism reaches beyond national borders or certain regions. The shift from a more traditional ideological (social-revolutionary) terrorism to religiously motivated forms coincides with a certain geographical shift from Europe and Latin America to Northern Africa, the Middle East and Central as well as South and South East Asia.[5] It also coincides with a number of new characteristics regarding organization, structures, membership and areas of operation. However, even September 11 and more recent events like the bombing attacks in Bali and Al Ghriba, Tunisia should not obscure the fact that ideological and ethno-national terrorism still exists in various parts of the world – not least South Asia – and that there are a number of groups (like Hamas and Hezbollah in the Middle East), which might fall into two or more categories. Yet we have to take into account that religion is more often the motivation for terrorist acts than it has been in the last few decades.

2.2.   THE GLOBALIZATION OF TERRORISM

Increasingly, terrorism goes global.[6] The most striking example, al-Qaida, is a truly global network, which cooperates more or less closely with national or regional groups like the GSFP in Algeria or the Jemaah Islamiyah in Indonesia. Furthermore, there is evidence of an ad hoc cooperation in various parts of the world with so-called non-aligned *mujahedeen*, individual persons or small groups, which are not part of the al-Qaida network and do not belong to any other, larger and hierarchically structured group. This globalization is not only a relatively recent phenomenon, it must also be seen as a dangerous development well beyond the more traditional forms of national or even international terrorism. National terrorism has a very long history and is characterized by at least two facts: perpetrators and victims are usually of the same nationality or are at least subject to the same authority, and the political aim is limited to changing certain political conditions within national boundaries or in a limited area under the rule of the attacked state (or colony or occupied territory). Typical European examples are or were the German Rote Armee Fraktion, the French Action Directe, the Greek '17th November', ETA and the IRA (Schneckener, 2002, p. 15) . Certainly, some or probably most of these groups had some international elements, ranging from ideology (international solidarity of the working class and so on) to financing, training and safe havens. Yet they were primarily national, with some international elements. Looking beyond Europe, in particular the Middle Eastern groups like the PFLP, Hamas and Hezbollah are good examples of internationalization – even if some of them currently confine their attacks to a limited geographical area. According to the RAND-St Andrews Chronology, international terrorism means incidents in which terrorists go abroad to strike their targets, select victims or targets that have connections with a foreign state (for example diplomats, foreign business persons, offices or foreign corporations), or create international incidents by attacking airline passengers, personnel or equipment. After all, it is less the difference in political objectives but in the selection of targets which distinguishes national from international terrorism. In order to achieve their aims, international terrorists systematically attack international targets so as to get more media attention and in the hope of receiving more support. The hijackings of several commercial airliners in the early 1970s were a quite successful terrorist strategy, bringing the occupation of Palestinian territories to worldwide attention through spectacular media coverage. International terrorism usually builds on a far more extended support network (including financing and logistics) than national terrorism. Good examples of these international support structures are the Sri Lankan LTTE, the IRA and certainly Hamas and Hezbollah. However, al-Qaida and the most recent developments go beyond mere internationalization on a number of counts:

1. the aim is to overthrow the international order, not just a government or an occupying power;
2. the ideology (in the case of al-Qaida Islamism) is by definition transnational;
3. the membership is truly international;
4. the structures are decentralized – networks rather than hierarchical organizations;
5. financing and logistics are maintained through worldwide legal and illegal sources, through related groups and contact persons, far less than in the more 'traditional' national and international terrorism through states.

It might appear paradoxical that al-Qaida, with its rather anti-modern ideas and its opposition to open society, went global whilst communist groups in the 1970s preaching international revolution had a rather parochial range of action. But that does not change the fact that the third millenium gave birth to global terrorism. And it does not change the fact that terrorists striving for a rather medieval world readily use all the achievements of globalization, like international telecommunication, unimpeded real-time money transfers, easily accessible flight schools, and so on. It seems that one of the downsides of globalization is the emergence of global or transnational terrorism.

2.3 MODERN, BUSINESS-LIKE LEADERSHIP STRUCTURES

A major characteristic of modern terrorist organization is the lack of central authorities, of clear hierarchies. Especially al-Qaida, but also a number of other groups, are only loosely connected, with very flat hierarchical structures and no military-style leadership structure. This lack of hierarchy is possible because – unlike in the more traditional forms of ideological and ethno-national terrorism – only a loose political, ideological or dogmatic framework exists. There are very few leading principles, as for example the hate against America, against Israel or against countries and governments supporting those states. Furthermore, there are some rather vague ideas of revitalizing basic religious values and – in the case of al-Qaida, but also Hamas and Hezbollah – the establishment of an Islamist empire, a Taliban-style Kalifat state as a response to the perceived dominance of the 'Western world'. Since there is no need for a detailed ideological or dogmatic framework there is also no need to gain the support of parts of the population of a certain country, or at least parts of the politically active layers of society. Consequently, there is no need to focus on certain limited targets, as for example leading politicians, members of the military and other key figures of the 'establishment'.

2.4 ASYMMETRIC WARFARE: THE VICTIM NOT AS TARGET, BUT AS PART OF A COMMUNICATION STRATEGY

September 11 has been a perfect example for asymmetric warfare. Only 19 suicide attackers and a financial input of probably only some US$500000 killed more than 3000 civilians and caused material damage of at least US$40 billion. But on top of that, the repercussions of September 11 resulted in a major decrease in world economic growth. On a smaller scale, Tunisia has witnessed a temporary decrease of income from tourism of up to 50 per cent after the bombing of the Al Ghriba synagogue, and Indonesia has suffered a tremendous economic setback after the murderous attack at Kuta Beach, Bali. Terrorists were thus able to inflict major damage on an enemy which was and is in terms of manpower, military equipment and money, vastly superior. But it is not only a matter of the (rather tactical) asymmetry of means available to terrorists on the one hand, and that of attacked states on the other hand. It is the asymmetry of warfare in a more strategic sense. Unlike in conflicts such as the Algerian independence war or the Chinese revolution, terrorism is no longer conceived as an inevitable (because of military weakness) preliminary stage to guerrilla warfare and then open war aimed at achieving a political objective against the will of an adversary. Modern terrorism seems rather to target through psychological effects (causing terror in its original meaning: instilling great fear) the economy, increasing the psychological burden and the economic costs for combating terrorism and finally forcing the attacked state(s) to give in.[7] Ideally – from a modern terrorist's point of view – an enemy vastly superior on all counts could be forced to accept the political claims of a relatively small group of non-state actors without even a short military conflict.

Recent events, as in Tunisia, Karachi, offshore Yemen and Bali, seem to indicate such a new tendency, if not strategy of international terrorism. Probably due to the hardening of targets especially in the United States, terrorist attacks on so-called soft targets like tourist or international trade facilities have increased. Since there are so many targets all over the world it is impossible to protect them sufficiently. Even with more sophisticated intelligence it will hardly be possible to predict the exact venue and time of a terrorist attack on a discotheque, a theatre, a container ship or an oil storage facility. Furthermore, a successful attack on a soft target might well entail the same overall results as an attack on a hard target. It sends a shock wave proliferated by international media all over the world, intimidating not only the local population or those geographically close to the scene of a terrorist attack, but also people thousands of miles away, deterring them from visiting or investing in the country where the actual attack took place. The media thus play a tremendously important role in almost any terrorist strategy. In fact the victims themselves have no particular importance for the terrorist, except as part of a communication strategy proliferated by the media, as conveyors of a triple message:

- that the government is not capable of guaranteeing security in the country;
- that tourists, foreign communities and investors should avoid the country;
- that the war against terrorism has not been and will not be successful, because the terrorists can select from a huge number of possible targets, all of them with major importance for local and regional economies, and because they have enough human and financial resources to attack those targets at almost any time.

European states (and not only they) face a particular dilemma in that respect, which has been reflected in the ASEAN leaders' declaration adopted in Phnom Penh on 3 November 2002: 'We call on the international community to avoid indiscriminately advising their citizens to refrain from visiting or otherwise dealing with our countries, in the absence of established evidence of possible terrorist attacks, as such measures could help achieve the objective of the terrorists.' And, indeed, many European countries have a legal obligation to advise their citizens properly on possible risks of travelling or investing abroad. On the other hand, an overreaction in terms of unnecessary warnings might – unwittingly – promote the objectives of terrorists who want to destabilize national economies. The dilemma is further accentuated by the fact that states have to take precautionary measures against terrorism on a permanent basis (if they fail once, it is perceived as a major defeat by the general public), whilst for terrorists one or a few successful attacks suffice to promote their agenda considerably.

2.5 INSEPARABILITY OF INTERNAL AND EXTERNAL SECURITY

September 11 has taught another terrible lesson. No country on our globe is immune against the scourge of modern terrorism. Even a mighty army, good relations with neighbours or vast oceans cannot protect our cities and citizens from major terrorist attacks. The security of any country is no longer almost exclusively in the hands of governments, in the hands of politicians, diplomats and generals, but increasingly in those of private actors. Terrorists, but also warlords and international organized crime pose more and more a direct risk for life and limb, health and wealth of average citizens on our globe. Whilst state-sponsored terrorism still exists, albeit on a much lower level than in the 1960s and the 1970s, it is more and more the threat by non-state actors which characterizes modern terrorism. This double challenge – inseparability of internal and external security, and non-state actors as a major threat for national and international security – has still not been tackled sufficiently. More than ever, a comprehensive strategy for preventing and countering terrorism on both the national and international levels is needed.

2.5.1 Preventing and Countering Terrorism

In the aftermath of September 11 most countries realized that terrorism is an international, in fact global challenge, and that at least in most cases, a merely national or even regional counter-strategy will not suffice. As a consequence, a number of unprecedented coalitions were forged and decisions taken in the international arena – on both the regional and global levels. However, some of the achievements in the post-09/11 period have been tainted by the failure of the international community to achieve consensus on the definition of terrorism. This lack of consensus is unfortunately not only a legal problem, limited to the august halls of the UN general assembly, but a practical one: state support for terrorist organizations (considered by their state sponsors as freedom fighters) has decreased, but not disappeared (the US National Strategy for Combating Terrorism names seven countries as state sponsors of terrorism). As a consequence, international cooperation in combating terrorism still is far from being satisfactory.

2.5.2   The Global Coalition against Terrorism

One of the most important achievements of post-09/11 US diplomacy was the creation of a global coalition against terrorism, including all five permanent members of the Security Council, the whole Western world, many states of the Arab world and of the G-77, including India and Pakistan. Even if this coalition is in fact rather a coalition against Osama bin Laden, al-Qaida and the Taliban, it is of tremendous importance for combating international terrorism. However, it is not an alliance based on common values, rather a coalition based on a limited convergence of interest for a given time. Therefore, one should not overlook that the coalition is fragile, and that for example unresolved regional conflicts, and the question how to deal with so-called states of concern or other political factors might overburden, imperil and finally destroy the coalition. Europe is certainly one of the more stable elements of that coalition, notwithstanding the rift between some EU members on how to deal with Iraq. On 21 September 2001 the European Council decided that 'the fight against terrorism will, more than ever, be a priority objective of the European Union'. The Council also declared that it is 'totally supportive of the American people in the face of the deadly terrorist attacks.'[8] Less than a month later, on 19 October, the Council again unequivocally stated its 'full support for the action taken against terrorism in all its aspects within the framework defined by the United Nations' and reaffirmed its 'total solidarity with the United States'. The Council underlined its determination to combat terrorism in every form, throughout the world. The Council furthermore vowed to strengthen the coalition of the international community to combat terrorism and requested to speed up certain measures and operations already envisaged on 21 September, such as a European arrest warrant.[9] In its Laeken meeting on 14–15 December the Council reaffirmed the 'total solidarity with the American people and the international community in combating terrorism with full regard for individual rights and freedoms.'[10] Finally, in the presidency conclusions of the EU summit in Seville (June 2002)[11] the contribution of the EU Common Foreign and Security Policy in countering the terrorist threat was highlighted, reinforcing the Council's decision of September 2001 to fight terrorism through 'a coordinated and interdisciplinary approach embracing all Union policies'.

   Declarations on the resolve to cooperate and join forces in the fight against terrorism are also found in the chairman's statement made at the fourth Asia–Europe meeting in Copenhagen on 24 September 2002, in the joint statement of the EU–Russia summit of 11 November 2002 and in a number of similar EU (or EU and international partner) documents. These declarations prove the increasing willingness of states and international organizations to cooperate globally in the struggle against international terrorism. It is also encouraging that most of these declarations and action plans take into account economic factors, and underline the importance of respecting international law including human rights.

2.5.3 Afghanistan

The success of Enduring Freedom and the destruction of the territorial bases of al-Qaida has been an important success in the war against terrorism. Afghanistan is no longer the training ground and meeting point for potential terrorists. It is no longer a potential laboratory for the development of weapons of mass destruction. But it is still a country with very fragile structures and far from being able to guarantee the safety of its own citizens. Much more needs to be done to build democratic structures, to firmly establish the protection of human rights and the rule of law, to extend the reach of the interim administration to all parts of the country, to have a functioning army and police force, to successfully combat drug cultivation and trafficking, and so on. Without successfully rehabilitating Afghanistan it might be impossible to win the war against terrorism. Furthermore, the success of Enduring Freedom has not led to a complete destruction of al-Qaida. To the contrary, as has been set out in an UN report, 'Al Qaida is fit and well and poised to strike again at its leisure.'[12] That is why the state community must look beyond Enduring Freedom and sustain a long-term engagement in Afghanistan in order to ensure that this country never again becomes a major hub for global terrorism. The European Union has declared its willingness to help the Afghan people and its new leaders rebuild the country and encourage as swift a return to democracy as possible.

2.6 IMPORTANT COUNTER-MEASURES OF THE INTERNATIONAL COMMUNITY

2.6.1 The United Nations

The shock of September 11 has sparked or sped up a number of counter-measures adopted by the international community. The Security Council of the United Nations has unanimously and unequivocally condemned the terrorist attacks of September 11 and has qualified in its resolution 1368 of 12 September 2001 that it regards 'any act of international terrorism as a threat to international peace and security.'[13] The Security Council has consequently recognized the inherent right of individual or collective self defence in accordance with the charter, if a state is the victim of a terrorist attack. The Security Council stressed also that those responsible for aiding, supporting or harbouring the perpetrators, organizers and sponsors of terrorist acts will be held responsible. With Resolution 1373 of 28 September 2001,[14] a number of mandatory decisions were taken on terrorist financing, obliging states to refrain from providing support to terrorists and to take the necessary steps to prevent the commission of terrorist acts, including by early warning, denying safe haven and by suppressing the financing of terrorist acts. With the same resolution the so-called Counter-Terrorism Committee has been established, to which all member states report on the steps they have taken to implement this resolution. The Committee has meanwhile received more than 180 reports and has not only set up a directory of available help, but also identifies the need for assistance, mostly in developing countries. Ideally it will match requests and offers for assistance. Furthermore, the Security Council has reshaped the sanctions regime directed originally against Afghanistan, the Taliban regime and al-Qaida. Whilst Afghanistan as a state has been removed from the target list, the sanctions regime under SC-Res 1267/1390/1455[15] now focuses entirely on the Taliban and al-Qaida, and particularly on the financing of those organizations. The sanctions committee established under Resolution 1267 has identified a considerable number of persons and organizations, whose bank accounts are frozen and who are prevented from entering or transiting the territory of UN member states.

Less encouraging is the situation in the UN General Assembly (GA). Whilst the GA has been able to unite in the condemnation of the September 11 attacks and of terrorism in general, its legal committee has so far been unable to agree on the so-called draft comprehensive convention against terrorism.[16] The reason for this is less a legal than a political one. The members of the Organisation of the Islamic Conference (OIC) wish to add an exemption clause to the definition of a terrorist act, which would exclude 'people's struggle including armed struggle against foreign occupation, aggression, colonialism and hegemony' from the scope of a terrorist crime. This far-reaching exemption is not only unacceptable to the Western world, but also to many G-77 members who believe that liberation wars fall under international humanitarian law, and that an exemption clause in the terrorism convention would at best be superfluous, at worst extremely dangerous. Unfortunately it was not possible for the OIC to agree on a more flexible approach at the summit meeting in Kuala Lumpur in February 2002, despite the efforts of Malaysian prime minister Mahatir. The chances of resolving this political stalemate are slim, even if the draft comprehensive convention remains on the agenda of the UN for the time being.

2.6.2 The European Union (EU)

The EU action plan of 21 September 2001, and the 'road map' emanating from it, is a living, permanently updated document, consisting of roughly 70 measures in the areas of justice and interior, foreign, traffic and transport, and financial policies. The most important achievements are an agreement on a EU-wide definition of a terrorist act, the harmonization of national penal codes in the area of international terrorism, the European arrest warrant which ensures automatic arrest in any EU state if one EU member state has made an arrest warrant, increased exchange of information and a number of measures with regard to freezing economic assets. In that context the EU member states created the so-called Clearing House which recommends to the EU ministers' Council the listing of certain persons or institutions involved in non-al-Qaida related terrorist activities. The Clearing House has been established in implementation of Security Council Resolution 1373 and deals with proposals by EU members and by third states. However, third states' proposals usually undergo an even more thorough scrutiny with regard to human rights and fail more often to meet the consensus requirement than those of EU member states. Despite the consensus requirement the Clearing House has successfully proposed more than 80 individuals and organizations for listing by the EU Council leading to the freezing of accounts and travel restrictions.

Other steps taken by the Council include the strengthening of EU instruments for long-term conflict prevention, the focusing of political dialogue with third countries on the fight against terrorism, the assistance to third countries in order to build counter-terrorism capacities (with Indonesia, Pakistan and the Philippines as the first countries selected for concrete measures), the inclusion of anti-terrorism clauses in EU agreements with third countries, and even re-evaluating relations with third countries in the light of their attitudes towards terrorism.

2.6.3 NATO

In its strategic concept of 1999, NATO had stated that acts of terrorism could have an impact on the security interests of the alliance. On 12 September 2001 NATO declared the attacks in New York and Pennsylvania to be directed against all 19 NATO members. For the first time in NATO's history, Article 5 of the Washington Treaty was invoked which states that an armed attack against one or more NATO member countries will be considered an attack against all. Thus both the UN and NATO recognized that an attack undertaken by non-state actors could pose a risk to international security equal or at least similar to that posed by states. It seems almost ironical that NATO, an alliance built 'to keep the Soviets out', never had to apply the core provision of Article 5 in order to defend itself against any state, but did so against a group of transnational terrorists. The old foes (the Soviet Union and Warszaw Pact) are now allies in the common fight against terrorism; the new NATO–Russia Council, established in May 2002, identifies terrorism as an important area for cooperation.

A number of practical measures were also taken by NATO after September 11, aimed at assisting the United States. They included enhanced intelligence-sharing, blanket overflight rights for the United States, sending elements of NATO's standing naval forces to the Eastern Mediterranean, and utilising NATO's airborne warning and control systems aircraft to help to protect the territory of the United States.

At NATO's Prague summit in November 2002, heads of state and government of the NATO member countries adopted a number of measures aimed at strengthening NATO's preparedness and ability to take on the full spectrum of security challenges, including terrorism.

2.6.4   G-8

On 19 September 2001 the G-8 heads of state and government unequivocally condemned the terrorist attacks in the United States. They underscored their determination to bring the perpetrators to justice, to combat all forms of terrorism, to prevent further attacks, and to strengthen international cooperation. Leaders called for rapid implementation of the 12 UN counter-terrorism conventions and asked all relevant ministers to identify and implement specific measures to enhance counter-terrorist cooperation in a range of key areas.

In response to that request, relevant G-8 ministers (of justice and interior as well as foreign affairs ministers, and G-7 finance ministers) developed and are implementing a large number of measures, elaborated by the so-called Roma and Lyon Groups of the G-8, consisting of diplomats and experts in counter-terrorism and combating international crime.

Priorities for the G-8 efforts and measures include actions to promote the global implementation of UN Security Council Resolution 1373, the close cooperation with the UN Counter Terrorism Committee to address the global threat of terrorism by monitoring and promoting the implementation of Resolution 1373, and the provision of technical and legal assistance to third countries for training and capacity-building in the areas covered by

Resolution 1373. The G-8 has furthermore developed recommendations on counter-terrorism, a series of principles and priorities that provide guidance to strengthen capacities to combat terrorism, by improving existing mechanisms, procedures and networks to protect societies from terrorist threats. The G-7 finance ministers' action plan of October 2001 (which has been endorsed by Russia) advanced efforts to immediately freeze assets of terrorists and to rapidly develop and implement international standards to prevent the abuse of the financial system by terrorists. G-8 members furthermore have been implementing new standards to ensure safety of travel for their citizens and to improve transport security. G-8 members share information and coordinate their activities to identify potential links between terrorist groups and criminal activities such as drug trafficking, smuggling of firearms and money laundering. G-8 members are sharing information on national capacities and techniques to respond in case of terrorist incidents involving chemical, biological, radiological and nuclear weapons. The most important achievement, however, is probably the 'G-8 Global Partnership Against the Spread of Weapons and Materials of Mass Destruction', adopted in Kananaskis, Canada on 27 June 2002. Under this initiative, G-8 partners will support specific cooperation projects, initially in Russia, to address non-proliferation, disarmament, counter-terrorism and nuclear safety issues. Among the priority concerns are the destruction of chemical weapons, the dismantlement of decommissioned nuclear submarines, the disposition of fissile materials and the employment of former weapon scientists. G-8 partners committed themselves to raise up to US\$20 billion to support projects over the next ten years.

2.6.5 OSCE

In their 'Bucharest Plan of Action for Combating Terrorism' (adopted by ministers in December 2001) the 55 participating states of the OSCE stood united against terrorism and resolutely condemned 'the barbaric acts of terrorism that were committed against the United States on 11 September 2001'. OSCE participating states committed themselves not to yield to terrorist threats, but to defend freedom and to 'protect their citizens against acts of terrorism, fully respecting international law and human rights'. At the same time OSCE participants adopted during the 'Bishkek International Conference on Enhancing Security and Stability in Central Asia' a programme of action which includes policing, border security, anti-trafficking measures (regarding small arms and light weapons, human beings and non-proliferation) and countering the financing of terrorism. The OSCE furthermore contributed to preventing and combating terrorism in a number of other ways, particularly with the promotion of democratic institutions, human rights and the rule of law. Finally, on 7 December 2002, the OSCE Ministerial Council adopted in Porto/Portugal an 'OSCE Charter on Preventing and Combating Terrorism', which *inter alia* recognizes the importance of the relevant United Nations conventions and protocols and reaffirms the commitment of all participating states to ratify and implement these international treaties.

2.7   THE LEGACY OF SEPTEMBER 11

The legacy of September 11 is not simple. It is a multiple challenge. It is about keeping the international coalition against terrorism alive, about rehabilitating Afghanistan, about taking all possible measures to counter terrorism, but even more it is the challenge of preventing terrorism. Obviously it is much more efficient to prevent people from becoming terrorists than to prevent terrorist acts from happening. However, referring to a remark made by the UN Secretary-General in autumn 2001, there will always be people who hate and kill, even if all injustice has been removed.[17] Prevention of terrorism cannot simply replace combating terrorism. But this is also true the other way round: combating terrorism cannot be successful if there is no meaningful prevention of terrorism. Again, it was UN Secretary-General Kofi Annan who described the other side of the challenge so pointedly: 'But if the world can prove, that she can continue, that she sustainably works to create a stronger, more just, more merciful and more international community across all borders of religion and race, then terrorism will fail to reach its targets'.[18] Prevention of terrorism and combating terrorism have to work hand in hand. Prevention of conflicts is always also prevention of terrorism. And even if the equation of poverty and injustice on one side and terrorism on the other is incorrect, one must realize that prevention of terrorism goes well beyond police, judicial or military measures. In order to stamp out breeding grounds for terrorism, a number of major political steps have to be taken:

- The political and social conflicts quite rightly emphasized in the UN Millennium declaration[19] have to be addressed urgently, as these often form the breeding ground for the emergence of terrorism. A fair and peaceful solution for regional conflicts, not only in the Middle East, is of utmost importance. History tells us that the best guarantee for successfully fighting terrorism is a viable strategy to deal with underlying factors.
- If we want the people in our countries to live in safety, freedom and without want, we need a system of global cooperative security, which

includes all levels of global policy relevant to security: taking into account the relations between great powers and their alliances, as well as the potential danger of regional crises and the threat posed by asymmetric conflicts. Since terrorism threatens world peace just as much as civil war and regional conflicts such a system must not be 'toothless', but must function in all three fields through reliable verification systems and enforceable sanctions mechanisms.[20]

- A comprehensive global policy is needed which includes classic foreign and security policy, but also development and structural issues. International trade, financial systems, global environment, migration and debt management have to be seen in a cohesive manner, as part of an enlarged concept of human security. ·

- We have to strengthen a meaningful dialogue between civilizations, aiming at peaceful solution of conflicts and replacing prejudice by confidence.

- Global security cannot work without respect for human rights. All efforts to secure peace will fail, if human rights are not protected and duly implemented. We need a binding global set of values to prevent and overcome conflicts that emerge due to inequality, injustice and deprivation of freedom. Combating terrorism must not be a pretext to violate human rights.

None of these challenges can be met without Europe. And none by a single European state. More than ever, European cooperation is a necessity in order to successfully combat international terrorism.

NOTES

1. The views in this chapter are expressed by the author in his personal capacity and do not necessarily reflect the views of the German government.
2. K. Annan, Statement by the UN Secretary General to the General Assembly, New York, 10 November 2001.
3. Asmus and Pollack (2002).
4. US National Strategy For Combating Terrorism, p. 1.
5. Waldmann (2002), p. 24.
6. U. Schneckener (2002).
7. H. Münkler (2002).
8. *Conclusions and Plan of Action of the Extraordinary European Council Meeting on 21 September 20*01, Doc. Nr. SN 140/01.
9. *Declaration by the Heads of State or Government of the European Union and the President of the Commission on 19 October 2001*, Doc. Nr. SN 4296/2/01 REV 2.
10. *Presidency Conclusions European Council Meeting in Laeken*, 14 and 15 December 2001, Doc. Nr. SN 300/1/01 REV 1.
11. *Presidency Conclusions Seville European Council*, 21 and 22 June 2002, Doc. Nr. SN 200/1/02 REV 1.

12. *Second Report of the Monitoring Group established pursuant to Security Council Resolution 1363 (2001) and extended by resolution 1390 (2002)*, UN doc. S/2002/1050, p. 2.
13. S/RES/1368 (2001) of 12 September 2001.
14. S/RES/1373 (2001) of 28 September 2001.
15. S/RES/1267(1999), 1390 (2002) and 1455 (2003) of 15 October 1999, 28 January 2002 and 17 January 2003.
16. *Report of the Ad Hoc Committee established by GA Resolution 51/210*, UN Doc. A/57/37 of 11 February 2002.
17. K. Annan, *Frankfurter Allgemeine Zeitung*, October 2002.
18. See note 17.
19. UN Millenium Declaration, Doc Nr. A/RES/55/2 of 8 September 2002.
20. J. Fischer (2002), 'Für ein System globaler kooperativer Sicherheit', Statement of the German Foreign Minister to the 57 General Assembly, 14 September 2002, in New York.

REFERENCES

Asmus, D. and K.M. Pollack (2002), 'The new transatlantic project', *Policy Review*, October/November.

Münkler (2002), 'Grammatik der Gewalt', *Frankfurter Allgemeine Zeitung*, 18 October.

Schneckener, U. (2002), *Netzwerke des Terrors*, Berlin: Stiftung Wissenschaft und Politik.

Waldmann, P. (2002), 'Terrorismus als weltweites Phänomen: Eine Einführung', in Hans Frank and Kai Hirschmann (eds), *Die Weltweite Gefahr*, Berlin, pp. 11–26.

3. Historical forces in international affairs and commerce: prospects for the international economy

Yusaf H. Akbar

INTRODUCTION

Is world trade and investment threatened by the need for enhanced security because of terrorism and the 'War on Terror'? Will certain regions of the world economy be cut off from world economic activity because of their high risk? Can capitalist economies maintain their openness in the face of continuous threats to the economic infrastructure of the world trading system? Do new attempts to regulate the flow of international capital threaten the liquidity of the global financial system? This chapter examines the events of September 11, 2001 (09/11) in a broader historical perspective. The central theme of this chapter's contribution is to examine the extent to which 09/11 was a new shift in the development of capitalism – the Huntingtonian-type 'Clash of Civilisations' – or whether the events can be explained by reference to existing experience. In doing so, the author attempts to examine the prospects for further intensification of economic relationships in the global economy.

The principal vehicle through which these issues will be examined will be to offer an analysis of the development of world trade in the face of other historical ruptures such as major wars and global economic shocks. As a rule, historical experience suggests that major conflicts reduce the intensity of economic exchange, leading to breakdowns in the functioning of capitalist economies. Similarly, global economic shocks such as a pandemic or oil price shocks slow economic growth, causing capitalist economies to become more inward-looking. Will 09/11 replicate this experience or does it offer something new and more threatening to the world economy? If 09/11 can be explained by reference to past events, it can be argued with a degree of confidence that the capitalist economies will recover and reach even higher levels of interdependence. If, however, 09/11 represents a new form of threat to capitalism, a number of potential problems could emerge over the long term. Given the fact that the War on Terror is not a conventional war in the sense of states fighting against each other, there is no guarantee of a peace treaty to hand out the spoils of war to the victors and to reorganize the societies of the losers. Moreover, there is no clear stated endgame by the protagonists who claim to be fighting the war, and certainly no clear vision for a post-War on Terror world. Thus, on this level, it could be argued that 09/11 brought a new kind of threat to the world economy: continuous disruption. This implies that new systems of world trade will have to be put into place to reflect that disruptive influence. Thus will there be an increase in the gap between the 'core' capitalist economies and the 'periphery' because of the need to protect the core from threats emanating from the periphery? The terrorist attacks in Bali, Kenya and Yemen in recent years suggest this. This is further reflected by the fact that al-Qaida have used countries which are at the very periphery of the world economy, that is, Afghanistan and Somalia, as bases for their operations. Is al-Qaida targeting the 'weakest link' in the capitalist world economy?

3.1　CONCEPTUAL FRAMEWORK

Since the very earliest forms of economic exchange, the relationship between security and trade has been paramount in the minds of people. On the one hand, free trade is believed to offer increased consumption opportunities in both quantitative and variety terms. On the other hand, opening a locality or community to trade increases the security risk that the community faces in terms of outsiders entering the area, public health risks of imported products and so on.

Today's world of highly interdependent markets in this sense is little different from the primordial local trading of centuries past. However, possibly the most important difference between the past and the current situation is the sheer intensity of economic exchange that currently takes place in a vastly larger area than ever before. As is well documented in the academic literature (Beck, 2000; Benn and Hall, 2000; Dollar and Kraay, 2002; Held, 2000; Hirst and Thompson, 1996; Rodrick, 1997; Rosencrance, 1996; Rothkopf, 1997; Sachs, 1998; Scholte, 2000; Stiglitz, 2002), the process of economic globalization, transnational transmission of technology and the increasing mobility of factors of production, especially capital, have increased the challenges facing states and regional entities in their attempts to monitor and control the flow of goods and services across jurisdictions. At the same time as increased liberalization has posed problems for regulators, it has offered unlimited opportunities for trade for economic agents. As the ideological shift in the late twentieth century towards favouring freer markets and reduced government intervention gathered pace, regulatory spaces left by retreating nation states were not readily filled by new transnational entities. A so-called 'Governance Gap' (Akbar and Mueller, 1997) emerged. Thus, while many people rejoiced at the increase in economic freedom that this brought, inevitably these changes created losers – territorially bounded, low-skilled workers, obsolete capital and uncompetitive industry.

For some, however, these changes merely confirmed a deep suspicion about the nature of capitalism that taken to an extreme, that is, a global level, it merely reinforced and strengthened inequalities between a core and a periphery (Wallerstein, 1976; Palan et al., 1996, and so on). Another aspect of the increased integration of world markets was the development, pre-eminence and spread of Western cultural values to all parts of the world, driven in large measure by the strength of the US economy in a post-Cold War world (Barber, 1996). This led some commentators to suggest that either a new 'Cold War' was emerging between Islam and the West (Huntington, 1998; Lewis, 2002) or that Western values had essentially triumphed over all others and we had reached a phase of perpetual historical stability (Fukuyama, 1992). The creation of the World Trade Organisation (WTO) and the increased deepening of integration among the 'Triad' economies of the US, EU and Japan certainly confirmed an increase in the linkages between economies forged by the presence of multinational enterprises (MNEs) and the increased demand by the latter for more open markets. Since the vast majority of the world's largest MNEs came from the G-7 economies, it was certainly understandable that a perception of the MNE as exporter of Western culture became dominant among those groups in non-Western societies who had seen their living standards fall and their degree of economic vulnerability rise as a consequence of globalization. For some, the late twentieth century thus represented a golden era in which economic growth could be sustained as long as economies remained open to technology, trade and investment. For others the process confirmed a neo-colonial domination which ought to be resisted.

It is in this light that the events of September 11, 2001 could be viewed. Indeed, as this book seeks to examine, the responses to 09/11 and their long-term implications are highly debatable and not necessarily clearly acceptable to all people. For international trade and investment, 09/11 has been viewed as an event that could radically alter the degree of openness of economies. This is due largely to a perceived change in the benefits of the trade-off between security and trade. Since 09/11, US public policymakers and their counterparts elsewhere in the world have been required to reconsider the degree to which free trade and investment is a desirable objective in itself, given the heightened security risks that liberalization poses. In particular, does the threat of international terrorism pose so high a risk that it is necessary to place restrictions on international trade? In terms of the financing for international terrorism, should governments pay closer attention to financial flows between banks? Is the current trade liberalization paradigm tenable in a world in which the foundations of capitalism are threatened? In particular, is there a potential for a vicious circle in that, by attempting to secure the West against threats from outside, policy-makers in the industrialized world restrict the ability of capitalist economies to expand, and further increase the gap between the core and periphery in the world economy? Would this not lead in turn to an increase in the degree of threat posed by terrorist groups based and organized in the periphery?

3.2   ANALYTICAL APPROACH

The main aim of this chapter is to analyse whether there is a uniqueness in the events of 09/11 that suggests future implications for international trade and investment are different from the past, or whether 09/11 has historical antecedents that can help policy-makers frame an appropriate response to the threats posed by 09/11.

  If it is likely that 09/11 is a repetition of previous historical shocks, then there are a number of exemplars that will help policy-makers respond, such as the process of trade liberalization after the Second World War in which the role of a hegemonic *Pax Americana* led to the development of a stable and largely extensive international trade expansion which contributed to the adoption and stabilization of democracy in many countries in the world. If, however, 09/11 is a unique event, and this chapter will argue that it is, the demand for continued and intensified liberalization may be contradictory with demands for increased security from society in the wake of 09/11. Moreover, the nature of the security threat as perceived by policy-makers is a non-traditional one. That is, terrorist activity is not confined to conventional armed combat and most, if not all, planning, preparation and of course targeting takes place in civilian milieus. This is further reinforced by the fact that the targets of terrorists are frequently economic in their nature, as the contestation of numerous terrorist groups is that capitalist institutions are the source of the problems that they are seeking to resolve through their chosen means. In short, does the pursuit of security undermine the very source of capitalism's success? In this context, it is worth returning to the core–periphery metaphor, in the sense that an obvious reaction to security threats that appear to emanate from countries on the periphery of economic development would be to close off trade and investment with them. Significant barriers to the movement of people from these countries could be imposed by developed countries, thus further hindering economic exchange between the core and periphery. Once again, a vicious circle could set in whereby states that have little or no control over activities in their territories, largely due to economic underdevelopment, may become ever more attractive locations for terrorist organizations. Current and recent examples of this include Somalia, Afghanistan and Rwanda. Indeed, in the immediate period since 09/11, decisions taken by G-7 and EU countries have been to significantly tighten control of their external borders; to propose and in some countries actively implement new immigration requirements for citizens from countries regarded as being high risk; and most contentiously, to put forward measures to track the flow of portfolio capital in and out of their countries in order to identify 'terrorist funds'. An indirect impact of 09/11 has been that security concerns have overshadowed attempts by the WTO to push through the latest round of trade liberalization measures under the Doha Round negotiations between senior decision-makers on both sides of the Atlantic. Ironically, one of the main thrusts of the Doha Round has been to engage the OECD countries in genuine trade liberalization in agricultural markets. It is these markets that are most likely to help the poorest countries to benefit from trade liberalization, and if the link between economic development and terrorism is taken seriously is likely to soothe one of the potential drivers of terrorism itself, that is, poverty.

3.3   ARE THERE ANY ANTECEDENTS TO 09/11 IN RECENT WORLD HISTORY?

Recent economic history is littered with major negative shocks impacting on economic performance of economies. Some of these shocks have come about by acts of nature such as major earthquakes or floods. Others have been due to the concerted actions of states and producers to control the availability of key inputs in the economy, such as oil. Most common of all has been the incidence of war or conflict that has disrupted the flow of goods and services. International public policy has also played a major role in economic disruption with the implementation of international economic sanctions with questionable results (Bojicic and Dyker, 1993).

Probably the most notable impact on the world economy has been the prevalence of major wars involving the most important economic powers at the time. Disruption has occurred at all levels of economic activity from local to global. In the nineteenth century, the Napoleonic Wars of conquest are largely believed to have caused the development of price inflation as the rise in aggregate demand fuelled by the requirements of fighting wars was not matched with an equivalent rise in aggregate supply (Ormerod, 1992). In the twentieth century, of course, the two world wars caused the most substantial dislocations of the world economy. The Vietnam War led to huge numbers of casualties on both sides, and on a macroeconomic level forced the US government to finance war expenditures through substantial monetary expansion. This led to an inflationary bubble which arguably contributed to the end of the Bretton Woods system of fixed exchange rates and the Gold Standard. In turn, the collapse of the Gold Standard reduced world trade as the highly volatile post-Bretton Woods exchange rate environment increased the risk of international trade operations. More generally, the slowdown in economic growth encouraged governments to erect a new range of trade barriers aimed at limiting competition that domestic firms faced.

A number of impacts on the economy were caused by the world wars. On the negative side, first, nations going to war meant that most men of working age were taken from civilian production and drafted into the armed forces. A horrific number of those drafted lost their lives and were therefore unable to contribute to economic activity once hostilities ceased. Second, in those areas where conflict took place the material and capital infrastructure was destroyed by the use of highly efficient and destructive weapons. Third, trade routes were disrupted as international commercial trade became effectively impossible across the major oceans and seaways. As a consequence, consumption patterns were affected, with rationing becoming commonplace in most countries involved in the war. Fourth, economic migration, an important source of economic growth, became almost impossible during war. Fifth, mass displacement of populations as war refugees also contributed to the destruction of economic and environmental infrastructure. While these effects of world war were clearly felt on a massive scale across the world, similar impacts of war were felt at all levels of conflict.

On the positive side, major war spawned a host of technological developments allied to the demands of military planners. Examples of successful innovation caused by war have been the development of radar, missile technology and the modern jet engine. After the end of hostilities, these technologies successfully crossed into the civilian realm and have transformed the economics of key industries such as international transportation and telecommunications. Those countries not directly affected by war on their territory (notably the United States) found that industrial production rose in line with the increased demand of the armed forces for weapons, munitions and other material required to wage war. Thus, in the case of the US economy, it exited the Second World War as the single biggest economy in the world, accounting for well over half of the world's GDP in 1945–47

(Calvocoressi, 2000). As a further boost, the US economy was uniquely placed to help rebuild the shattered economies of the countries involved in the war. Moreover, a concomitant feature of *Pax Americana* was that the post-war world economy should be built on a free-trade, multilateral framework. Democratic societies should eschew protectionism in favour of open economic relations. Proponents of the multilateral free trade system argued that this was the single greatest safeguard against the re-emergence of world war; that is, economic interdependence reduced the possibility of war. Functionalist idealism of this kind (Mitrany, 1933) was replicated at a European level with the creation of the European Coal and Steel Community and the European Economic Community in the 1950s (Milward, 1993).

After both the First World War and the Second World War, there was significant pressure by the US government on the European colonial powers to relinquish power over their colonies, for both idealist Wilsonian reasons, as well as more cynical self-interested motives. National self-determination meant not only that free peoples could democratically decide their futures, but the dismantling of colonial 'preference' would open up markets to US-produced goods and services. The net result of decolonization was in part an increase in trade openness with a certain degree of trade diversion away from intra-colonial trade patterns towards multilateral, third-country trade. While critics can rightly point to the long-standing legacies of post-colonial dependence, there can be little doubt that one of the benefits of the world wars was an end to colonial rule in many parts of the world.

What this analysis suggests is that previous major world conflicts and their post-conflict environments have led to important and long-lasting structural changes to the world trading system and world economy that have generally mitigated in favour of a more open, liberal world economic order. Largely driven by the economic and political interests of the US, the world trading system has been incrementally liberalized in spite of the security risks posed by openness. It is important to stress that of course structural change emerged as a consequence of the ending of conflict as much as the conflict itself. Thus, in the midst of the Second World War, it would have been difficult for all but the most liberal idealists to recognize that an end to conflict would lead to the creation of a multilateral political system.

This brings the analysis to the salient question as to whether anything that has been outlined above bears any similarity to a post-09/11 world. We believe that the current situation resembles more closely the four decades of Cold War hostilities rather than the 'hot' wars of the twentieth century. This is because the post-09/11 security situation is more akin to the deterrence nature of Cold War military and security planning. In using the word 'deterrence', we mean several things. First, security focuses on the prevention of future conflict rather than fighting actual conflict. Second, the subversion of enemy organizations and the role played by espionage is central to the prevention of conflict. Third, deterrence implies a degree of preemptive action in order to prevent future conflict. Fourth, an emphasis on internal security would imply the need for monitoring citizens' activities in their own countries. The human rights issues here are manifest.

On an economic level, the Cold War effectively closed off the Soviet Bloc of East and Central Europe, parts of communist Africa, Asia and Latin America from trade with 'Western' economies. An absence of technology transfer, know-how and foreign investment arguably contributed to the eventual demise of communist economic planning in these countries after 1989. It also meant that the consumption opportunities for people living in the Soviet Bloc were significantly constrained by the absence of foreign trade and investment (Dyker, 1991). For business in the industrialized countries, government measures outlawed trade with Soviet Bloc countries for 'security' reasons. Industrial espionage linked to development of military hardware was a topic of much controversy; trade in products with a linkage between civilian technologies and potentially military applications led to prosecutions of companies involved in this kind of commerce. Despite these similarities between 09/11 and the Cold War, the differences are equally striking. The Cold War was 'fought' by two protagonists with well-defined enemies and objectives – principally based around containment. This meant that the control of economic activity was set up to respond to these objectives. First, capital flows that were already restricted as part of national macroeconomic policy objectives, could also be controlled in the name of security. Nor had technological progress in the financial sector reached such a stage as to permit the volume of transactions that occur today on a daily basis. Second, until the completion of the Uruguay Round in the 1980s, international trade still faced a significant number of trade barriers. The presence of physical barriers to trade, such as the maintenance of customs posts within the EU for example, meant that it was still possible for governments to control the flow of goods across borders. Third, the growth of the service sector only began to rise exponentially in the 1990s, again in line with rapid developments in telecommunications and Internet technologies. Prior to the 1990s it was possible to control and monitor the activities of organizations perceived by governments to be subversive, through accessing the limited communications channels available to them. With the growth of the Internet, it is considerably more difficult to monitor the activities of terrorists and, moreover, the propaganda effort of terrorist groups and their supporters is much broader in scope because of the Internet. By contrast, the 'War on Terror' is supposedly fought between governments and an ill-defined enemy that does not have the same kinds of institutional characteristics of a traditional enemy. There is no organized army; no elected or appointed representatives; the scope of terrorist activity does not limit itself to conventional conceptions of warfare; most of all, terrorists are perceived to be as much 'the enemies within' as they are 'foreign' foes. There is no clear endgame or timeframe in which this 'war' will be fought. Advocates of the War on Terror, especially in the US administration, argue that the war will end when all terrorism is ended. This is arguably a rather vague and probably unachievable objective – especially unless there is a workable definition of terrorism accepted by the international community.

Unlike the Cold War, there is no consensus among the international community on which should be the legitimate targets for action nor is there agreement on the degree to which legitimate economic activity should be restricted in order to catch the flows of terrorist funds and related trade in services and goods. Moreover, cynics might argue that states choose to label resistance movements as terrorist in order to justify policies of internal repression.[1]

3.4   WHAT ARE THE IMPLICATIONS OF THIS FOR THE POST-09/11 WORLD ECONOMY?

If we accept that the War on Terror is sufficiently different from previous historical events including the world wars and the Cold War, the implications for the international economy are substantial. In particular, the current consensus on the need for an evolving and liberalizing world economy will be brought into question. While critics of globalization correctly point to the peripheral participation of sub-Saharan Africa and parts of South Asia in the world economy, there can be little disagreement that trade liberalization has led to net gains for the world economy. Indeed, the next and most crucial stage of trade liberalization at the WTO is agriculture, where the poorest countries could benefit substantially from the removal of trade barriers and the reform of distorting subsidy regimes in European and US agricultural policy. A major problem could be that a convergence of interests in the developed world could lead to a derailing of the Doha Round in favour of more 'pressing' issues on security and terrorism. These converging interests are among those who genuinely believe in the need to fight terrorism; those groups who stand to lose from agricultural liberalization; and policy-makers who wish to divert attention from trade to other issues where they can make political gains more readily or avoid having to take difficult decisions on trade. Increased vigilance at borders could also slow down the flow of goods and services. More generally, a slowdown in the world economy engendered in part by less dynamic world trade growth may increase the pressure on governments to protect domestic firms from competition from abroad. There is the possibility of the return to 1970s New Protectionism. Last but not least, greater uncertainty among consumers caused by security fears could have serious impacts both on a sector and on a macroeconomic level. Industries such as tourism (dealt with in more detail by Frédéric Dimanche in Chapter 9 of this volume) will clearly be transformed by fears of terrorism and the generally higher costs imposed on insurance companies and travel companies. On a macroeconomic level, increased uncertainty among consumers has the effect of dampening aggregate demand and hence economic growth.

Global capital markets could face difficult times ahead, too. This is because governments are being pressed to take more effective control over the flow of terrorist funds, and in particular they are being pressed to examine the role of confidentiality clauses on bank accounts and transactions. Offshore banking centres should also consider their role in the financial system if it is perceived that they have become conduits for the laundering of terrorist funds. Greater scrutiny of electronic transactions is thus inevitable if governments wish to be sure of their nature. This of course poses a huge problem for policy-makers, as global capital markets are vast and the sheer volume of transactions through myriad channels would require multilateral cooperation to be effective. Given the difficulties encountered by the EU in its attempts to tackle money laundering,[2] it is likely that a wider multilateral forum would find it more difficult to reach agreement.[3] Moreover, there are issues of national competitive advantage that some governments may be reluctant to surrender in the name of a nebulous War on Terror. Certain locations such as London, Luxemburg and Zurich could lose their competitive edge as financial centres, based on low regulation and client confidentiality, if they were required to implement more stringent rules. It is also worth pointing out that there are considerable political interests among the financial services community that would resist new legislation aimed at restricting capital flows.

Indeed, it is likely that successful control of terrorist funds will come not so much through direct monitoring from governments, but through voluntary acceptance and implementation of the rules by the private sector.

Equally noteworthy is the reality that in fact the liberalization model is a durable one that has become well established in the minds of policy-makers and business people. It is not clear that an alternative model of the relationship between regulation and economic benefits has been sufficiently well formulated to question the benefits of market liberalization. Moreover, while the costs of removing existing national barriers were relatively low in administrative terms, the construction of new regulatory systems could prove to be both a costly and a time-consuming process. The author of this chapter believes what is likely to emerge is that countries will be morally pressured to agree to blacklisting certain activities and a group of rogue countries, those that refuse to do so, will be cut off from access to global financial markets. This represents a 'path of least resistance' solution as those countries who refuse to abide by the rules will be the ones to face being left out of the global financial markets.

In terms of international labour migration, it is likely that certain countries will be singled out as high-risk sources of immigration. It is reasonably well accepted on the basis of past experience that migratory flows are important mechanisms for the functioning of labour markets in the world economy. A steady flow of educated and uneducated migrants to the US, the UK, Germany, France and the Netherlands in the twentieth century has been a significant boost to economic growth, and to ensuring that bottlenecks in labour markets could be relieved (Aldcroft, 2001). Indeed, it is the steady flow of low-skilled workers who are employed in many basic service industries and agriculture during the 1960s that has helped promote economic stability. Moreover, highly skilled engineers, scientists and medical staff often come from developing countries and work in the industrialized countries.

In the current context, Islamic countries are seen as the obvious case where immigration restrictions are likely to be the harshest. It is here that US immigration authorities have increased their vigilance by requiring fingerprinting and registration for visitors to the US.[4] Thus, we should expect that longer term, it will become increasingly difficult for citizens of Islamic countries to be able to travel and work with the same degree of freedom, if any, that they may have enjoyed in the past. While officially, most governments do not admit to the idea of introducing 'profiling' of individuals, the clear implication of current changes to US immigration laws, as an exemplar, is that certain foreigners are less welcome than others because of the potential security threat they pose. More worryingly, it appears that in the US at least, the more stringent controls are impacting upon almost anyone applying for a visa, even outside of the list of Islamic countries.[5] Moreover, the potential for being rejected may act as a significant deterrent to applicants for visas to the US, the UK and Schengen countries. The problems facing the EU economy are possibly more worrying than those of the US economy. This is because labour market rigidities in continental Europe appear to be more severe than in the US and where migration could be most effective (Heitger, 2000).

3.5   TOWARDS AN INCREASING GAP BETWEEN CORE AND PERIPHERY IN THE WORLD ECONOMY?

As discussed above, a post-09/11 world is one in which security concerns and the War on Terror as enunciated by the US administration are likely to have significant long-term impacts on the world economy. From trade in goods and services, to banking and labour migration, increased restrictions in international economic exchange justified in terms of the need for height-ened security could lead to a slowing down of the world economy. This is likely to be compounded by increased uncertainty caused by the fear of ter-rorism, and the political economy of protectionism which may lead govern-ments to increase trade barriers to protect industries hurt by recession.

Clearly, governments in industrialized countries will find it difficult to justify long-term restrictions against commerce if the perception among citizens is that the threat of terrorism is as much illusion as it is reality. In response, future governments may change the emphasis of their policy over time away from a knee-jerk security response – especially if the negative impact on the economy becomes significant. Moreover, the embedded liberal trade regime at a regional and international level may offer checks and balances against an over zealous reimposition of trade and investment barriers. It will be difficult for individual countries to impose new rules in the face of potential prosecution at the WTO. In this sense, there is cause for optimism that a post-09/11 world will not be allowed to backtrack on the progress of the last few decades.

However, one of the more worrying aspects of the current discussion of the War on Terror is the 'us and them' perception being forwarded by a number of leading politicians.[6] The current view is that if we can seal off threats to security by closing economies and societies to the threat from outside, we can continue our tradition of international trade liberalization. Thus currently, and understandably, the US and UK administration's emphasis on the threat posed by Islamic terrorism suggests that attempts to seal off the Islamic world from the West may portend the future of the War on Terror.[7]

While in the short term this may bring significant political gain by dem-onstrating the earnest nature with which governments are tackling the ter-rorist threat, it is not seeking to address arguably one of the main causes of terrorism: global economic inequality. Indeed, we believe that while a post-09/11 world is unique in history, one of the possible ways to resolve this 'war' can be found in replicating the experience of the past. While terror-ism cannot be explained solely by reference to the presence of a core and periphery in the world economy, as there are countless cases of where extreme poverty and perceived economic injustice do not engender violence of this kind, history suggests that where concerted efforts are made to engage societies in the mainstream of the international economy, where multilateral institution-building offers possibilities for the reconstruction of devastated economies, and where the perception that the multilateral system is set up to respect all parties to the system and that the benefits of multilateralism are seen to be distributed fairly, there is a greater likelihood that international conflict can be reduced.

The most notable exemplar is that of the Marshall Plan where a dominant US economy and society decided both in the interests of the multilateral system and in its own interests to provide resources to reconstruct Europe after the Second World War. The parallels with the current situation are clear. Today, the US is the only remaining superpower, its hegemonic power in both the economic and military sphere is largely unquestioned. One of the central motivations of the Marshall Plan was to ensure that democracy and multilateral cooperation in Western Europe could take hold in order to contain the perceived threat that communism posed at the time. In opening up European markets, it was believed by US policy-makers that one of the central beneficiaries would be American businesses (Hufbauer, 1990).

There is a perception that despite years of liberalization, the developing world has not gained as much from this process as has the developed world. The post-09/11 world offers an unrivalled opportunity for the developed world to demonstrate that multilateral trade liberalization can work for all by embracing an inclusive policy towards the periphery by opening up agricultural markets. Rather than closing off the industrialized world to some of the poorest countries in the world, where poverty has the potential for being a breeding ground for terrorism, we believe it is better to open markets to these countries. It is a frequently cited refrain among political scientists that 'democracies do not fight wars with each other'. Moreover, there is also arguably a link between free trade and democracy: that is, free trade reinforces democracy (Weart, 1998; Weede, 1984; Wright, 1965). Once economic linkages between civil societies become strong, the political pressure to maintain and enhance them becomes compelling. There can be few who would not argue that the EEC has contributed to peace in Western Europe by ensuring that mutual economic dependence of France and Germany would make it hard for them to fight a war. Moreover, Spain, Portugal and Greece's membership of the EU has cemented and reinforced the democratic structures in these countries. What are the impediments to a similar programme in those countries which could benefit from economic reconstruction, and whose participation in the world economy is central to their successful democratization? The main criticism of adopting a Marshall

Plan-type solution is based largely upon the contention of the non-existence and cultural and religious unsuitability of these societies for democracy and therefore inclusion in a liberal world economy. First, there is the contention that whilst there was a clear set of pre-existing democratic structures in Europe before the Second World War, there are similar institutional characteristics present in those places regarded as 'terrorist' countries. Much more significant institution-building and democratization would be required prior to their entry into a multilateral trade and investment framework.[8] A second argument is that while there are clear economic spillovers into the democratic realm in Western Europe, there does not appear to be such a strong functionalist argument among the group of countries that are regarded as being high risk sources of terrorism. Third, culturally, Islamic countries are not suitable for Western forms of democracy and that therefore we cannot expect these societies to adopt behaviour that we expect from European and Anglo Saxon societies. Moreover, the link between religion and the state is different in Islamic countries, and this absence of secularism is the main problem facing democratisation. Fourth, the current political borders of these countries reflect a post-colonial imposition of territorial boundaries and therefore there are not sustainable and easily identifiable polities. Fifth, there is the *realpolitik* of the current War on Terror that needs to be explicitly addressed. With the exception of Arab Gulf states that have significant oil supplies, a number of the states which are regarded as being terrorist countries are on the periphery of the world economy, playing little role in international trade, receiving negligible amounts of foreign direct investment and being non-existent sources of international capital.

An important but related explanation for why the current US administration, as sole superpower, is reluctant to play a proactive economic role is that, unlike in the Second World War in which the US was practically unaffected by warfare on its territory, the 09/11 attacks hit directly at the US mainland. This could arguably have a different psychological impact on American society where a demand for isolationism may be stronger. This is compounded by the fact that the Second World War ended with a Democrat president in office who shared a liberal multilateral vision for the world system, whereas in the current political landscape, neither the Republicans nor the Democrats have strong internationalist coalitions. Indeed, an almost universal reaction to the 09/11 attacks in the US has been to accept that war is an inevitable consequence of what happened.

Taking all these issues into account, the most likely outcome in the short to medium term is that rather than focusing on an inclusive and constructive dialogue, the foreign policies of the industrialized world will seek to isolate terrorism from the mainstream world system, thereby further relegating some of the poorest societies further into the periphery.

3.6 CONCLUSION

This chapter has sought to examine the potential impact on the world economy of the 09/11 attacks and the subsequent decision to launch a War on Terror. The central question has been whether the impact of 09/11 is a repetition of previous world economic history or whether it is a new rupture with historical experience. I believe that the closest historical parallel to the War on Terror is the Cold War. Yet we can find that the differences between the current situation and the past are also compelling. The current degree of technological and economic interdependence in the world economy is largely unprecedented. The scale of regulatory demands on governments in light of technology and globalization more generally is higher than ever before. At the same time, the dominance of liberal economic paradigms demands a liberalization logic which once begun is hard to reverse. The spaces in which 'subversive' political activity can flourish beyond the control of governments have also proliferated with the use of the Internet and the liberalization of capital markets.

In this context, the events of and initial responses to global terrorism should be understood. The initial policy response of the industrialized world has been to tighten security, especially against countries that are perceived to be sources of terrorism. This has occurred across all sectors of the economy from financial markets to labour migration, as well as in the trade of goods. The pursuit of the War on Terror has placed the crucial Doha Round of trade negotiations lower down on the political agenda and undermined the chances of achieving trade liberalization in agricultural markets. This has been compounded by the insistence of the major player in the world system, the US government, on pursuing a relatively monotonic military–security-based solution to the threats posed by terrorism, that is, tackling the symptoms rather than the underlying causes of terrorism. This chapter argues for a more nuanced approach to managing the post-09/11 world. While strengthening the most obvious weaknesses of the current security framework and developing a specific strategy to pre-empt terrorist attacks is clearly necessary, the danger of ignoring the underlying causes of terrorism such as poverty, inequality and a lack of democracy in many parts of the developing world is damaging. Thus by bringing developing countries into the mainstream of the world economy, by pushing trade and investment liberalization into those sectors where developing countries have the best opportunities of succeeding, the developed world could go a long way towards minimizing the risks of multiple terrorist networks developing.

It is also worth emphasizing that those constituencies that wish to frustrate trade liberalization in order to shelter their interests from the impact of trade liberalization could also benefit from a security-based justification for limiting free trade. If the Doha Round falls below the political radar screen, it could put off desperately needed reforms to the world trading system that will benefit economic nationalism at the expense of developing countries.

As a final reflection, it is worth noting the durability of international liberal trade regimes that since 1945 have managed to embed a liberalization process in the international economy that has been hard to undermine. In this sense, we are optimistic that even if in the short term security considerations may be paramount, the ability of the multilateral framework to prosper is unlikely to be threatened. It is also worth noting that while the current US Republican administration has committed itself to a military response to terrorism, it is possible that future presidents could pursue more nuanced strategies in the interests of both the US economy and the world. The underlying strength of multilateral institutions will weather the initial threat posed by international terrorism. Trade liberalization, while generating considerable opposition by groups who have fundamental disagreements about globalization, has increased consumption possibilities for billions of people in the world, and it has brought productive and technological benefits to a number of regions of the world economy. Crucially, it has undermined the power of economic nationalists to argue for trade protectionism. There is a lot more work to be done in the world economy. The WTO has to tackle seriously its critics' claim that it protects the interests of the industrialized world. It has to cajole the EU and the US to tackle honestly the problems of agricultural protectionism and to open these markets to developing country producers. It also has to broaden the trade agenda in order to consider the impact of free trade on the environment, and the protection of social and cultural systems in the light of globalization. While current purveyors of conventional wisdom tend, for their own interests, to focus on security, the long-term stability of the world economy and the widest possible participation in a fair and open trading system is likely to outlast terrorist issues. It is a return to matters of global economic importance that the post-09/11 world must consider in the medium to long term.

NOTES

1. Kaldor (1990) pointed to a similar phenomenon during the Cold War where both sides used the external threat as justification for internal policies of repression and human rights violations.
2. EU legislation is governed by the Amended EU Directive on money laundering (91/308/EEC). The EU Commission proposed amendments in 1998 that were finally adopted in November 2002, more than four years later.
3. The OECD has also developed legislation, largely on a recommendation rather than a

mandatory basis, on money laundering. The Financial Action Task Force (FATF) of the OECD has also drawn up a list of 'non-cooperating countries and territories' who do not actively seek to control money laundering. At the end of 2002, these were the Cook Islands, Egypt, Grenada, Guatemala, Indonesia, Myanmar, Nauru, Nigeria, the Philippines, St Vincent and the Grenadines, and Ukraine. In October 2001, the FATF produced a set of 'Special Recommendations on Terrorist Financing'.
4. Citizens of the following mainly Islamic countries; Afghanistan, Algeria, Bahrain, Eritrea, Lebanon, Morocco, North Korea, Oman, Qatar, Somalia and Tunisia, the United Arab Emirates, Yemen, who were not officially resident in the USA were required to register with Immigration and Naturalization Service by mid-February 2003.
5. 'Chinese seeking visas to study in US are being rejected in greater numbers', *Chronicle of Higher Education*, June 2002; 'Fortress America', *The Week (India)*, 9 December 2001.
6. At even the very highest level of government. Few will forget George W. Bush's claim that countries are 'either with us or against us' in the 'War on Terror'.
7. The 'Barbarians at the Gate' metaphor is apt here – if civilization can be kept apart from the savages, we can continue life as normal.
8. The current official view held by the US Republican administration is that US foreign policy is not about nation building. Therefore an investment in spreading democracy would not be high on the agenda.

REFERENCES

Akbar, Y. and B. Mueller (1997), 'Global competition policy: issues and perspectives', *Global Governance*, **3** (1), Jan–April, pp. 31–50.

Aldcroft, D. (2001), *The European Economy 1914–2000*, London: Routledge.

Barber, B. (1996), *Jihad vs. McWorld: How Globalism and Tribalism Are Reshaping the World*, New York: Ballantine Books.

Beck, U. (2000), *What is Globalization?*, Oxford: Blackwell.

Benn, D. and K. Hall (eds) (2000), *Globalization, a Calculus of Inequality: Perspectives from the South*, Kingston, Jamaica: Ian Randle Publishers.

Bojicic, V. and D. Dyker (1993), 'Sanctions on Serbia: sledgehammer or scalpel?', *SEI Working Paper Series*, No. 1, June.

Calvocoressi, P. (2000), *World Politics since 1945*, 8th edn, London: Longman.

Dollar, D. and A. Kraay (2002), 'Spreading the wealth', *Foreign Affairs*, January/February.

Dyker, D. (1991), *Restructuring the Soviet Economy*, London: Routledge.

Fukuyama, F. (1992), *The End of History and the Last Man*, New York: Avon Books.

Heitger, B. (2000), 'Unemployment and labour market rigidities in OECD countries; the impact of taxes', *Kiel Institute of World Economics Working Paper Series*, No. 985.

Held, D. (2000), *A Globalizing World? Culture, Economics, Politics*, London and New York: Routledge.

Hirst, P. and G. Thompson (1996), *Globalization in Question: The International Economy and Possibilities of Governance*, London and Cambridge: Polity Press.

Hufbauer, G. (1990), *Europe 1992: An American Perspective*, Washington, DC: Brookings Institution.

Huntington, S. (1998), *The Clash of Civilizations and the Remaking of World Order*, New York: Touchstone Books.

Kaldor, M. (1990), *The Imaginary War: Understanding the East-West Conflict*, Oxford: Blackwell.

Lewis, B. (2002), *What Went Wrong: The Clash Between Islam and Modernity in the Middle East*, New York: Harperperennial Library.

Milward, A. (1993), *The European Rescue of the Nation State*, London: Routledge.

Mitrany, D. (1933), *Progress of International Government*, New York: Elliot's Books.

Ormerod, P. (1992), *The Death of Economics*, London: Penguin.

Palan, R., J. Abbot and P. Deans (1996), *State Strategies in the Global Political Economy*, London: Pinter.

Rodrick, D. (1997), 'Sense and nonsense in the globalization debate', *Foreign Policy*, Summer.

Rosencrance, R. (1996), 'The rise of the virtual state', *Foreign Affairs*, **75** (4).

Rothkopf, D. (1997), 'In praise of cultural imperialism?', *Foreign Policy*, Summer.

Sachs, J. (1998), 'Unlocking the mysteries of globalization', *Foreign Policy*, Spring.

Scholte, J.A. (2000), *Globalization: a Critical Introduction*, London: Palgrave.

Stiglitz, J.E. (2002), 'Globalization and its discontents', *American Prospect*, **13** (1), January.

Wallerstein, I. (1976), *The Modern World-System: Capitalist Agriculture and the Origins of the European World-Economy in the Sixteenth Century*, New York: Academic Press.

Weart, S.R. (1998), *Never at War: Why Democracies Will Not Fight Each Other*, New Haven, CT: Yale University Press.

Weede, E. (1984), 'Democracy and war involvement', *Journal of Conflict Resolution*, **28** (12), 649–64.

Wright, Q. (1965), *A Study of War*, 2nd edn, Chicago, IL: University of Chicago Press.

4. Terrorism and international business: conceptual foundations

Michael R. Czinkota, Gary A. Knight and Peter W. Liesch

INTRODUCTION

Terrorism has emerged as an important threat to the international firm. It reflects the risk of violent acts to attain political goals via fear, coercion or intimidation. Key concepts on terrorism are reviewed and then linked to the international activities of the firm. Key units of analysis, actors and facilitating factors are highlighted in the relationship between terrorism and international business. A model that ties these elements together and conclusions are offered with suggestions for future research.

4.1 CONCEPTUAL FOUNDATIONS

While terrorism has existed throughout history, its global impact has increased markedly in recent years. For example, the September 11, 2001 attacks in the United States killed citizens from a total of 78 countries (US Department of State, 2002, p. v). Terrorism has contributed to a decline in the global economy (for example, European Commission, 2001), and has affected entire industries such as tourism, aviation and retailing on a global level. New government policies in many nations have altered the global environment of business.

Scholars have written on terrorism in many domains that include anthropology, criminology, economics, history and international relations. Nevertheless, in the domain of international business, there does not yet exist a systematic theory on terrorism. Yet, terrorists attack international businesses far more than any other target. For example, since 1996, well over 300 attacks have been conducted against businesses each year (US Department of State, 2002). In 2001, international terrorists targeted a total of 397 business facilities worldwide, while military or government facilities were targeted in a total of 35 events. Since 1996, Latin America has been the site for the greatest number of international attacks, followed by Western Europe, Asia and the Middle East. Bombing is by far the most common type of event, followed by armed attack, and kidnapping, vandalism and hijacking (US Department of State, 2002). Terrorists typically target innocent bystanders rather than 'hard' military or government targets. For example, even when victims of the 09/11 attacks are excluded, the great majority of the 4655 casualties of terrorist attacks in 2001 were civilians.

In the context of growing globalization and the expanded international activities of the firm, research is needed now more than ever on the nexus of terrorism and international business. International business research is generally conducted at the firm level and investigates cross-border firm-level activities and their interrelationships with the external environments in which the firm operates. When companies traverse specific stages of increasing foreign involvement on their way to becoming fully internationalized (Bilkey and Tesar, 1977; Johanson and Vahlne, 1977; Cavusgil, 1980; Czinkota, 1982), exporting and importing are often the first in a series of international entry modes. Foreign direct investment (FDI), in which the firm establishes regional headquarters, factories or marketing subsidiaries abroad, is generally considered the ultimate stage of internationalization. Other entry modes such as licensing, franchising and interfirm cooperation (for example, joint ventures) involve partnering between home-country and foreign firms.

Each one of these international business modes is affected by terrorism. Yet, the specific effect is likely to be very different for each mode. Also, the response to terrorism will differ, depending on the activity of the firm. In the next section we present an overview on terrorism concepts, key constructs and linkages. We then link terrorism to the international activities of the firm and discuss the relationship between terrorism and political risk. We conclude with suggestions for further research.

4.2   TERRORISM: KEY CONCEPTS AND CHARACTERISTICS

Terrorism is mentioned in the Bible and was a characteristic in the Roman Empire (Morris and Hoe, 1987; Schlagheck, 1988). However, contemporary terrorism emerged in the 1960s and exhibits a range of specific characteristics. Terrorism is a complex, emotionally powerful phenomenon that challenges scholarly efforts aimed at its definition and conceptualization. A range of subjective interpretations has appeared in the literature, often driven by political rather than scientific purposes. Schmid and Jongman (1988) identified more than 100 definitions in extant literature and Laquer (1996) laments the lack of a comprehensive, detailed definition of terrorism. The phenomenon is often subsumed under political risk, guerrilla warfare and criminal activity. Furthermore, it may be employed to achieve ends that are considered legitimate by some governments or other audiences around the world.

Most definitions of terrorism converge around the notion that violence, or the threat of violence, is employed to frighten or intimidate people. Their fears, in turn, exert pressures on governments that may help terrorists achieve goals that are unrelated to the violence itself. Terrorism emerges within situations of conflict as reflected by repressive governments and economic inequalities, as well as ideological, ethnic or religious rivalry among states or other groupings. For the purposes of our discussion here, we combine key aspects of a variety of analyses (Alexander et al., 1979, p. 4; Crenshaw, 2001; United Nations, 1999), and define terrorism as 'the systematic threat or use of violence to attain a political goal or communicate a political message through fear, coercion, or intimidation of particular persons or the general public'.

4.2.1 Types of Groups

Terrorist groups can be divided into three major categories: non-state supported, state-sponsored and state-directed groups (US Army, 1987; Seger, 1990; US Department of State, 2002). Non-state supported groups traditionally have been small special-interest groups that usually lack substantial support and are often apprehended due to a lack of skills and training that larger-scale terrorists typically receive (US Army, 1987; Seger, 1990; US Department of State, 2002). Nonetheless, recent trends reveal that ideological zealotry combined with the ability to collect funds from sympathizers globally, and augmented by individual supporters with very large personal wealth, can make such groups very dangerous.

State-sponsored groups receive training and weapons, as well as logistical and administrative support from sovereign nations in the Middle East, Asia, Africa and elsewhere. Training of these groups may take place in a third country away from the sponsoring state. Groups in this category are responsible for as much as 70 per cent of the international terrorist incidents occurring today (US Department of State, 2002). They frequently target corporate facilities, operations and personnel.

State-directed groups are organized, supplied and controlled by a nation. State-sponsored and state-directed terrorism has significantly elevated the terrorist threat around the world today. Most of today's groups are much better armed, trained and supported than in earlier times (Hanle, 1989; Seger, 1990; US Department of State, 2002).

4.2.2   Phases of Terrorism

Terrorist incidents are usually well planned, often rehearsed, and may be carried out with military precision. There are several distinct phases to a terrorist attack (US Army, 1983; Hanle, 1989; Seger, 1990). In the pre-incident phase, the intelligence needed to plan the event is gathered by a cell charged with this task. This information is communicated to the command cell for target selection and a plan of attack is developed and rehearsed. In the initiation phase, after a target has been chosen and an attack plan has been devised, the tactical cell is activated. The members of the tactical cell may travel to the target using different routes, coming together only at the last minute. The climax phase is when the attack takes place, the bomb goes off, the victim is assassinated, or the hostage event is concluded. At this point the terrorists either escape or are captured or killed.

Each of these phases involves varying terrorist activities. By the same token, they lead to different types of involvement with potential targets. For example, in the pre-incident phase, terrorists may recruit or place low-profile confederates inside firms in order to gather intelligence, while during the climax phase, high-profile assassins start to slaughter people. Since there are likely to be substantial differences between the types of terrorists involved in each of the phases and their activities, the defences to be built against them also must differ. For example, personnel selection and hiring procedures may be key to repelling terrorists in the pre-incident phase, while the hardening of targets may be much more useful for the latter phase.

4.2.3   Facilitating Factors

Several key factors have affected the way terrorists can operate today. Among them, urbanization and the concentration of people, government offices, businesses and industrial facilities have facilitated the efforts of terrorists. Cities bunch people into confined spaces, usually providing them with fewer means of escape, while terrorists can find more places to hide and plan their violent activities.

The media also has seemingly increased the pay-off from terrorism, with rapid, widespread global reporting bringing to the world the fear and ever-present possibility of a local attack. The global reach of a message is now more easily achieved, since television and other instant communications allow people worldwide to learn about a terrorist incident within minutes of its occurrence. Competition among media outlets also encourages the broadcast of information that facilitates diffusion of terrorist messages, sometimes inciting support that might not otherwise have eventuated. Terrorism's main impact, and that which is intended, is the fear and stress that it engenders among people around the world. It is this psychological response that in turn alters the macro economy, affects consumption, and leads to widespread panic or obsessions that can have harmful long-term societal effects. By putting terrorism on a global stage, the media also may provide the means to inspire and instruct other terrorist groups, leading to further or escalating terrorism (Schlagheck, 1988; Weimann and Winn, 1994).

Today, terrorist group members can communicate with each other with great efficiency, using modern communications systems, such as international telephony and the Internet. Such communication allows terrorists to plan and activate attacks with unprecedented efficiency and maximum impact (Crenshaw, 1990; Seger, 1990). In response to these developments, many security agencies have undertaken great efforts to tap into these communication efforts in order to receive information about planning and timing of attacks, and to interrupt them if possible. Systems such as 'carnivore' are able to rapidly process large quantities of data and search for specific threat patterns. However, terrorists often have been found to use quite primitive communications systems, such as runners or motorcycle couriers. Whether they do so in response to the monitoring mechanisms or due to insufficient resources, the result can be the same: despite increased use of interception technology, many communications between terrorists remain impervious to penetration.

Modern transportation systems also have proven critical to terrorist activities. They provide the means for terrorists, in a timely manner, to arrive at and depart from the sites of attacks. Sophisticated transportation also facilitates the often unaccompanied movement and delivery of weapons and other supplies used in terrorist attacks (Schlagheck, 1988; Crenshaw, 1990).

A final and more recent distinction of terrorists is the availability to them of new tools. Terrorist leaders are dedicated to their cause and, if objectives regarding publicity, retaliation or penetrating well-protected facilities are sufficiently warranted, the leadership may commit the cell knowing that they have little chance for survival, often by means of suicide bombing. Perhaps the most worrisome of contemporary developments is weapons of mass destruction (WMD), including nuclear, biological and chemical weapons, that hold the potential to kill thousands of people in a single event. With a goal of exercising indirect pressure on governments, ensuing from widespread citizen concerns, terrorists can use WMD and suicide bombing to wield higher levels of derivative influence than ever before.

4.3   TERRORISM AND INTERNATIONAL BUSINESS: UNITS OF ANALYSIS AND ACTORS

A critical research stage in any field is the establishment of a theoretical base on which further research can be built. Requirements for successful research into the link between terrorism and international business are the identification of key variables, their interrelationships and operationalization for future research. This task may be challenging in that terrorism is a relatively nebulous or imprecise construct, whose nature, antecedents and consequences may be difficult to conceptualize or distinguish from other events that occur in the macro environment of business.

In an effort to clarify the research task, we distinguish three levels of analysis – the primary level, the micro level and the macro level. From the scholar's perspective, the primary level refers to research conducted on terrorist threats at the level of the individual person and firm, including the firm's operations located abroad. It deals with actual or threatened damages or destruction of physical plant, property or equipment, and/or injury or death. A primary-level terrorist event directly affects the ability of an individual or firm to function along established patterns. This level of analysis is useful for gaining very detailed knowledge about how terrorism affects individuals and the individual firm.

The macro level refers to the effect of a terrorist attack on the global environment, and emphasizes the impact on variables such as the world economy, consumer demand for goods and services, and reactions by supranational organizations such as the United Nations. At this level, the consequences of terrorism are analysed with regard to their impact on the global macro environment. One shortcoming of the macro level is that it may be too broad. The effect of terrorism may be difficult to distinguish from those of other macro events, such as economic downturns, wars and large-scale environmental disasters.

At the micro-level of analysis, terrorism is investigated with regard to its effect on specific regions, industries or levels in international value chains. This reflects perhaps the most useful possibility for analysis because here the effects of terrorism are more significant than at the primary level, and can be distinguished and analysed more readily than those of the macro level. For example, at the primary level, the bomb explosion in Bali affected a night-club, some surrounding hotels and several hundred visitors. At the macro level, the attack had severe implications on Indonesia and nearby countries, particularly in terms of their perceived security. At the micro level, the analyst would evaluate the effects on tourism to Bali and other places heretofore thought of as safe, and would also include tighter transportation security measures and the resulting slowdown in logistical activities.

It is also useful to distinguish terrorism's direct and indirect effects. Direct effects comprise the immediate and direct economic and business consequences of terrorism. That is, the direct effect of terrorism includes the panic and consequent changes in typical activities (such as a decline in spending) that it engenders in consumers and investors, as well as the immediate actions taken by businesses, industries, local government agencies and non-governmental organizations and associations to deal directly with the event. From the business perspective, the main, albeit temporary effect here is usually a decline in consumption that such events often engender. On the other hand, indirect effects are longer-term actions and new policies enacted by national governments as well as national and supranational governmental organizations (for example, Centers for Disease Control in the US, United Nations, World Bank) over the longer term in response to terrorist events. There may be an enactment of new rules and regulations intended to improve security conditions, but which simultaneously impact upon the efficient operation of the firm. These responses alter the business environment in ways that are often more harmful to business interests than the terrorist events that provoked them. It is often through such new regulations that governments make the terrorist intent come true by transmitting effects across the world and far beyond the industries and regions that were the original targets of terrorist acts. These externality effects might well be the most difficult to identify, to analyse and to adjust into corporate decision-making and strategy formulation.

Lastly, we distinguish the major actors relevant to research on terrorism: the terrorists themselves, producers, consumers and governments. Producers are firms of all sorts that are both affected by terrorism and employ managers who devise approaches to deal with terrorism. Consumers reflect all buyers of goods and services whose purchasing behaviour may be affected by terrorist events. The mass-psychological implications of terrorism can be substantial and impact upon buyers' propensity to consume. Producers suffer due to reduced revenues from falling consumer demand, and expenses may rise from a variety of causes directly and indirectly related to terrorism. Short-term shortages of input goods may occur if, as a result of attacks, certain externally-obtained resources are delayed or become unavailable. Producers may attempt to recoup decreasing sales via increased advertising and other promotional activities, all of which incur unplanned expenses. Business insurance rates in various industries may rise as insurance providers put up premiums to account for additional risk.

Governments impose new regulations and restrictions intended to avert or deal with terrorism. For example, increasingly complex customs clearance and international logistical requirements or specific requirements imposed to enhance security systems, such as airlines in several countries have experienced, all combine to increase the costs of doing business, particularly business across national borders. Moreover, creeping government-imposed security measures will tend to lessen the efficiency with which international business channels can function. These imperfections, akin to the more traditional imperfections experienced in international business, reduce efficiencies in the functioning of international systems of exchange.

Overall, producers, consumers and governments, at the macro, micro and primary levels, are all influenced by, and need to respond to, the actions of terrorists. These actors also interface among themselves via processes that may be subject to change, often unplanned and unintended. All of these linkages suggest that terrorism will impose significant impediments to international trade and international investment, and as a result, these impediments will increase the transaction costs of doing business internationally. Just like predations by thieves or corruption (Anderson and Marcouiller, 2002) terrorism generates price mark-ups equivalent to a hidden tariff or tax. With appropriate and sufficient data, it should therefore be possible to assess the extent to which anti-terrorism measures encourage trade and increase welfare, and to delineate parameters for the level of investment into such repellent measures.

4.3.1   Uncertainty and the International Business Environment

Uncertainty is a characteristic of the business environment and strongly associated with terrorism. It has been defined as 'a lack of information about future events so that alternatives and their outcomes are unpredictable' (see Friedmann and Kim, 1988, p. 64). Terrorism increases the level of uncertainty in the business environment in the following areas:

1.   consumer demand for the firm's goods and services, which tends to decline due to the fear and panic that ensues in the wake of terrorist acts;
2.   supply of needed inputs, resources and services;
3.   government policies and laws enacted to deal with terrorism, thereby altering the business environment and especially the ease with which business is conducted;
4.   macroeconomic phenomena, exacerbated by terrorism;
5.   the nature of relations among countries, as affected by terrorism.

The first three components listed above reflect processes that are critical to international business. Consumer demand for goods and services is affected perhaps most directly by terrorist events. However, the supply of needed organizational inputs can be altered as well, either directly or in conjunction with other effects, such as new government policies and deteriorating macroeconomic indicators. Governments impose new regulations and policies in order to counteract terrorism or its effects. Macroeconomic variables are affected, as when, for example, the value of a nation's stock market falls in response to terrorist activities through its mass-psychological impact. Finally, particularly in the case of state-sponsored terrorism, the quality of international relations among involved nations suffers. Many of these effects reflect indirect consequences of terrorism, which are often those most pre-eminent in the master terrorist's mindset. The actors, factors, phases, outcomes and units of analysis involved in terrorism and international business are portrayed in the general typology in Figure 4.1.

4.3.2 Terrorism and Political Risk

Terrorism resembles political risk in some aspects, but not in others. We use the political risk definition of Wells (1998) which focuses on risks faced by investors that are principally the result of forces external to the industry and which involve some sort of government action or, occasionally, inaction. Political risk implies the occurrence of unwanted consequences due to the political behaviours of governments and other public entities. Both political and economic events engender political behaviours that result in political risk. Traditional views on political risk emphasize that it occurs primarily due to (usually host) government interference with business operations after an investment has taken place, and that it is usually directed at firms and their managers which employ the FDI mode of foreign market entry (for example, Simon, 1984; Friedmann and Kim, 1988; Makhija, 1993; Butler and Joaquin, 1998). However, these two conditions often do not apply with regard to terrorism. In contrast to political risk, terrorism has more macro-level consequences, and can affect all types of foreign entry modes. While political risk is typically confined within national borders, terrorism's effects tend to be felt more broadly in business activity that crosses borders. There is a substantial difference in timing wherein political risk tends to build up gradually, sometimes lying nascent, until it finally emerges. In contrast, terrorism strikes suddenly, often without premonition or warning.

When dealing with foreign firms on their home turf, governments have the upper hand and are usually quite effective in achieving the political behaviour goals associated with political risk. Terrorism, on the other hand, is not particularly effective in achieving its intended goals. Indeed, many governments tend to respond to terrorism with a resolve to minimize its impact. In contrast

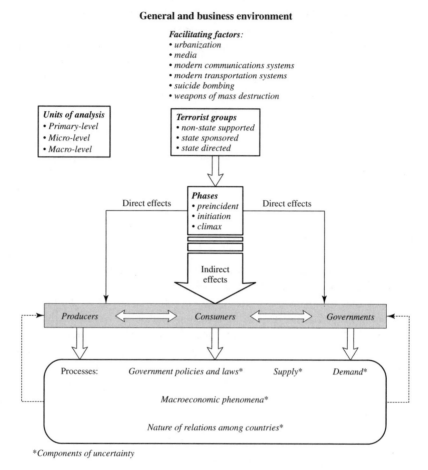

*Figure 4.1   A general typology for the analysis of terrorism and
                international business*

to the political behaviours inherent in political risk, terrorism is not normally conducted as an officially sanctioned activity of national governments. It might be supported, indirectly and covertly, by some governments, but terrorism is rarely conducted as visible government policy.

Moreover, political risk is usually linked to a locale and tends to be less of a factor in politically stable countries. Firms unhappy with political developments can (at least eventually) redirect their activities to a different country. By contrast, terrorism can strike anywhere and, thus, the political stability of terrorist-targeted countries is often not relevant, nor can firms make a choice in terms of their exposure to terrorism.

Political risk typically targets specific objects, such as firms and their managers. However, the targets of terrorism are often symbolic, and the victims represent a much more random and unsuspecting audience. To achieve its maximum shock effect, terrorist violence is usually provocative and dramatic. Acts are usually carried out covertly by small bands of extremists who lack the means to execute larger-scale military campaigns or to target their opponents more openly (Crenshaw, 2001). These characteristics contrast sharply with those of political risk.

Terrorists often assert that they are waging war, in which case terrorist acts might then be considered war crimes, breaches of the rules of war or, occasionally, legitimate fighting approaches. The victims of terrorism are often different from the target audience, which may comprise entire nations or regions of the world, or particular religious or ethnic groups. Indeed, the connection between the victims and the targets may be quite tenuous. The specific victims may even be irrelevant to the terrorist cause. 'Pure terrorism' as wholly indiscriminant violence mostly focuses on ratcheting up the pressure on governments to take or consider actions. With political risk, firms may respond to the political behaviours imposed on them (for example, tariffs) by employing other political behaviours (for example, lobbying the central government). Political behaviours associated with political risk are generally legal, at least in the context of the countries where these behaviours take place. From the perspective of most observers, however, terrorism is generally illegal, as well as immoral.

When governments decide to change policies they may encounter some unintended consequences. These consequences may be particularly unforecastable when governments intend to quell terrorism. Efforts aimed a protecting the most vulnerable targets, such as civil aviation, ports or embassies in high-threat countries, may motivate terrorists to simply substitute easier targets for less accessible ones (Crenshaw, 2001). Given typical scarcity of resources for terrorists, they are rationally likely to respond to higher price conditions (due to increased protections enacted by firms or governments) by allocating their resources to those modes or missions of attack which are less costly – that is, more likely to succeed (Sandler et al., 1991). For example, if foreign terrorists can no longer find their way into the United States, they may attack US symbols and representatives abroad with greater frequency. Similarly, if the embassies of a country are more secured and fortified, terrorists may find attacks on that nation's individuals and companies more attractive.

Research on political risk implies that it is an international phenomenon, yet its international aspects primarily affect firms that are operating internationally. The political behaviours leading to political risk are generally confined to individual countries and lack the macro-level consequences

that involve numerous countries simultaneously and characteristic of terrorism (for example, Cosset and Suret, 1995). Its effects are not confined
within particular national borders.

Political risk tends to occur with a degree of certainty or objective uncertainty and can therefore be predicted with considerable accuracy (for
example, Kobrin, 1979; Fitzpatrick, 1983). Terrorist events, on the other
hand, are by their nature clandestine and typically occur quite suddenly. As
we have seen, not even the world's best intelligence agencies excel at predicting specific terrorist events. Terrorism greatly increases the (perceived) level
of uncertainty for international business and therefore raises risk more
than do political shifts.

Political risk occurs within individual countries at the primary level (for
example, expropriation of corporate assets) and micro level (for example,
tariffs and taxes). By contrast, terrorism's effects are often experienced
much more at a macro level, potentially involving numerous countries
simultaneously. It tends to produce both direct effects (that is, the terrorist
act itself, experienced at the primary and micro levels) and indirect effects
(for example, the consequent imposition of new government regulations
and controls, as well as the exacerbation of tensions between countries).
Accordingly, terrorism's consequences are potentially much more broad-
based and far-reaching than those of political risk. This, combined with the
greater challenges involved in measuring and predicting terrorism, implies
that the managerial task required to deal with terrorism (before and after
terrorist events) is highly complex.

Overall, the location, the timing, the sources and targets of terrorism are
substantially different from those of political risk. Therefore, the effects of
terrorism on international business require investigation and theory-build-
ing separate from those of the existing political risk literature. While this
literature might provide a point of departure for investigations into terrorism, new approaches are needed to accommodate the fundamental differences that terrorism brings to the environments in which firms do business,
and in which managers guide those firms. Frameworks and analytical
approaches might need be constructed from hitherto unknown, or little
used, constructs and assumptions to investigate this phenomenon.

4.4   CONCLUSION

The paucity of terrorism research reported in the international business literature may have resulted in part because terrorism has proven difficult to
define and conceptualize. The concept itself and the various ways – at the
primary, micro and macro levels – in which it affects international value

chain activities are undoubtedly difficult to investigate and model. While the study of terrorism has been approached within various perspectives, including political science, psychology and sociology, it may be more useful for international business researchers to define terrorism more narrowly as an act, to enable more theoretically objective approaches and quantitative analyses using empirical data. Business scholars should focus on research that ultimately leads to normative approaches that can be practically applied by managers. Various methods can be employed to gauge terrorism's effects, including surveys directed to managers and consumers, along with measures from secondary data of its impact on specific industries, such as the airlines and tourism. Noticeably, governments have been able to define terrorism sufficiently to take action against it.

When conceptualizing the effect of terrorism on international business, it is useful to distinguish the most vulnerable links in firms' value chains. While an attack can destroy an entire firm, such events are relatively rare. From the individual producer's perspective, it is more useful to view terrorism at the micro level wherein input sourcing, manufacturing, distribution, and shipping and logistics are likely to be the most vulnerable areas. At the consumer unit of analysis, management and marketing are perhaps the most important organizational functions for dealing with the before and after of terrorist events. To the extent they affect buyer confidence and spending levels in the national and global economies, all terrorist incidents are ultimately macro as a result of their negative externality effects. As the September 11, 2001 attacks revealed these negative externality effects can have global implications, regardless of where the terrorism occurs.

Management's ability to maximize profits in the face of terrorism is a function of its effectiveness in stabilizing risk and ensuring sufficient revenue in exchange for any remaining exposure. Within the international value chain, efficiency derives primarily from the optimal sourcing of inputs (for example, factors of production) and the minimization of costs associated with distribution and logistics. Terrorism moderates the links between value-chain activities (in which managers seek to optimize effectiveness and efficiency) and firm performance (for example, profitability). Terrorism's effects will pose a drag on these linkages and managers will seek to overcome terrorism's effects via judicious management of resources, strategies and processes.

Future empirical research into the effects of terrorism on international business should identify the types of terrorist events likely to affect the firm's operations, the primary- and micro-level conditions under which they are most likely to do so, and the nature of the specific processes through which these effects occur. In-depth case studies on firms directly affected by terrorism also will serve to provide grounded information as to the nature of relationships between types of terrorism and their specific effects, and facilitate the development of models and theory. This research is important because of the dire consequences that terrorism potentially poses. Panicked efforts to deal with suddenly unfolding events are less likely to sustain firm performance in the absence of thoughtful planning and the application of empirically verified methods for dealing with terrorism.

REFERENCES

Alexander, Y., D. Valton and P. Wilkinson (1979), *Terrorism: Theory and Practice*, Boulder, CO: Westview Press.

Anderson, J.E. and D. Marcouiller (2002), 'Insecurity and the pattern of trade: an empirical investigation', *Review of Economics and Statistics*, **84** (2), 342–52.

Bilkey, W.J. and G. Tesar (1977), 'The export behavior of smaller Wisconsin manufacturing firms', *Journal of International Business Studies*, **9**, Spring/Summer, 93–8.

Butler, K. and D. Joaquin (1998), 'A note on political risk and the required return on foreign direct investment', *Journal of International Business Studies*, **29** (3), 599–608.

Cavusgil, S.T. (1980), 'On the internationalization process of firms', *European Research*, **8** (6), 273–81.

Cosset, J.-C. and J.-M. Suret (1995), 'Political risk and the benefits of international portfolio diversification', *Journal of International Business Studies*, **26** (2), 301–18.

Crenshaw, M. (1990), 'The causes of terrorism', in C. Kegley (ed.), *International Terrorism: Characteristics, Causes, Controls*, New York: St Martin's Press.

Crenshaw, M. (2001), 'Terrorism', in N. Smelser and P. Baltes (eds.), *International Encyclopedia of the Social and Behavioral Sciences*, vol. 23, Amsterdam: Elsevier, pp. 15604–6.

Czinkota, M. (1982), *Export Development Strategies: US Promotion Policies*, New York: Praeger Publishers.

European Commission (2001), *Overview of EU Action in Response to the Events of 11 September and Assessment of their Likely Economic Impact*. Brussels: Commission of the European Communities, European Union.

Fitzpatrick, M. (1983), 'The definition and assessment of political risk in international business: a review of the literature', *Academy of Management Review*, **8** (2), 249–54.

Friedmann, R. and J. Kim (1988), 'Political risk and international marketing', *Columbia Journal of World Business*, **23**, Winter, 63–74.

Hanle, D. (1989), *Terrorism: The Newest Face of Warfare,* London: Pergamon-Brassey's.

Johanson, J. and J.-E. Vahlne (1977), 'The internationalization process of the firm: a model of knowledge development and increasing foreign commitments', *Journal of International Business Studies*, **8**, Spring/Summer, 23–32.

Kobrin, S.J. (1979), 'Political risk: a review and reconsideration', *Journal of International Business Studies*, **10**, pp. 67–80.

Laqueur, W. (1996), 'Postmodern terrorism', *Foreign Affairs*, **75** (5), 24–36.

Makhija, M.V. (1993), 'Government intervention in the Venezuelan petroleum industry: an empirical investigation of political risk', *Journal of International Business Studies*, **24** (3), 531–43.

Morris, E. and A. Hoe (1987), *Terrorism: Threat and Response*, London: Macmillan Press.

Sandler, T., W. Enders and H.E. Lapan (1991), 'Economic analysis can help fight international terrorism', *Challenge*, February, 10–18.

Schlagheck, D.M. (1988), *International Terrorism*, Lexington, MA: Lexington Books.

Schmid, A.P. and A. Jongman (eds) (1988), *Political Terrorism: A New Guide To Actors, Authors, Concepts, Databases, Theories, and Literature*, Amsterdam: North Holland.

Seger, K.A. (1990), *The Antiterrorism Handbook*, Novato, CA: Presidio Press.

Simon, J.D. (1984), 'A theoretical perspective on political risk', *Journal of International Business Studies*, **15**, 123–43.

United Nations (1999), *United Nations General Assembly Resolution 51/210 Measures to Eliminate International Terrorism*.

US Army (1983), *Countering Terrorism on US Army Installations*, Fort Monroe, VA: Headquarters TRADOC.

US Army (1987), *FC 100-37 Terrorism Counteraction*, Fort Leavenworth, KS: US Army Combined Arms Center.

US Department of State (2002), *Patterns of Global Terrorism 2001*, Washington, DC: United States Department of State.

Weimann, G. and C. Winn (1994), *The Theater of Terror: Mass Media and International Terrorism*, White Plains, NY: Longman.

Wells, L.T. (1998), 'Good and fair competition: does the foreign direct investor face still other risks in emerging markets?', in T.H. Moran (ed.), *Managing International Political Risk*, Malden: Blackwell, pp. 15–43.

5. The complexity of the geopolitics dimension in risk assessment for international business

Gabriele G.S. Suder

INTRODUCTION

John Agnew (1998) in *Geopolitics: Re-visioning World Politics* argued that world politics stem from Europe, evolving to a global power position, imposing patterns on the rest of the world in the pursuit of primacy of competing nations through colonization (from the late eighteenth century on), naturalization (1875–1945) and ideology (after the Second World War). The post-Cold War era was marked by the development of theories about in-between structures, originating in the search of cultural and polit-ico-economic primacy.[1] The belief in the hegemonial dominance of the US failed to materialize in the1990s, and geopolitical theory was comple-mented by global conservatist, corporatist, left and reformist, and neo-lib-eralist models that look at the world order in terms of control and power, culture and civilization, modernization, or globalism and anti-globalism.[2] September 11, 2001 has given way to a new era that is characterized by com-plexity, vulnerability and uncertainty in all fields of world politics and eco-nomics.[3] Containment is a probable strategy that will consequently be adopted, but it is not the aim of this chapter to erode its alternatives. Rather, we acknowledge that global space and territory have become seem-ingly uncontrollable. This geopolitical and economic challenge is what we will examine: a flux of change that challenges and is challenged by the tran-sitivity of this globalization, of vulnerability and of threat. A number of profound certainties, of fixed and barely questioned realities in the interna-tional business environment, have to be complemented, or they have disap-peared, or they are in question (see all chapters of this book) through terrorism. Part of this process of alteration is the awareness that assess-ments of geopolitical forces and the nature of relations between states, nations and regions have a vital impact on global corporate activity. Conventional wisdom is replaced by new analysis and reflection about the possible long-term implications of September 11, 2001. But cause and effect in the social sciences is always a problematic phenomenon. In the field of international political economy, the agency-structure debate rages on unabated. Many try to understand the fundamental shifts of the post-09/11 era.[4]

This chapter aims to examine trends in the geopolitical debate and its nexus to international business. It assesses both classical and contemporary theory in order to develop the basis of discussion. It attempts also to conceptualize a part of risk management that complements traditional approaches through the emphasis on the notion of 'geopolitical turmoil' or 'risk' under which we will term terrorism. While classical international business theory includes terrorism under the classification of the legal and political environment, associated to political risk, Czinkota, Knight and Liesch demonstrate (see Chapter 4) that this category is not sufficient. We need to conceptualize a complementary model as a tool for normative risk assessment and analysis. While only a relatively small group of firms is potentially brought to complete breakdown through international terrorist attacks, the impact of the particular era of (post-)09/11 terrorism on the vast proportion of international corporate activity is potentially vaster in space and time than in the pre-09/11 era. Traditional risk assessment through the examination of the legal and political forces in countries in which a firm operates are therefore insufficient: the assessment of geopolitical turmoil itself needs to become global; but relevant qualitative and quantitative measures are needed that tackle this global challenge. Indeed, William Thornton labels (post-)09/11 terrorism, in term of neo-realist theory of pro- and anti-globalization, 'geoterrorism'.[5]

In order to develop the non-material explanations for shifts in geopolitics in a post-09/11 world, it is necessary to examine other literature on geopolitics – especially that considering concepts such as normative force and power that transcend the currently emerging consensus. A material examination of geopolitics enlarges the attempts to problematize the underlying assumptions of risk assessment, that provide critical information to CEOs, managing directors, lawyers, risk managers, insurers, reinsurers, business development executives, brokers, underwriters, claims officers and others.

5.1 THE HISTORICAL ORIGINS OF POST-09/11 SCHOOLS OF THOUGHT

The study of the political distribution of space is an ancient concern – based deep in concerns of the distributive consequences of social and economic activity. Machiavelli's *Il Principe* is probably the most famous work of geopolitics. Traditional concepts are also based on writings such as those of Aristotle and Confucius. Geopolitical study as a discipline started with the nineteenth century, at the end of the 'Age of Exploration' after Europe explored and colonized the inhabited parts of the world. At the Renaissance, the modern world economy had started to emerge with the concept of the nation-state, with certain interdependencies that were studied.

The birth of geopolitics took place in Europe, due to the fact that at the end of the Middle Ages, most European nation-states were already in existence (France, England, Portugal, Spain, the Netherlands, Scandinavian countries). The discipline allowed each state to situate itself in the world and draw decisions based on the concept developed thereby. Systems studied therefore involved mainly the world economy (interdependencies), world empires (the systematic conquest and subjugation of other nations) and mini-systems (small, isolated, and lacking trade relations with the outside).

The nineteenth century, marked by the industrial revolution, completes the exploring and mapping of the earth and much of its resources. At this point we recognize a clearly structured border-transcending stream of goods, services, news and travel (still mostly Eurocentric). While the discipline spread with European influence to different continents, the world wars definitively exported the discipline on a global level, and in particular to North America.

A twentieth-century tradition of thinking about statecraft included such strategists as Friedrich Ratzel, Alfred Mahan, Rudolf Kjellen and Halford Mackinder. This developed in the inter-war period with Karl Haushofer's German *Geopolitik* and Nicholas Spykman's 'rimland' theories, and finds expression in contemporary writings like that of Henry Kissinger and Zbigniew Brzezinski.[6]

Halford Mackinder wrote an essay entitled 'The Geographical Pivot of History' which incorporated three geopolitical approaches, at a time when various groupings of imperialist powers were emerging. Mackinder's (1904) essay explored whether the age of overseas expansion had ended and that the world was becoming a closed political system where a political activity in one place produced a response in another, 'every explosion of social forces, instead of being dissipated in a surrounding circuit of unknown space and barbaric chaos, will be sharply re-echoed from the far side of the globe, and weak elements in the political and economic organism of the world will be shattered in consequence'. The fundamental claim made in his analysis was the continual struggle throughout European history to achieve and prevent control of an area known as the 'pivot area'. Mackinder claimed simply that the potential for world domination lay in land-based, rather than maritime-based, powers. He saw that the majority of the world's population was concentrated in Eurasia and Africa and argued that whoever could control this area would be able to dominate the world. Mackinder also saw that the key to this supremacy lay in the pivot area, since dominance of this guaranteed self-sufficiency through an abundance of resources, provided the occupier with natural defences to attack, namely the sea, and was an important strategic position since it had a lot of boundaries ideal for launching an invasion. Around the pivot area was an inner crescent of marginal states and an outer crescent of oceanic powers, namely Britain, the USA and Japan. The threat identified by Mackinder and his heartland theory forced him to come to two strategic conclusions. First, whoever controlled the pivot area should be prevented from expanding into the marginal states because this would provide the basis for world domination. Second, in the event of such a threat becoming reality, an alliance of overseas powers should support armies in bridgeheads such as France, Italy, Egypt, India and Korea. Elements of Mackinder's analysis were used in Nazi Germany's legitimization of the concept of *Lebensraum*.

Three approaches generally characterize the study of geopolitics:

- The normative approach is taken generally by more conservative analysts. It sees power as the necessary feature of international politics and trade relations.
- The historical-dialectic position interprets international relations as an interlinking of history and society that show the contradiction of work and capital; this policy approach has particularly influenced research on development aid for the Third World and on disarmament.
- The empirical-analytical position is the contemporary mainstream approach taken in research of international relations and of trade theory. It is a quantifying, heterogene position that attempts to come to scientific conclusions on the basis of the description of facts and microanalysis.

The term 'geopolitics' has been historically dedicated to examining and analysing the relative importance of countries within the global geopolitical order by utilizing the three complementary and competing frameworks labelled as:

- the power approach,
- the ideological approach, and
- the political economy approach.

The power approach looks at the relationships between nations by examining their ability to influence or change the behaviour of others. Essentially, this emphasizes the importance of agency in the international system. Since the middle of the twentieth century, this approach has arrived at an analysis that accounts for a dramatic shift of power relations in the international system. The bipolarity of the 1940s and 1950s, with the USA and USSR superpowers dominating, was replaced by the loose polarity of the 1960s and the development of newer and stronger industrial nations, and finally into the growth of the multipolarity stage with the emergence of the European Union, Japan and China as significant economic powers following the US. In this case, geopolitical analyses argue that while structures may have changed, the geopolitical equilibrium has been preserved by a hierarchy of powerful states developing at the expense of smaller and weaker nations. Thus state power remains supreme and relative power relations maintain a complex balance of power in the world. The normative 'Darwinian' implications of the classical approach to geopolitics is that strong states will therefore inevitably have control in the world system, relegating weak states to subservience.[7]

The ideological approach is used as a basis upon which the state can justify territorial actions, domestically and globally. In the case of the USA in the nineteenth century, it expanded its frontiers by 'going on a mission to civilize the wilderness', hence gaining the territory that increased its geopolitical significance. The USSR also used ideological reasoning to vindicate military intervention whenever socialism was threatened from a source within its boundaries. It is this ideological approach that led S.B. Cohen, in his book *Geography and Politics in a Divided World* (1964), to formulate his hypothesis on shatter belt regions, an extension of the work done by Fairgrieve on his 'crush zones'. Here Cohen describes a shatter belt as 'a large, strategically located region that is occupied by a number of conflicting states and is caught between the conflicting interests of adjoining Great Powers'. This region therefore includes South-east Asia and the Middle East which, because of resources, means its political and economic fate is of vital concern to other emerging powers. However, within these regions there is an instability of culture, history, environment and politics that makes the area very unstable and hence may cause the emerging powers to engage in territorial action. Irredentism can be part of the cause and the consequence.

The political economy approach assumes that geopolitics cannot be understood without fully considering the distribution of wealth in the global economy. Wallerstein (1974) considered the links between processes of capital accumulation, resource competition and foreign policy, a study which thrust the USA into the leading role and downgraded the USSR since it had far more limited economic capabilities. Thus the failure of state planning and its subsequent dramatic collapse in 1989 was explained by the inability of socialist planners to maintain levels of productivity and capital accumulation in the face of an increasingly expensive arms race. As the ability of the US government to fund its increases in military expenditure began to outstrip that of the USSR, economic conditions in planned economies worsened with economic shortages becoming commonplace. Paradoxically, increased defence expenditure by the US and its NATO allies allowed a Keynesian virtuous circle of growth to emerge. Increased public expenditure on armaments[8] created employment, which in turn raised incomes and generated consumer demand. Combined with the relative productivity and innovative capacity of the defence industry, the US government was able to maintain the arms race and avoid economic stagnation.

5.2   THE PAST AND FUTURE OF THE STATE

For Shapiro (1994) recent events reflect the development of the modern state system that was the beginning of the geopolitical imagination, for geopolitics is traditionally space as organized by the state. He argues that the state system as a horizontal organization of space, around the principle of state sovereignty, is innately a moral geography, 'a set of silent ethical assertions that pre-organise explicit ethico-political discourses' (Shapiro, 1994, p. 482). Following this logic, geopolitics could be suspected to be a practical problem-solving approach for the conceptualization and practice of statecraft. A label for a variety of traditions and cultures of theory and practice, it is then an instrumental form of knowledge and rationality, which explains the differences in the geographically as well as politically diverse schools of thought.

The study of distinct schools of geopolitical thought illustrates this diversity in developed countries.[8] Figure 5.1 offers a general historico-geopolitical summary of five schools of geopolitical thought.

The essential basis for geopolitics is, as Figure 5.1 demonstrates, traditionally based on a rational apportionment of space and territory, and depends on the perspective adopted. In line with this rational approach, modern mainstream geopolitics has complemented classical geopolitics with notions that help to understand the impact of geography, politics and history on international (business) relations, comparing different geographic approaches to geopolitics throughout the world, as well as mentalities and concepts. This presupposes the assessment and prioritizing of international knowledge of social, economic, political, cultural

Country	Origins of historico-geopolitical concepts
France	Nation-state by the Renaissance. Classical French school of geopolitics contrasted West (cooperation and flexibility) and East from fear of Germany (authoritarianism and rigidity). Geopolitics centre around European position in the world, until Europe is devastated by world wars. Strong support of international cooperation on peace.
Germany	Until mid-19th century (Bismarck's Prussia) very fragmented; land-based power. Strives for unification of nations and protection against vulnerable position through expansion in both world wars. 'Battlefield' of the Cold War for the US and Soviet Union.
GB	Nation-state by the Renaissance. Dominant power of British Empire through control of the seas. Classical Theory: Mackinder, heartland (Germany, Eastern Europe, Russia), control of 'world island' (Europe, Africa, Asia), with Britain to balance the threat of Continental dominance by retaining Russia as an ally against Germany.
US	European colonial outpost developing into leading military and economic power. Cyclic foreign policies (introversion and extroversion). After Second World War, geopolitics centre around Cold War. Individualist, democratic, universal, seeking to overcome boundaries by power and via technological expansion.
Russia	Empire under Czars peripheral, backward, isolated until Peter the Great, attacked by invaders; feudal society. After Second World War, geopolitics of Soviet Union centre around Cold War. Focus on cultural divides and struggles for identity.

Source: Assembled from Agnew (1998), Braden and Shelley (2000), Tunander et al. (1997), Picht (1995), Suder (1994).

Figure 5.1   Schools of geopolitical thought (selected countries)

and environmental forces, that analyses the relationships between locations and the global marketplace, taking into account (geographically speaking) location, distance, direction, diffusion, place and regions.

Geopolitics takes existing power structures as given but not everlasting, and works within these to offer advice to decision-makers. By nature, it reifies a transparent and objectified world which is commonly based on truth systems such as ideology, religion or scientized versions of religion. Its dominant narrative is based around concepts of the global balance of power and the need for actors to place themselves strategically in a fundamentally anarchic and ephemeral world.[9]

5.3 THE CONCEPTS OF ENEMY, SPACE AND LEGITIMACY

The 'Millennium Special Edition' of *The Economist* (December 1999) instructed us: 'The world map has always been shaped not by science alone, but by religion, politics, art and obsession. Themes such as divine power, the natural elements, secular ambitions, recur constantly and express more than pure geography.' Today, we map the world mostly on the basis of the political and economic priorities of the region or pattern that we belong to. We are innately subjective, and need to assess and prioritize assets that it is useful to examine. But who are 'we'? Figure 5.1 gave us a first hint about the complexity of a possible assessment of the 'us' and the 'other' – potentially, the 'enemy'. Geopolitics is almost mythical when it offers clarity and insight in a complex world. It may reduce openness to the geographical diversity of the world and repress questioning and difference, or open up these questions. International relations are characterized by a multitude of decision-making bodies. They are polycentric and have been interpreted as an 'anarchy of politics' due to the many different bodies that are influenced by very different geopolitical forces. Through the discipline of geopolitics, the plurality of the world may well be reduced to certain 'transcendent truths' about strategy, or help analyse, assess and predict events. This is where the challenge lies.

The state is a political unit. States are separated by boundaries drawn between them, sometimes consistent with the territories inhabited by particular nations; for instance, most French live in France, but France also contains minorities of other nations, like the Basques in France and Spain. We also find states that divide nations, or that are constituted of several nations. The state is built on a monocentric basis. It may channel and represent the interests of its citizens and industry through engaging in international relations, interacting with other decision-making bodies and their interests.

The state is also characterized by its right to control territory within its boundaries. Territory has three aspects: a piece of land, seen as sacred heritage; a seat of power; and a functional space. These aspects define identity, authority over a population defined by its residence, and efficiency (administrative or economic). Sovereignty is the recognition of these rights, implying jurisdiction of this state within its boundaries.

A nation is here defined on the basis of culture, religion, language, ethnicity, sharing common cultural traits and a sense of self-identification. A nation can be distinguished from other groups of people, for instance the Scottish, French and Welsh. States with many nations within their boundaries include Canada, Switzerland, Belgium, South Africa, and especially

Russia and India. Many nations are divided among different states, like Arabs, Kurds, Germans and Koreans. The permeability of borders and the quantitative rise of non-governmental and non-national actors has marked contemporary geopolitical analysis profoundly.

These characteristics are the basis of global geopolitical analysis. Through such analysis, rational decision-makers can generate measurable results on the basis of well-specified calculations of risk, resources and space, in foreign policy as well as in international business. The following section attempts to examine the impact of current and future events in the light of 09/11 from a geopolitical perspective on risk assessment.

5.4   THE GEOPOLITICAL IMPACT OF SEPTEMBER 11

Important literature was added to the classical literature on geopolitics, engaging in a discussion of power and ideology, of the strength or of the decline of the US 'empire'.[10] This literature explores the 'clash of civiliza-tions',[11] or a global anarchy to come, with a weak Europe and an increas-ingly strong US,[12] or the division of the rich democratic nations, with a nation-state focus of the US, and a desire for an international community focus by the majority of the EU.[13] The European Union, born from the ashes of two world wars, arose from the belief of a handful of diplomats, statesmen and businessmen in the force of economic collaboration for peace between nations. Norman Stone argues that Europe exists because the US wants it to, in order to prevent the historical 'Euro-anarchy'.[14] Through the many phases of Euro-pessimism and Euro-optimism, member states have achieved the highest degree of international integration yet con-cluded on the globe.

5.4.1   A Watershed in Geopolitics

September 11 is commonly recognized as one of the most significant geo-political events of recent years, a watershed of similar degree to the world wars, the Cold War and the collapse of the Soviet Union. It is also the first momentum of geopolitical change in the new millennium. The fundamen-tal concepts of geopolitics, the notion of the nation, the state and the nation-state, have been subject to great changes ever since the end of the Cold War, the last phase of what Bobbitt argues to be the twentieth-century-long epochal war. Sovereignty, as well as boundaries and territory, shifted simultaneously with the transfer of primarily economic power structures due to globalization and economic integration of structures all over the world. At the same time, we recognize a counter-shift towards strong localization; nations have become more conscious about their identity, roots and differentiation from other nations.[15]

Bobbitt and Howard (2002), from the political economy approach, argue that the future will see markets struggle under US hegemonic leadership to counteract uncertainty and global threat under US-created universal law. Through the geopolitical move towards globalization and the subsequent reinforcement of localization, nations have become important actors in geopolitics, comparable to the wave of non-governmental organizations in the 1980s. These actors supplement the power position long exercised by the state or political system, by functional international organizations, functional regional organizations and also federal global organizations (like the UN). Associations or alliances between sovereign states (like NATO, but also military *ad hoc* coalitions, as we have observed against Iraq) have, with the new wave of warfare against terrorism, become essential to the redesigning of world order. The international economically and politically predominant situation of the US, since the end of the Cold War, has been complemented and reinforced by its supremacy in the military sphere. But vulnerability has not decreased in terms of national security.

The end of the Cold War dramatically changed the geopolitical situation[16] of the main 'battlefields' of this era – Western Europe, Eastern and Central Europe, but also the Third World and developing countries. Globalization challenged development prospects: alignment with superpowers was superfluous. Western foreign investment started to divert into better-developed Eastern European countries. Economic and increasing political stability accompanied this trend in the new EU candidate countries, but not in the developing world. Arguably, the political economic approach submerged ideological theory. But in nationalism (encountered in less-developed economies and in poverty more than in the rich ones) there is additionally challenged stability of the latter regions: the failure of a balance of rights for minorities and nationalist desires for homeland have resulted in increasing civil conflict or cultural genocide in these regions.[17] Political risk focused hence on on-the-spot trade relations and corporate activity, rather than a global approach, yet too rare in a globalized and vulnerable world. Does this mean that poverty is a main creator of the kind of terrorism that we came to know on 09/11? Henwood states that this would mean ignoring that East Asia and Latin America have not produced major currents of this new terrorism, despite the important global capital flows of the last decades.[18] Laqueur argues that terrorism also exists without inequalities.[19] While poverty and social inequality have historically been a feeding ground for fanaticism and extremism, they are not exclusive or essential for the breeding of terrorist activity.

Preparing for the demands of the future means taking into account that the world adds 200 000 people every day. The world is divided between 'haves' and 'have nots' that are exposed to the transitivity of a continuous rise in globalization, of systemic vulnerability, and of threat. This underlines the political economy approach.

5.4.2 A Watershed for International Business?

The internationalization of business continues as part of both phenomena: business plans are prepared on a multinational scale, and need to take into account geopolitical and cultural diversity, and to tackle foreign competition and transnational collaborations. Sustainable growth needs to be intertwined with social responsibilities, and risk and disaster management need to be recognized as an integral part of international strategy formulation. The difference in economic structure of less-developed countries relative to developed countries is stunning: a high dependency on primary and secondary sectors of the economy, with the obvious different degrees of efficiency and ambiguity of development in the poorly developed tertiary and quaternary sectors. While the European Union is the most important donor of development aid, less than one-third of FDI goes into the developing world, due to instability and other unfavourable external factors of the markets.[20] What has really changed is that the risk that we are assessing:

- is diversified and global;
- increases the focus on geopolitical turmoil and global terrorism;
- potentially impacts upon international business anywhere in the world, not necessarily directly but indirectly through the consequence of uncertainty curbed by the inter-connectability of corporate activity to the domestic and international business environment.

Huntington, certainly the political scientist with currently the strongest ideological impact on US foreign policy, was quoted after 09/11 expressing his views about today's world:

> It is a dangerous place, in which large numbers of people resent our wealth, power, culture, and vigorously oppose our efforts to persuade or coerce them to accept our values of human rights, democracy and capitalism. In this world America must learn to distinguish among our true friends, who will be with us and we with them, through thick and thin; opportunistic allies with whom we have some but not all interests in common; strategic partner-competitors with whom we have a mixed relationship; antagonists who are rivals but with whom negotiation is possible; and unrelenting enemies who will try to destroy us unless we destroy them first.[21]

While Huntington nuanced his words, explaining that his aim is to possibly avoid a clash of civilizations, well aware that this clash is the aim of al-Qaida,[22] his wording[23] raises questions about the cited values and the methods of spreading them. The quote firstly requires a reflection about the often-used analogy on geo-strategic priorities by some EU members, by the US in the times of Nazi Germany. Secondly, a deeper look at geo-economic forces that are part of international politics is needed. Thirdly, what are the implications of change in geopolitical thinking for international business?

5.5 GEOPOLITICAL CHANGE SHAPING THE INTERNATIONAL BUSINESS ENVIRONMENT

The analysis of an analogy between Saddam Hussein's Iraq and Nazi Germany demonstrates that we can assume resistance to Hitler had waited too long. A pre-emptive strike of the kind we saw against Hussein's regime in Iraq, at the time of Munich, would have been the end of the terror of that time.[24] Does this imply that 09/11 is cause and consequence of the expansion of the 2001/2002 warfare, first targeting Afghanistan, to legitimate the 2003 Iraq war and the possibility of prospective wars? Nazi Germany at the time had a strong industrial base, military allies and one 'Aryan' mobilization against the Jewish part of the population in particular. This was not the case in Hussein's Iraq. The ex-regime was linked to tyranny, the abuse of the rule of law and human rights, the breaking of UN rules, and its link to terrorism had to be condemned. The international communities' resistance to military intervention at the time chosen by the US reflects the general belief in Europe and elsewhere that these issues could have been solved through the UN. However, the European voice is not united, and lacks power.

The means used in counter-action to 09/11 can be claimed as dangerous, insofar as peripheral states without the same democratic and humane values as the US might well take the same intrusion as their right. Also, the war against Iraq dealt with the defiance of UN resolutions on weapons of mass destruction. These weapons have, at the time of writing this analysis, not been found. But the same threat is also valid in other countries such as Israel, Pakistan and North Korea. Human rights abuse is equally not reserved to the Iraqi regime, but is known in many other countries of the world. Links to al-Qaida can be found in Saudi Arabia and elsewhere.

The critical geopolitical theory emphasizes the inter-twining of geography, politics and political economy factors. Geo-economists turn to an analysis of resource factors in this 09/11 war scenario for an explanation, and therefore attempt to look at visible and often consequences of geopolitical

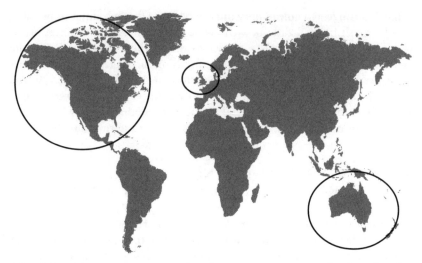

Map 5.1   A hegemony scenario (circles represent centres of political and economic power)

change to the international business environment. Iraq possesses the second-biggest oil reserves in the world, which are technologically easy and economically low-cost to exploit. Access to this resource in addition geographically frees the way between the Caspian Sea and the Mediterranean for oil export logistics. This transforms the world energy market completely. It has the potential to revive the US and thus benefit the world economy. At a downturn of the beginning of the twenty-first century, this may open the Middle East to major investment flows from international business. It also reduces dependence on OPEC and Saudi Arabia. On the other hand, FDI may stagnate or decrease due to uncertainty and risk factors prevailing in the region (see Chapter 8).

On the basis of changes in the geopolitical order, alternative future structure scenarios can then be developed. This scenario development could help in risks assessment by the corporation. For instance, a first scenario (see Map 5.1) assumes that the US dominates the world as a hegemony. The hegemony succeeds in installing its law and values as universal. It is then a power that the rest of the world become vessels to. Ramonet (2002), for example, states that under pressure from the US 'to sign up against Iraq, we see nominally sovereign states allowing themselves to be reduced to the demeaning status of satellites'. He argues that the US national security strategy re-established the rights of preventive war as used in 1941. It abolishes, under this perspective, the international law principles in a Westphalian international system.

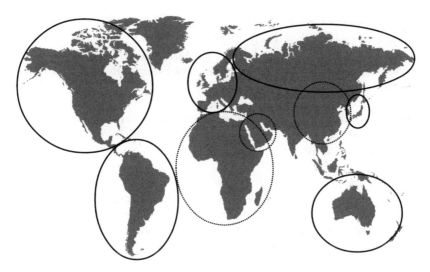

Map 5.2   A multipolar scenario

A second scenario (see Map 5.2) imagines a multipolarization of the international community in which Europe, China and Russia play an essential role next to the US, in which the UN does not (*ex-post*) legalize the war against Hussein's Iraq. The UN would thus regain power and credibility.

In terms of geopolitical risk assessment, scenario 2 provides more complexity but a higher degree of diversity. These and other scenarios, based on different post-09/11 terrorism perspectives, need to tackle the complexity of assessment that will only be useful tools if not potentially self-fulfilling prophecies of disaster assessment that could be tools to international business and terrorists, that may see terrorists substitute easier targets for less accessible ones (Crenshaw, 2001). Would their impact still be the same? We will discuss this point below.

For quantitative and qualitative risk assessment and research, it will be useful to define and narrow the criteria on which the risk ratio of alternative future geopolitical scenarios can be calculated for corporate purposes, as a basis for the extension of loss-modelling to operational resilience planning in international business.

5.6   WAR, TERRORISM AND GENERAL SECURITY RISK ASSESSMENT

Technology has globalized the economy, and changed the face of risk and emerging threat. When we study the main types of war and conflict, as classified by the United Nations, we notice that interstate wars (state-to-state wars such as Iran–Iraq) are mostly about territory and resources, unresolved boundary issues (often on a historical basis) or the artificial imposition of boundaries by outside forces (through modern or past colonialism), when either:

(a) nations are artificially united, resulting in civil wars (Nigeria) or genocide; or
(b) nations are divided (Somalia).

Civil wars, in which groups within a state fight, often between nations, ethnic groups or separatist movements (Northern Ireland, Afghanistan, but also terrorism and secessionism like the Basque region or Corsica), reveal the instrumentalization of culture or religion for mainly social, political or economic aims of groups in the population that do not benefit from the same opportunities and advantages.[25] In both types of warfare, irredentism is a supplementary cause: it is the desire to bring into the state all areas that were once part of it and make a frontier. World wars that take place between blocs of states often resulted from alliances that formed according to politico-economic interests. We may include the Cold War in this category, in which superpower competition was the impetus to establish spheres of interest. German public opinion in particular, which has been traumatized by centuries of warfare and guilt, has feared since 09/11 that a world war may be triggered through the US reaction to terrorist intrusion. Uncertainty, going further than assessable risk, is linked to the threat of terrorism, the act of terrorism itself, and the threat that the aftermath of terrorism bears in political reaction.

Following ASIS International (2003), general security risk assessment guidelines could be encouraged to follow a process flowchart that has been adapted to the argument, as illustrated in Figure 5.2. This framework model can be applied to geopolitical scenario planning and political risk assessment, and incorporates the quantitative and qualitative assessment of effects on international value chain activities. Terrorism as a risk for the international corporation can be clearly categorized into three levels of analysis (as are discussed in this chapter): it is useful to distinguish terrorist threat, act and aftermath. The three components help assess the direct and indirect impact on competitive advantage, comparative advantage and return on investment (discussed by McIntyre and Travis in Chapter 8).

This necessitates a clear and objective identification of assets and actors at the start, and of the feasibility of options in correlation to potential loss and disruption and their cost. The frequency of events, although difficult to define due to an apparent 'random' nature of terrorism, can nevertheless

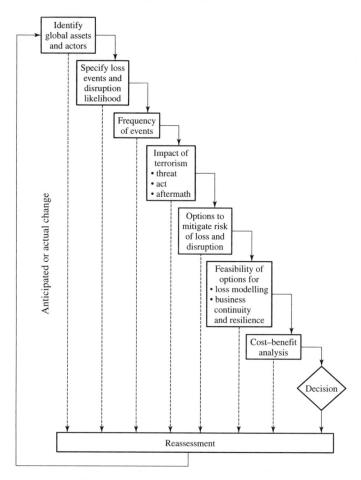

Figure 5.2   Geopolitical security risk assessment: a general framework

be pinned down through empirical data accessible from police, security or insurance companies. ASIS International proposes the equation of $P = f:n$, with P defined as the probability of event, f as the number of actual occurrences of that event, and n as the total number of experiments seeking that event, then ranked on a chart ranging from highly likely to barely likely. [26]

You want to evaluate the impact of the threat on the company. A big threat that has a small probability of appearance might be considered to be as important as a small threat that has a big probability of appearance. For better understanding, for instance, consider what is more sensitive for your company: to have 300 dead in a plane crash every six months or 300 dead on the roads every day? Is the likelihood of your CEO dying on the road bigger than him or her dying in a plane? Will this risk entail a geopolitically significant aftermath because of certain conditions prevailing in the event?

The risk is the probability (P) multiplied by the impact (I),

$$R = P \times I$$

with impact being the amount of money you will lose, and the probability of operational resilience. This means the best-operations-scenario for your firm to work under the impact of terrorist threat, act and aftermath in the international business environment. If the geopolitical impact is small and the probability low, you will not consider a mitigation of risk feasible, because you will not encounter a cost–benefit ratio that would lead you to reassess the way you operate internationally even in times of crises. If the risk is high, assets can be redistributed in a manner that ensures operational resilience throughout the crisis.

Firms cannot entirely redirect their operations away from a global risk. UN Resolution 1368 of 12 September 2001 stated that any terrorist activity must be considered as a threat to international peace and security.[27] The concept of the 'enemy', the other, the different and the one that 'merits hate' (as exploited through the instrumentalization of religion in all warfare, immoral as the concept appears), creates interior instability and public support necessary for warfare. This is the blaming of somebody on the outside or inside of structures, with a certain artificial indifference to reality, and is used in all conflicting scenarios. The concept is a profound force in the mythical quality of classical geopolitical theory. 'Place death' is the destruction of a civilian area or strategic location in order to undermine the morale of the public. It is an instrument that has been used ever since war has been known. It is this aspect of terrorism that has the most direct impact on business: since 09/11, the strategy of place death has complemented terrorism to a dimension as yet unknown.

Nevertheless, the number of companies that were brought to a complete halt was relatively small, relative to the indirect impact on international business as examined in the chapters of this book. (Post-)09/11 terrorism may well, in the long run, continue to target companies, tourist business and financial centres, as easy targets.

5.7   CONCLUSION

The world has never been as organized (into state, international, inter-governmental and non-governmental structures) as it is at the beginning of this millennium. This network of regional and quasi-universal legal order has shown a capacity for conflict prevention hitherto unachieved, but does not decrease vulnerability and threat through inherently asymmetric terrorism.

This is where the discipline of geopolitical risk assessment could play an increasingly meaningful role in offering a new model aiming at loss-modelling followed by operational resilience planning in international business. Avoiding explicit Machiavellian attempts to provide advice, geopolitics in risk assessment must deconstruct superficial ways in which we may read the world political map, but become a useful tool to prioritize risk, assets and operations in the diverse risk scenarios, in preparation for direct and indirect rupture effects. Geopolitics is by its nature a victim of subjectivity – looking at the world from one perspective. Knowledge is always situated knowledge, articulating the perspective of certain cultures and subjects, but it must not ignore that of others. The author of this chapter argues that the threat of terrorism, the act of terrorism itself and its aftermath can be classified in complementarity to political risk, but rather under the label of 'geopolitical risk' or 'turmoil'. Geopolitics can be useful for corporations to assess risk on a scale comparable to that used by post-09/11 terrorism for threat.

Underlying geopolitics in the post-09/11 era does not argue that territory is constituted of nature and is organic. Deeper reading of such assumptions lead to dangerous extensions of the nature-based concept of geography, that is, certain parts of the world are underdeveloped, or 'backward' because of their spatial location on the earth. In this discourse, 'history' and 'geography' serve as *deus ex machina* explanations for conflict. Of course, a more considered view of geography, and its politics, is that in fact most geography is man-made and defined.[28] Thus geopolitics as a discipline can only ever be subjective in its methodology. Once the fundamental subjectivity of the discipline is accepted, and the analysis prioritized, it becomes highly useful as a tool for decision-making in international business risk assessment that goes deeper than quantitative analysis of a 'global' political risk.

For sociologists Anthony Giddens and Ulrich Beck, industrialization has been so successful that it has created a new form of modernity, a reflexive modernity of 'risk society'. Industrial society is a victim of its own success: 'high-powered industrial dynamism is skidding into a new society without a bang of a revolution, bypassing political debates and decisions in parliaments and governments' (Beck, 1996, p. 26). Industrial society is attempting to confront globalized techno-scientific risks. International business tries to deal with a different, more complex and vulnerable environment that contains direct and indirect threats to its operations.

Overall, international business operations must transcend the classical opposition of interior and exterior, of public and private, of political and social, and of national and international in geopolitics in order to assess risk through transitivity. This is the basis for the conceptualizing of risk management on a global level today that, akin to the traditional market imperfections that international business faces, reduces inefficiencies in the case of rupture.

NOTES

1.   Compare amongst others Tunander et al. (1997) and Huntington (1993) pp. 22–49.
2.   See in particular Huntington (1996), Kaplan (2000) and Gray (1995).
3.   See also Bailey (2003), pp. 49–65.
4.   See Kaplan (2002), Barber (2003).
5.   Thornton (2002), p. 3.
6.   For a discussion of these figures see O'Loughlin (1994). For a consideration of traditions of geopolitics see Dodds and Atkinson (1999).
7.   For a study of power politics and offensive realism, see for instance Mearsheimer (2001).
8.   This diversity is more drastic between less-developed and developed countries; LDCs nevertheless traditionally have less nuanced historically influenced schools of political thought.
9.   Spengler (1990) in 1918–20, in an attempt to shape a philosophy that would predict the main historical events, criticized the traditional conception of history as a series of independent processes divided in periods, but argued that world history (and amongst it the West) consists of cultures that pass through different phases of cyclic levels, in a life cycle from youth through maturity and old age to death. The last one is here called 'civilization', a period of decline from which there was no escape. Spengler upheld the ideal of obedience to the state and supported German hegemony in Europe. His refusal to support Nazi theories of racial superiority led to his ostracism after the Nazis came to power in 1933.
10.   For instance Todd (2002).
11.   Huntington (1993; 1997; 1998), *The Clash of Civilizations* has been a 2002/03 bestseller for *Foreign Affairs*, the journal that had published the article and book in the 1990s.
12.   Kaplan (2002).
13.   Algieri (2003).
14.   Stone (1992).
15.   Braden and Shelley (2000), Friedmann (1990).
16.   Kaplan (2001) states: 'The Cold War had . . . been won. [by the West]'. It might be more precise to state 'the Cold War was lost by the East', which is not the same.
17.   For more information on this issue, see www.geoscopie.com and www.un.org.
18.   Henwood (2001).
19.   Laqueur (1987), p. 381.
20.   Economist Intelligence Unit (2002).
21.   Kaplan (2001).
22.   See Thornton (2002), p. 4.
23.   It may remind somewhat of Frederick the Great of Prussia's 'Diplomacy without arms is like music without instruments'.
24.   Fallows (2002).
25.   Chenu in *Le Monde Diplomatique* (2003).
26.   ASIS International (2003), p. 16.
27.   S/RES/1368 (2001) of 12 September 2001.
28.   The word itself, geography, means 'earth writing', which implies a superimposition of artificial lines on the earth.

REFERENCES

Agnew, John (1998), *Geopolitics: Re-visioning World Politics*, London: Routledge.
Algieri, Franco (2003), 'Europa am Ende der Unschuld', *Sueddeutsche Zeitung*, 11–18 April.
Almond, G. et al. (2000), *Comparative Politics Today: A World View*, London: Longman.
Anderlini, S.A. (ed.) (2000), *The European Union, Conflict Prevention and NGO Contributions*, Brussels: FEWER.
Arquilla, J. (1997), *In Athena's Camp: Preparing for Conflict in the Information Age*, Santa Monica: RAND Corporation.
Arquilla, J. (2001), *Networks and Netwars: The Future of Terror, Crime and Militancy*, Santa Monica: RAND Corporation.
ASIS International (2003), *General Security Risk Assessment Guideline*, Alexandria, VA.
Bailey, M.N. (2003), 'The year in review: a turning point?', in Peter K. Cornelius, Michael E. Porter and Klaus Schwab (eds) (2003), *The Global Competitiveness Report 2002–2003*, World Economic Forum, New York and Oxford: Oxford University Press.
Barber, Benjamin R. (1992), *Jihad vs. McWorld*, New York: Ballantine Books.
Barber, Benjamin R. (2003), *Fear's Empire: War, Terrorism and Democracy*, New York: W.W. Norton.
Beck, U. (1996), *The Reinvention of Politics: Rethinking Modernity in the Global Social Order*, London: Polity Press.
Bloomfield, L.P. (ed.) (2002), 'Global markets and national interests: defending the US Home – the new geopolitics of energy, capital and information', *CSIS Significant Issues Series*, July 2002.
Bobbitt, P. and M. Howard (2002), *The Shield of Achilles: War, Peace, and the Course of History*, New York: Knopf.
Braden, K.E. and F.M. Shelley (2000), *Engaging Geopolitics*, Harlow: Pearson Education.
Cohen, S.B. (1964), *Geography and Politics in a Divided World*, 1st edition, Oxford: Oxford University Press.
COFACE (2002), *The Handbook of Country Risk*, London: Kogan Page.
Cole, L. (1996), *The Eleventh Plague: The Politics of Biological and Chemical Warfare*, New York: W.H. Freeman.
Commission of the European Communities (2000), *Single Market Scoreboard 2000*, Brussels: CEC.
Cornelius, Peter K., Michael E. Porter and Klaus Schwab (eds) (2003), *The Global Competitiveness Report 2002–2003*, World Economic Forum, New York and Oxford: Oxford University Press.
Crenshaw, M. (2001), 'Counterterrorism policy and the political process', *Studies in Conflict and Terrorism*, **24** (September–October), 329–37.
Dodds, K. and D. Atkinson (eds) (1999), *Geopolitical Traditions: Critical Histories of a Century of Geopolitical Thought*, London: Routledge.
Economist Intelligence Unit (2002), *The World in 2003*, London: The Economist.
Fallows, J. (2002), 'The fifty-first state?', *Atlantic*, November, **290** (4), 53–62.
Falkenrath, R., R. Newman and B. Thayer (1998), *America's Achilles Heel: Nuclear, Biological and Chemical Terrorism and Covert Attack*, Cambridge, MA: MIT Press.

78   *The geopolitical and geo-economic environment*

Friedmann, Jonathan (1990) 'Being in the world: globalization and localization', in Mike Featherstone (ed.), *Global Nationalism, Globalization and Modernity*, London: Sage.

Géopolitique (2001), *Après le 11 Septembre*, No. 76, December, Paris.

Giddens, Anthony (1994), *Beyond Left and Right*, Cambridge: Stanford University Press.

Giddens, Anthony (2002), *Runaway World: How Globalization is Reshaping our Lives*, New York: Routledge.

Gray, John (1995), *Enlightenment's Wake: Politics and Culture at the Close of the Modern Age*, London: Routledge.

Henwood, D. (2001), 'Terrorism and Globalization', *The Nation*, 21 November.

Hoffman, Bruce (1999), *Terrorismus, der unerklaerte Krieg. Neue Gefahren politischer Gewalt*, Frankfurt: S. Fischer.

Huntington, S.P. (1993), 'The clash of civilizations?', *Foreign Affairs*, **72** (3), 22–49.

Huntington, S.P. (1996), *The Clash of Civilisations and the Remaking of World Order*, New York: Simon and Schuster.

Huntington, S.P. (1997), 'The Erosion of American national interests', *Foreign Affairs* **76** (5), 38–40.

Huntington, S.P. (1998), *The Clash of Civilizations and The Remaking of the World Order*, New York: Touchstone.

Innis, H.A. and J.O.M. Broek (1945), 'Geography and nationalism', *Geographical Review*, 301–11.

Isaak, Robert A. (2000), *Managing World Economic Change: International Political Economy*, London: Prentice Hall.

Kagan, Robert (2003), *Paradise and Power: America and Europe in the New World Order*, London: Atlantic Books.

Kaplan, R. (2000), *The Coming Anarchy: Shattering the Dreams of the Post Cold War*, New York: Vintage Books.

Kaplan, R (2001), 'Looking the World in the Eye', *Atlantic*, December.

Kaplan, R. (2002), 'The World in 2005', *Atlantic*, March.

Klare, M. (1995), *Rogue States and Nuclear Outlaws*, New York: Hill and Wang.

Larçon, J. and B. Ramamantsoa (2000), *Europe's Strong Suit*, European Business Forum.

Lampton, D. (ed.) (2000), *Major Power Relations in Northeast Asia: Win–Win or Zero-Sum Game*, Washington, DC: Brookings Institution Press and Tokyo: Japan Centre for International Exchange.

La Decouverte (ed.) (2001), *L'Etat du Monde 2002*, Paris.

Lagadec, P. (1993), *Preventing Chaos in Crisis*, Maidenhead: McGraw-Hill Europe.

Laqueur, Walter (1987), *Terrorismus*, Frankfurt/Main and Berlin: Ullstein; translated from *The Age of Terrorism*, London: Weidenfeld & Nicolson.

Laqueur, Walter (2003), *No End to War: Terrorism in the Twentyfirst Century*, New York and London: Continuum International Publication.

Le Monde Diplomatique (2003), *L'Atlas du Monde Diplomatique*, Paris: Le Monde.

Lewis, B. (2002), 'What went wrong?', *Atlantic*, January.

Livingstone, Neil C. (1990), *The Cult of Counter-Terrorism*, Lexington, MA: Lexington Books.

Mackinder, H.J. (1904), 'The geographical pivot of history', *Geographical Journal*, **23** (2), 421–42.

Mann, M. (1993), *The Sources of Social Power. Volume II*, Cambridge: Cambridge University Press.

Mearsheimer, John J. (2001), *The Tragedy of Great Power Politics*, New York: Norton.

Micklethwait, J. and A. Wooldridge (2000), *A Future Perfect*, London: William Heinemann.

Morabia, A. (1993), *Le Gihad dans l'Islam médiéval*, Paris: Albin Michel.

O'Loughlin, J. (ed.) (1994), *The Dictionary of Geopolitics*, Westport, CT: Greenwood.

Ó Tuathail, G. (1999), 'Deterritorialized threats and global dangers: geopolitics, risk society and reflexive modernization', *Geopolitics*, 3 (3), 17–33.

Picht, R. (ed.)(1995), *Agir pour l'Europe: Les Relations Franco-Allemandes dans l'Après-Guerre Froide.*

Pwblf (1998), 'Business as partners in development' and 'Building competitiveness and communities'?, www.pwblf.com.

Ramonet, I. (2002), 'Servile states', *Le Monde Diplomatique*, October.

Revel, Jean-François (2002), *L'Obsession Anti-américaine: son fonctionnement, ses causes, ses inconséquences*, Paris: Plon.

Rosser, B. and M. Rosser (1996), *Comparative Economics in a Transforming World Economy*, New York: Irwin.

Shapiro, M. (1994), 'Moral geographies and the ethics of post-sovereignty', *Public Culture*, 6, 479–502.

Short, J.R. (1982), *Introduction to Political Geography*, London: Routledge.

Spengler, Oswald (1990), *The Decline of the West*, vols 1 and 2: 1918–22 and 1926–28, Oxford: Oxford University Press.

Stone, Norman (1992), *The European* 14–17 May, 21.

Suder, Gabriele (1994), *Geopolitical Management: The Case of Eurocopter*, Cranfield: European Case Clearing House Case Studies.

Thornton, William H. (2002), 'Balance of terror: the geopolitics of empire vs. jihad', *Perspectives on Evil and Human Wickedness*, 1 (2), 109–15, www.wickedness.net.

Tunander, O., P. Baev and V. Einagel (eds) (1997), *Geopolitics in Post-Wall Europe: Security, Territory and Identity*, London: Sage.

Todd, E. (2002), *Après l'Empire*, Paris: Gallimard.

Wallerstein I. (1974), *The Modern World-System: Capitalist Agriculture and the Origins of the European World-Economy in the Sixteenth Century*, New York: Academic Press.

Weigert, H.W., H. Brodie and E. Doherty (1957), *Principles of Political Geography*, New York: Appleton Century – Crofts.

PART II

The trade and investment environment

6. The impact of geopolitical turmoil on country risk and global investment strategy

Michel Henri Bouchet

INTRODUCTION

One of the conclusions of this chapter is that the September 11, 2001 terrorist attack coupled with the Afghan and Iraqi pre-emptive wars coincide with a major and probably long-lasting reassessment of country risk. The global terrorist threat catalyses a number of emerging risks that stem from higher and wider volatility in the global economy, including in the economic, financial and socio-political spheres. More than ever, market globalization coincides with risk globalization.

September 11 and the Afghan and Iraq wars have a two-pronged impact. First, geopolitical turmoil reactivates and globalizes containment, given that terrorism replaces communism as a widespread security threat. Second, it feeds a perverse dialectic between stateless violence and enhanced security measures, both within the 30 Organization for Economic Cooperation and Development (OECD) countries and in the developing nations. In addition, the combination of mounting global terrorism, tighter banking regulations and a worldwide economic slowdown reduce market access prospects for emerging countries and increase the scope of liquidity difficulties. Foreign direct investment (FDI) flows have shrunk since their peak of 2000 and trade tensions are mounting between Europe, North America, Japan and the emerging market countries (EMCs). In the OECD, the protracted impact of the Internet bubble reinforces the negative wealth effect of the stock market decline and prospects of a housing market value correction. The Japanese banking system is in need of a thorough restructuring with a solid capital base and a sound portfolio. Japan is thus no longer a regional growth engine. In the US, the banking system faces a rise in consumer debt equal to more than 100 per cent of annual private income. Any rise in short-term interest rates will increase the spectre of mounting non-performing loans. The European banking sector, notably in Germany, remains fragile. All in all, developed and developing countries face a number of long-standing impediments to growth and their impact is compounded by geopolitical turmoil.

These negative trends pave the way for a gloomy economic outlook. What fully modifies the scope of risk the global economy faces is precisely that it is global. Strong and lasting global growth belongs to the past, given the many risks and vulnerabilities that spill over and create volatility. Slower and more erratic growth might in fact be the new reality. As the global economy becomes an 'echo chamber' that propagates and accentuates imbalances, it is doomed to face cycles of stop-and-go. Investors and lenders are worried about the reliability of corporate governance and accounting statements. The absence of institutional stabilization mechanisms, such as a 'lender of last resort' fund, makes the global economy vulnerable to shocks like never before. Worldwide income inequalities within and among countries impede the conditions of stable and sustaining growth. They feed social disorder, migrations and political upheaval. Whereas economic planning gets more and more refined and sophisticated, and the ideology of economic development, as a vector of progress, becomes the dominant paradigm, many face the loss of their future.

Rising risks without traditional warning signals thus require the risk analysts to be more agile, broad-minded and innovative than in the past. Volatility and complexity make quantitative assessment of country risk, including ratings and rankings, at best partial tools and at worst recipes for simplistic outlooks. The shortcomings of ratings and panel-based market consensus methods has been exemplified on the eve of the Asian crisis. They are still larger in the aftermath of 09/11. Only an array of converging analytical approaches can lead to a more rigorous examination of the economic, institutional and socio-political fabric that holds or distorts a country's development path. The latter can be defined as economic growth coupled with those conditions that make it sustainable. These conditions include a legitimate political power base, social mobilization, sound institutions and robust infrastructures.[1]

6.1   THE END OF INNOCENCE AND THE SANCTUARY LOSS

For some time after the 1865 Civil War, the US government attempted to pursue its traditional policy of isolationism. But Americans, gradually and maybe reluctantly, turned their attention from internal events to active participation in international affairs and overseas expansion. By the beginning of the twentieth century, the United States had finally emerged as a world power. Furthermore, after the Second World War, the US adjusted to the systemic 'imperatives' for 'there was no other nation capable of establishing a balance in a new world order characterised by the collapse of Europe, Soviet expansion, Chinese resurgence, and the birth of a multitude of new nations in the Third World between East and West'.[2]

Our view is that 09/11 will mark a global extension of the 1947 'containment policy'. The latter was developed in the aftermath of the Second World War, when US foreign policy had to meet the Soviet challenge. When George Kennan, the Foreign Service's foremost expert on the Soviet Union, developed his conceptual framework, he stressed that the Soviet Union had no community of interest with the capitalist states, thereby managing its relationships with the Western powers in terms of deeply-rooted innate ideological antagonism. The latter would continue until the capitalist world had been destroyed. There was no peace horizon: 'Like the Church, communism is dealing with ideological concepts which are of a long-term validity, and it can afford to be patient. It has no compunction about retreating in the face of superior forces. The main thing is that there should always be pressure, constant pressure, toward the desired goal.'[3] To pursue the analogy, the Truman 'Doctrine', coined in the President's speech on 12 March 1947, can also be put in parallel with George Bush's 'axis of evil' and 'rogue states' doctrine that he elaborated on in the course of 2002. The United States and the Western nations, Truman emphasized, could survive only in a world in which freedom flourished. And the US would not realize this long-term objective without being willing to help free peoples to maintain their institutions and their national integrity against aggressive movements that seek to impose upon their totalitarian regimes. This is so because the latter undermine the foundations of international peace and hence the security of the United States.

The September 11, 2001 terrorist attack reactivated and globalizes US containment policy, thereby maintaining the pendulum far towards the interventionist posture of the United States. In many instances, 09/11 raises a global threat similar to that of the Soviet Union back in the late 1940s. Today, terrorism replaces communism as the driver of containment. This containment strategy has been revived at a time when the Iraqi crisis is nothing more than a milestone after 09/11 and the Afghan crisis in the long-term US strategy to eradicate terrorism. Other military interventions are likely, and permanent 'vigilance' is the new posture. The ultimate objective is a global extension of President Theodore Roosevelt's 'Big Stick' policy, aimed at 'making the world safe for democracy'. The dialectic between transnational violence and pre-emptive containment has a deep impact on the global economic outlook.

6.2   GEOPOLITICAL TURMOIL, TERRORISM AND COUNTRY RISK: ONE-TIME SECURITY EARTHQUAKE OR PROTRACTED SEISMIC DAMAGES?

What are the long-term implications of 09/11 for global investment strategies? Terrorism – premeditated, politically motivated violence perpetrated against non-combatant targets by subnational groups or clandestine agents[4] – is certainly on the front burner of cross-border investment strategies. For the risk analyst, the twofold question is (1) whether global terrorism and political violence are salient and lasting risk parameters, and if so, (2) how to take this into account, anticipate it and cover it.

There are two ways to look at the rising threat of globalized terrorism. There are those who think that the 09/11 attacks' unintended result was to test the resilience of the global financial markets. They also consider the Iraq war purged the global tensions and has cut through the midst of uncertainty. The Federal Reserve System's flexible response with its liquidity injection, as well as the concerted actions of official monetary institutions, are proofs of the ultimate resistance of the capitalist system, reportedly. Though September 11 was an unprecedented exogenous shock, the terrorist attack on the largest economic nation did not trigger any financial meltdown nor any major economic recession worldwide. Terrorism did not achieve a systemic crisis in the global economy. Clearly, terrorist-related uncertainty in emerging and industrialized countries involves a cost, both direct and indirect, that affects private business activities. However, this cost can be covered by a range of political risk insurances, both private (for example OPIC, Coface) and public (MIGA). Moreover, the attack on the United States has prompted the US foreign policy's pendulum to shift decisively toward unilateral global interventionism, with a view to eradicate terrorism and the 'axis of evil' in the 'rogue states'. The inescapable conclusion is that terrorism and geopolitical turmoil will impose concerted international action to make the world safer for democracy under US military supremacy and ideology guidance. This is the price to pay for preserving a sustainable globalization process. Federal Reserve chairman Alan Greenspan expressed robust optimism observing there is still considerable scope for expansion in international trade and capital flows, despite signs that financial globalization is nearing maturity.[5]

On the opposite side, there are those who think the terrorist attack will mark a turnaround in the global economy and that 'things will never be the same again'. The attack is symptomatic of a deeply-rooted fragmentation of the international system, that is increasingly polarized by ideology, income gaps and religious beliefs. According to this view, a 'clash of civilizations' looms on the horizon as Samuel Huntington puts it.[6] Contrary to a superficial reading of mere abstracts, Huntington does not take major intercivilizational wars for granted. He suggests the avoidance of such wars requires core states (that is, the US, *inter alii*) to refrain from intervening in conflicts in other civilizations. In other words, spheres of influence must be clearly drawn and rigorously respected. This would mark the return to a strict reading of the Monroe Doctrine as well as the long-term unfolding of US post 09/11 unilateral military interventionism. What Huntington announces, however, is the emergence of mounting tensions coming from 'torn countries', that is, those in which two or more civilizations coexist within their borders. Given the global dissemination of Western market-oriented values, the number of torn countries is about to grow and politico-cultural tension is about to rise.

This second school considers 09/11 as a watershed that has and will have deeply-rooted effects on globalization. This is Ulrich Beck's standpoint. The German social scientist considers the terrorist attack will stand for many things in the history of humanity.[7] According to Beck, the risk of transnational terrorist networks is the third of three major risks along with ecological crises and global economic crises. The attack tragically illustrates the concept of a 'world risk society'. In a nutshell, the perverse effect of technological development is to set off unpredictable, uncontrollable and incommunicable consequences that endanger modern civilization. Those who argue that the 'peace dividend' is elusive, given the new era of scattered conflicts, and given more sophisticated and destructive terrorist groups, share this view.[8] Faced with this formidable challenge, Beck considers that a solution lies in enforcing global cooperation with a new alliance between states to restore security.

Our view is less sanguine, however. The 'clash of civilisations' is a romantic and catchy term. Cultural battlefields conjure up global clashes between Civilization versus Barbarism, which are more appealing than GDP gaps, access to water and capital flow volatility. Terrorism is certainly an advanced symptom of cultural clashes. Beyond the arena of geopolitics and international relations, mounting terrorism will have a deep and long-lasting impact on the global economic system. September 11 erupted, indeed, at a time when the world capitalist economy is facing a twofold unprecedented challenge. On the one hand, the market-based economic system confronts a legitimacy challenge. What is of concern is the rising and costly volatility of the global economy and the unfairness of the distribution of its benefits. The anti-globalization demonstrations constitute a clear-cut illustration of widespread discontent. On the other hand, the global economy also faces a regulation challenge. The post-Second World War era has witnessed a number of financial and economic crises amplified by a ramification effect that threatens to transform a country's financial difficulties into a regional recession and, at worst, a systemic crisis. This challenge has been acute during the Asian crisis of 1997–98 and, more recently, in the Argentine crisis of 2001–2. The developed countries are also confronted with major governance challenges, as illustrated in the Enron, WorldCom, and Putnam cases. Many of the financial storms of the 1990s and 2000s have been unexpectedly severe and have caught the international financial institutions (IFIs) off guard, in particular the IMF. The Bretton Woods institutions have responded to the upheaval with tighter macroeconomic surveillance, early-warning signals, improved transparency and a tighter regulatory framework embodied in the upcoming Basel II banking capital adequacy regulations. In this volatile environment, the enhanced threat of global terrorism affects risk management and global investment strategies in many ways. One can distinguish eight main consequences.

First, global terrorism reminds risk analysts that there is no 'sanctuary' in the global economy. So far, country risk was perceived as a matter of emerging countries at the fringe of the global markets. Most of the analysis was focused on endogenous risk causes, such as political upheaval, social tensions, guerrilla action and coups d'état. September 11 exemplifies that even the largest and strongest economy in the world is vulnerable to exogenous and abrupt shocks. The rise in commodity prices and the Iraqi crisis have taken their toll throughout the global economy. Employment declined sharply in early 2003 in the US, while fears about homeland security and global terrorism chill consumer and investor confidence, depress spending and result in excess capacity following the 1990s investment boom and the marked productivity gains. Business confidence suffers from the negative 'triple wealth effect', that is, from depressed stock prices, global markets slowdown and a looming housing market bubble. As a result, industrial production is flat and there are no reliable signs of recovery in capital spending. Weak demand and overcapacity, combined with high domestic debt, will keep depressing the struggling corporate sector. Despite upbeat forecasts of US economic growth in 2004, questions remain about the sustainability of the recovery.

Second, the Iraq war will not be enough to place the US economy on a path of self-supporting growth. The US$450 billion defence outlay will prevent the US from sinking into a double-dip recession without lasting positive impact. Defence spending as a share of GDP reaches 'only' 4.1 per cent in 2003, compared with 4.8 per cent during the 1991 Gulf War, 9.4 per cent during Vietnam, 14.1 per cent during Korea and 37.9 per cent during the Second World War. The only obvious winners are Lockheed Martin's shareholders, given the rise in the company's equity value following the award of two US Air Force contracts in mid-March 2003 worth nearly

US$10 billion. However, the top US defence contractors such as General Dynamics, Northrop Grumman, Boeing and Lockeed Martin strive to survive the industry's shake-out of the 1990s. Following the first Gulf War, annual defence procurement has been cut in half. Though the September 11 attacks led to substantial increases in defence outlays, actual procurement spending came in lower than expected. All in all, over 2002, the S&P's aerospace and defence index has declined 32 per cent, compared with a 23 per cent drop for the S&P 500-stock index.[9] The industry clearly benefits from the Iraq War, that requires replenishing the stocks. But while the bulk of the industry's profit margins will stem from the electronic upgrades related to network-centric and high-tech warfare, the shift of focus away from the contractors' traditional businesses falls short of reactivating the US economy's growth engine. The combination of defence and security spending, with tax cuts and other fiscal stimulus, will not suffice to boost durable growth in the US without a reactivation of global economic dynamism. The negative impact on airlines and tourism will more than offset any defence-related stimulus.

Third, the dialectic between global terrorism and US military unilateralism fuels political upheaval. In the United States, terrorism is reinvigorating the interventionist foreign policy stance that was weakening since the fall of the Berlin Wall. The world is getting increasingly polarized, both on income grounds but also on cultural and ideological grounds. The erosion in secularism cannot but add fragmentation in the global arena. Geopolitical turmoil imperils trade liberalization and increases uncertainty. The US decision to put steep tariffs on steel imports and to boost farm subsidies, in the context of a cheaper dollar, exacerbates trade tensions with Europe and Asia.

Fourth, the terrorist attack is a symptom of the globalization of 'private', compared to nation-state, violence that does not spare any territory. It thus creates a Sword of Damocles on investment strategy, in a world where disorder and upheaval are the norms. As such, it acts like a tax on cross-border investment. Clearly, the global system is currently more volatile than during the Cold War years, when symmetric and bilateral tensions managed to create a sort of tense equilibrium. The latter benefited many states that drew Cold War dividends stemming from their specific position between the Western and the Soviet blocs, including in Africa and the Middle East. The major powers patronized their clients with subsidies and aid money, a substitute for economic and social reforms. The collapse of the Soviet bloc in 1990 created a short-lived optimism around the concepts of new world order, the end of history, and 'Washington consensus'. Many countries, however, lost overnight their privileged status of subsidised proxies of the Cold War. Their role of geopolitical stakes in the balance of power between the two blocs, gave them a position of 'parasites' in the international system. Many countries turned into free-riders. The collapse of the Berlin Wall sent these countries back to their objective situation: poor, corrupt, socially fragmented and structurally weak. Institutional weakness and bad governance could not resist the removal of the Cold War safety net. Many of these states have comprehensively collapsed in Africa, Eastern Europe and Asia. They become the home of corrupt regimes and criminal networks.

Fifth, 09/11 sheds light on the United States' overall vulnerability, well beyond the global terrorist threat. In particular, the twin external and budgetary deficits put a renewed emphasis on the question: For how long will the US economy keep living beyond its means? The US Congressional Budget Office projects a fiscal deficit close to 5 per cent of GDP in 2004. In addition, the protracted current account deficit, over US$400 billion per annum, raises the spectre of external financing challenges as well as a long-term decline in the dollar exchange rate. The traditional Keynesian policy tools are not at hand. Regarding monetary policy, the Fed has lost most of its interest rate ammunition. Any further cut would trickle down too slowly to be effective or would show the Fed's last card and could open a liquidity trap, as in Japan. Export-led growth could only materialize with further trade subsidies and a steep decline in the value of the dollar, which would trigger sharp tensions with US trading partners and the WTO. Regarding a budget deficit-led economic reactivation, the financing of a growing deficit would be limited by investors' risk appetite, given the weaker dollar and low interest rates. All in all, at a time when the United States claims 'hyperpower' status in the geopolitical arena, combined signs of economic and financial vulnerability cast doubts on the stability of the world's largest economy. Investor confidence began to take a battering in the US as a consequence of the terrorist attacks, followed by a series of legal investigations affecting such companies as Enron, WorldCom, Arthur Andersen, Citigroup Putnam and Merrill Lynch. The emerging geopolitical vulnerability of the US coincides with mounting questions on the quality of corporate governance in many developed economies, with potential impact on the health of the domestic and global financial systems.

Sixth, 09/11 exemplified the speed of crisis transmission in the global markets. The spillover effect was well known since the 1994 'Tequila' crisis in Mexico and the subsequent Asian crisis of 1997–98. However, the crisis contamination worked then from the periphery to the centre. In the 2001–03 period, however, in an already depressed world economy, the deflationary forces at work in the OECD were reinforced by the terrorist impact on investment and consumption. A flexible and accommodative monetary policy in the United States did not fully succeed in changing the markets' negative expectations. Risk-averse investors were hit by the 'herd instinct' syndrome, which tends to put all emerging market countries into a similar asset class, that is, the most risky, without much discrimination. As O'Brian writes: 'The increased ease of communication and sophistication of risk management models injects greater market volatility by allowing traders to respond instantaneously to events in distant countries, which they often understand only vaguely.'[10]

Seventh, global tensions cast light on the absence of effective global economic coordination, despite the supervision mandate of international financial institutions, such as the IMF, the World Bank and the Basel-based BIS. Central banks with their total reserves of hardly $2600 billion are not armed to convincingly stem destabilizing short-term capital flows. The IMF, with a total of less than $90 billion in financing arrangements for 52 countries, is not equipped for offsetting recessionary forces in the global economy. Its financing support is often deemed too modest to lead country governments to adopt tough belt-tightening stabilization measures. Worse, the IMF intervention under the form of post-crisis 'bailout packages' is often criticized as increasing moral hazard by rewarding bad policies by governments and excessive risk-taking by private creditors and investors. Barro observes that with help from the US, the IMF encourages bad economic policy by rewarding failure with showers of money.[11]

Last, the global terrorist threat and its broad consequences call for a necessary and thorough reappraisal of risk assessment methods that must incorporate the disruptive projections of ideological antagonism on both sides. Risk management software has been caught totally off guard by these new risks. The worldwide network of illicit organizations of global reach casts light on a complex web of transnational risks that traditional assessment methods are unequipped to take into account. As Moisés Naim notes: 'The illegal trade in drugs, arms, intellectual property, people and money is booming. Like the war on terrorism, the fight to control these illicit markets pits governments against agile, stateless, and resourceful networks empowered by globalization'.[12] In particular, the political risk definition, usually limited to national government interference with private business operations,[13] requires a comprehensive reappraisal. The classical approach to country risk remains nation-state focused – including GDP, balance of payments, economic infrastructure, liquidity and solvency and the socio-political system. Today powerful decentralized networks that ignore national borders add a new risk element to cross-border investment.

In conclusion, country risk assessment is made increasingly complex, as volatility is everywhere, in the economic, financial and geopolitical realms.

6.3   THE SHORT-TERM FINANCIAL EFFECTS OF POST-SEPTEMBER 11

The terrorist attacks on the United States on September 11, 2001, traumatized the nation and sent a shock wave all over the world, illustrating the
global nature of risk and the absence of sanctuary. The attacks exacerbated an already weak economy in New York City.[14] The short-term financial cost can be estimated at over US$36 billion, including earnings losses,
property damage, public infrastructure and the clean-up of the site.[15] This
cost does not include the attack's effects on employment and consumer
confidence as well as the city's reduced productive capacity. The near-term
cost comprises the increased public- and private-sector homeland security
outlays, estimated at roughly US$72 billion per year, strictly in the US
economy, with a more prolonged impact on reduced overall productivity,
resulting from tighter security controls and reallocation of research and
development spending.[16] In the United States, the terrorist attacks had a
relatively modest incidence on security and national defence outlays that
account for 3.8 per cent of GDP in 2003, a share much below the 1947–92
average, thereby preserving the 'peace dividend' of the collapse of the
Soviet Union in the early 1990s. This figure, however, does not include the
cost of US military intervention in Asia and in the Middle East.

These financial costs, however, are short-term in nature and do not take
into account the ramifications in other countries' security outlays. The IMF
estimated that tighter security precautions in the wake of the attacks will
cost the world about US$75 billion, with a long-term cost of the order of
0.75 per cent of world GDP.[17] Regarding the US economy, economic scenarios calculations find the cost of the 09/11 terrorist attack to be 1 per cent
of GDP in each year, between 2001 and 2003.[18] But all in all, the terrorist
attack did not jeopardize the global economic system. The interbank
payment network resisted, thanks to the concerted intervention of central
banks that prevented any substantial and lasting disruption of payments
systems. In particular, the Federal Reserve responded quickly and efficiently to stem the risk of a liquidity crisis and to restore payments coordination. There were no runs on commercial banks in the United States and
elsewhere. More importantly, there was no major impact on the exchange
rate of the US dollar compared with other international currencies such as
the euro and the yen. As illustrated in Graph 6.1, the value of the dollar
compared to the euro did not fall in the aftermath of 09/11. The negative
market correction was short-lived. No lasting bearish market nor any concerted speculative attacks affected the dollar exchange rate. In fact, the
dollar gained strength during the last quarter of 2001. Its value was nearly
constant between the beginning and the end of 2001. The nearly 10 per cent

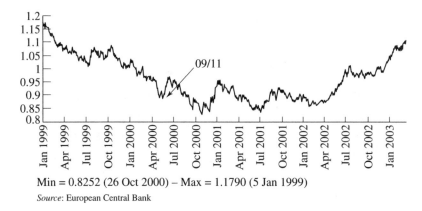

Min = 0.8252 (26 Oct 2000) – Max = 1.1790 (5 Jan 1999)

Source: European Central Bank

Graph 6.1   Exchange value, US dollar vs. euro

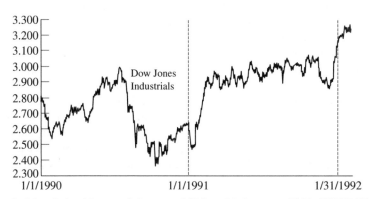

Graph 6.2   Price history, 1 January 1990 to 31 January 1992 ($INDU)

fall of the dollar on a trade-weighted basis in 2002 thus started well after the terrorist attack. It has nothing to do with the Twin Towers and is due to a combination of interest rate differentials and a certain 'benign neglect' of the US Fed's dollar exchange rate management, aimed at stimulating exports and correcting the current account deficit.

Finally, the two crises, that is, 09/11 and the Iraq wars, did not have any lasting negative impact on the stock markets. In the former, the Fed intervened jointly with central banks to prevent any large-scale herd instinct. As the Graph 6.2 illustrates, the terrorist attacks were followed by a short stock market contraction that gave rise to a price increase.

Regarding the second Iraq War of April 2003, the absence of an abrupt

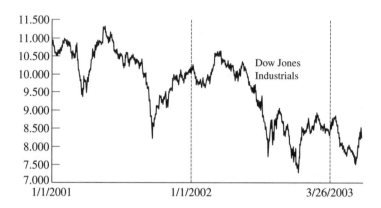

Graph 6.3   Price history, 1 January 2001 to 26 March 2003 ($INDU)

oil price hike and the short-term nature of the US military intervention prevented a rise in inflationary pressures as well as a global slump. The Iraq war did not trigger any stock market depression, as shown in Graph 6.3. Given the protracted build-up to war in late 2002 and early 2003, the destabilizing surprise effect did not happen and the beginning of the military intervention even led to a 'relief rally'. The most important consequence of the war from a growth perspective is the increase in the US trade and fiscal deficits. The combination of the import surge that reflected the jump in oil prices preceding the Iraq War, the dollar's fall and flat exports, given the slowdown in global economic growth, place the US trade deficit on track to hit US$500 billion in 2003. Graph 6.3 shows that no abrupt stock market contraction followed the US military intervention since it was well anticipated by the markets.

6.4   COUNTRY RISK: A NECESSARY RECONSIDERATION

The growing preoccupation with country risk was catalysed by the post-9/11 global security concerns coupled with the Afghanistan and Iraq wars. Following the short-lived peace dividend of the fall of the Berlin Wall, there is widespread concern that the world is inherently dangerous and unstable. Globalization is vulnerable. Innovation and dynamic growth requires a predictable economic and political environment with robust institutions. Socio-political upheaval, civil disorder, armed conflicts and terrorist networks are embedded into weak institutions. They exemplify a crisis of mediations. Social infrastructure, comprising political parties, unions, civil

society associations, judiciary and parliamentary bodies altogether constitute channels for expressing discontent and mobilizing civil involvement.
When such institutional channels are missing, because they are too weak,
repressed or not credible any longer, the vacuum is filled by uprising, arbi-
trary violence and civil disorder. Most of the countries that suffer from
institutional deficits belong to the 70 or so nations (from a world total of
roughly 190), regarded by the World Bank as 'Low-Income Countries
Under Stress' (LICUS category). The CIA expects transnational terrorism
to find prime breeding grounds in 'states with poor governance; ethnic, cultural, or religious tensions; weak economies; and porous borders. In such
states, domestic groups will challenge the entrenched government, and
trans-national networks seeking safe havens'.[19]

Civil disorder is not new. In the late fourteenth and early twentieth centuries, national terrorism was widespread in many European countries,
most noticeably in Tsarist Russia. American history itself is punctuated by
terrorism, notably when anarchists exploded a bomb on Wall Street on 16
September 1920. Civil disorder was then animated by nihilist doctrines that
Camus analysed so thoroughly in his *Homme Révolté*. Bakunin and his
fellow anarchist revolutionaries focused their passionate hatred against the
state as the domination force that repressed the people. Revolution was the
good, whereas the state was the crime.[20] In the mid-twentieth century,
national armed conflicts were often limited by national boundaries. The
uprisings in the post-Second World War era were aimed at the political and
economic emancipation of colonized nations from the rule of Western
powers, mainly British and French. Thus, until the late 1980s urban violence was targeted at national governments and at their repressive military
and police forces. This was basically intra-nation violence. Terrorism was
for the most part both secular and nationalist. Its ideological substratum
was the Leninist and Trotskyite revolutionary ideologies, aimed at self-
determination and decolonization. The Cuban guerrilla forces sent by
Castro into Angola and Mozambique in the mid-1960s were not terrorist
groups. Their mission was strengthening anti-imperialist resistance against
Portuguese domination. Likewise, Guevara's guerrilla warfare in Bolivia
fought US-assisted national army forces. The goal was the collapse of the
'bourgeois' state under the aegis of US imperialism. Contrary to terrorism,
that involves 'the intentional use of violence against civilians in order to
attain political targets',[21] guerrilla warfare involves military or security personnel. Similar examples can be found in decolonization uprisings in many
developing countries, which strived to substitute a national state (often
socialist) to an imperialist one. The result was a swelling tide of nationalism in Asia, Africa and Latin America.

However, socialism is not a legitimate driver of international violence any longer. There is currently no credible system challenge, following the collapse of the Soviet bloc. Religion-based ideology constitutes the new front against market-driven consumerism and capitalist materialism. What global terrorism exemplifies in the beginning of the twenty-first century is a violent rebellion against an economic and ideological colonization by market-based forces under an overwhelming US influence. As Cohen writes: 'Behind the veil of nominal independence, imperial dominance continues with a different form. Control is now exercised informally, rather than formally, and the main form of this control is economic penetration – connections of trade and investment'.[22] The specific nature of stateless and cross-border terrorist violence today is that it is globalized, precisely because the neo-liberal Western-inspired market forces it fights are globalized too.

September 11 abruptly illustrates the nihilist 'fight to the death' of powerful and decentralized terrorist groups who do not aim at the collapse of the state but at that of a system. Global terrorism targets all the institutional representations of a global economic system that is increasingly challenged as being illegitimate. Accordingly, private businesses face new operational challenges, as they can become hostage to a global struggle where the end justifies the most violent means.

Thus country risk analysts must cope with a three-pronged volatility. The first one is financial by nature. New technology and the global integration of financial markets make possible sharp capital flow reversals, destabilizing speculation, exchange rate crises and an abrupt liquidity crunch. Financial volatility causes havoc in the affected emerging market countries. The transmission speed of financial imbalances has vastly accelerated over the last 20 years. As a result, country financial problems get quickly transformed into regional crises. The Asian crisis of 1997–98 is a clear-cut example of the ramification process that engulfed a whole region in economic recession before touching almost every emerging market country, including Russia. These middle-income economies are lumped together by investment fund managers and bank creditors, into one single asset class. Herd instinct is at the root of undifferentiated cross-border exposure strategy, resulting in crisis propagation.

The second type of volatility is mainly economic, through trade relations and exchange rate variations. Competitive devaluations and shock therapy-based stabilization policies lead to spillover effects. This contamination through balance of payment channels boils down to exporting recession to neighbouring countries. Joseph Stiglitz is one of the most vocal critics of trade and capital market liberalization promoted by the IMF's 'market fundamentalism'.[23] Stiglitz points out that excessive trade openness increases the vulnerability of developing countries to external shocks.

The third type of volatility is politico-ideological – this risk can spread through worldwide terrorist networks and geopolitical turmoil. As terrorism thrives on poverty and institutional weakness, political volatility focuses attention on the role of institutions and governance in the development process. This is an area that traditional country risk approaches have not tackled sufficiently. In particular, political instability breeds on corruption and bad governance. It erodes confidence in public institutions and government policies. It cuts into government revenues and leads to large spending. It penalizes private sector initiatives. It makes investment returns much more uncertain. Whereas liquidity and solvency ratios can be measured and predicted with relative ease, political stability requires an in-depth analysis of the country's socio-cultural drivers, including history, religion, ideology and, more broadly, values.

Including political risk and governance in risk assessment can lead to a sharp reversal of risk exposure strategy. For example, the California-based Calpers decided to divest from four emerging market countries in February 2003, namely Indonesia, Malaysia, the Philippines and Thailand. This strategy stems from a revised framework for evaluating emerging market countries, combining country and market factors. Calpers's rationale is that 'without strong country infrastructures, including social, to support the capital markets, the latter cannot be truly viable'.[24]

Country factors focus on three types of criteria that support a conducive environment for productive private sector investment:

- political stability (civil liberties, independent judiciary and legal protection, political risk);
- transparency (freedom of the press, accounting standards, stock exchange listing requirements, monetary and fiscal transparency); and
- productive labour practices (enabling legislation, institutional capacity).

6.5 THE LONG-TERM IMPLICATIONS OF GEOPOLITICAL TURMOIL REGARDING COUNTRY RISK AND GLOBAL CAPITAL

Even though the 9/11 attacks and the Afghan and Iraq wars did not endanger the institutional and economic roots of the global capitalist system, the ongoing terrorist threat's long-term impact can be considered as a 'tax' on investors, exporters and creditors on the global markets. This tax increases the uncertainty, hence the risk and cost of cross-border investment. The most affected economic sectors are the tourism industry, insurance and reinsurance, banking and airlines. Even Qantas, one of the most profitable and resilient airlines, warned that fears of terrorism and the Iraqi crisis had caused its forward bookings to slow considerably, resulting in a sharp fall in share prices.[25] Many insurance companies and commercial banks, including in Asia and Europe, have seen their share prices plunging under the weight of falling global stock markets and mounting losses. This is so because the global economy works like an 'echo chamber' that propagates, enlarges and distorts signals, creating waves of volatility. Let us consider for instance the global impact of SARS (severe acute respiratory syndrome) during 2003. Even though the epidemic grabbed the headlines due to the 1000 or so people killed, this must be compared with malaria, that kills 3000 people every day, mostly children in Africa. Close to 500 million people contract malaria every year and at least a million of them will die, according to the WHO and UNICEF. The difference between malaria and SARS is that the latter affected a strong regional global engine of growth. SARS contaminated mostly Asia, while malaria spreads across Africa. Accordingly, the World Bank shaved a 0.5 percentage point from an earlier 5.5 per cent in the 2003 economic growth forecast for East Asia. CDC Ixis went a step further and cut the growth in Asia by 0.7 per cent to only 3.8 per cent for the region in 2003, due to a severe impact on domestic consumption.[26] Indeed, the outbreak of SARS has inflicted the greatest blow to the Chinese economy since Tiananmen in 1989, causing a plunge in retail sales, a slump in demand for exports and a near collapse in domestic and foreign tourism. As roughly 25 per cent of Asia's exports go to the USA, the combination of a weaker dollar and SARS created a brake on regional economic growth.

All in all, what fully modifies the scope of risk that the global economy faces is precisely that it is global. Strong and lasting global growth belongs to the past, given the many risks and vulnerabilities that spill over and create volatility. The toll of rising global uncertainty and volatility, however, is much heavier on emerging countries than on the OECD group. Global risk aversion has a large impact on the international allocation of resources and thus penalizes the emerging countries, which were about to recover from the protracted 1998 crisis. The greater risk of large-scale terrorism increases the prudence of risk-averse creditors who must also face the new Basel II regulations on banks' capital ratios. The proposal for a new rating-based capital requirement framework might lead to procyclicality, to crisis and contagion sensitivity. Regarding past financial crises, linking capital requirements to ratings would have drastically increased the banks' capital cost on emerging market lending.[27] Portfolio managers, exporters and lenders will increasingly look twice before allocating assets outside the

OECD countries' perimeter. In early 2003, Calpers decided to withdraw much of its assets from emerging countries, given the unacceptable risk levels.

Following the 1982 debt crisis, international banks have cut their exposure on emerging market countries. They have concentrated on specific-purpose financing and they have left official creditors, both bilateral and multilateral, to fill balance of payment gaps with a mixture of new money and debt relief. In a second stage, during the mid-1990s, private financing in the form of bonds rather than loans has played a greater role, similar to that during the 1890s. At that time, the bulk of country financing took the form of bond issues on the international capital markets, mainly in Europe and North America. A wave of bond defaults dried up countries' market access well after the Great Depression. Today, an overall re-examination of risk versus opportunity in cross-border exposure, combined with tighter regulation and shareholder pressure for short-term profit maximization, open a new stage in the activity of international capital markets. In addition, the spectre of collective action clauses in foreign bond contracts or the prospect of a sovereign debt restructuring mechanism under the IMF's auspices further erode market access for the majority of emerging countries. The name of the game is risk differentiation and portfolio diversification.

A limited number of investment-grade countries will keep access to capital and banking markets for infrastructure financing and market-driven development purposes. These countries mainly belong to the OECD group, together with new industrialized countries that exemplify dynamic, diversified and balanced growth, mainly in Asia and Latin America: Korea, Chile, Mexico, Brazil, the Czech Republic, Hungary, Slovenia, the Slovak Republic, Poland, Taiwan, Hong Kong and Singapore. A second group of middle-income countries will access short-term trade and specific-purpose financing, working capital lines as well as structured financing with guarantees and collateral. These countries are oil and raw material producers, as well as developing countries with little diversified export base: Algeria, South Africa, Tunisia, Morocco, Jordan, Colombia, Costa Rica, Peru, Romania, Thailand, the Philippines, Indonesia and Venezuela. For the vast majority of remaining developing countries, including those severely indebted low-income countries, official creditors will be the unique channel of external funding, under the form of low-interest, long-term credit and development aid.

As Graphs 6.4, 6.5 and 6.6 illustrate, countries with a weak institutional base and a volatile political situation have witnessed a sharp reduction in market access since the late 1990s. Many have suffered a further cut in short-term credit lines since 09/11. Two groups of countries can be differentiated. The first group comprises high-risk countries that have faced a

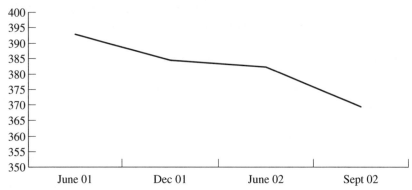

Graph 6.4   Short-term bank claims on developing countries (in US$ billion)

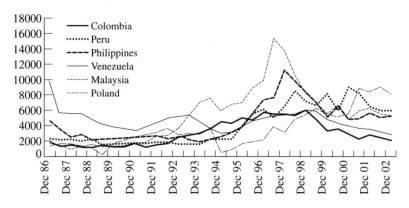

Graph 6.5   Decline in short-term bank exposure (in US$ million)

growing reluctance of the banking community to increase risk exposure beyond traditional moderate levels. Trade lines and working capital lines are kept to the minimum, cash collateral is often required, and any exposure increase would be penalized by discounts in the secondary market, and taxed by heavy loan-loss reserves and expensive aside capital. These low-income countries should have never tapped the capital markets to finance development projects in the first place. This is the case of the Côte d'Ivoire, Cameroon, Morocco, Ecuador and Nigeria. A second group of middle-income countries has suffered from a sharp reversal of short-term capital flows resulting from the global liquidity crunch in the aftermath of the Asian crisis in late 1990s.[28] This group includes Indonesia, Russia,

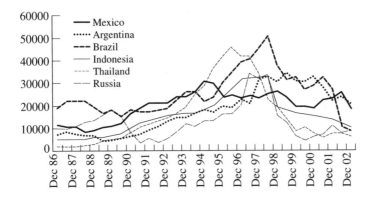

Graph 6.6   'Double-drop' in short-term bank lines (in US$ million)

Brazil, Argentina, Peru, Thailand, the Philippines, Venezuela and Colombia. In many of these countries, short-term debt dropped back to 1990s levels. In particular, international banks' claims shrunk due to three converging factors:

1. the protracted impact of the Asia crisis and the related spillover effect;
2. capital adequacy guidelines that penalise emerging market countries; and
3. a reassessment of political risk since 09/11.

Graph 6.4 illustrates the decline in the international banks' short-term risk exposure relating to two developing countries. Two inflections can be observed. The first took place at the time of the Asian crisis and was a factor of crisis acceleration and propagation. The second took place between mid-2001 and late 2002, in the aftermath of 09/11. It reinforces the capital reversal impact of the decline in FDI in emerging market countries. Graphs 6.5 and 6.6 show the decline in bank exposure on developing countries.

Graph 6.5 illustrates the sharp decline in short-term bank exposure on a selected group of 'moderately' middle-income countries that experienced a sharp drop at the time of the Asian crisis and again following 09/11. This group includes, in particular, Colombia, Poland, Peru, Malaysia, Cameroon and Nigeria.

Graph 6.6 casts light on the 'double-drop' in short-term bank lines in the aftermath of the 1997 Asian crisis and 09/11 for several 'high' middle-income countries, most noticeably Brazil, Mexico, Argentina and Russia. The marked decline in bank exposure shows the country risk reconsideration under way in international banks. The risk aversion trend has been accentuated by the Basel II capital adequacy regulatory framework that penalizes emerging market countries compared with investment-grade and OECD countries.

Emerging market countries are likely to face tougher market access conditions. Risk aversion for lenders, exporters and creditors alike will lead to close scrutiny of return prospects, coupled with short-term oriented exposure as well as guarantees and collateral. Craig Karmin notices: 'History supports a sceptical view [regarding portfolio diversification in emerging markets]. Emerging-market companies have been among the most volatile stocks during the past decade. They have been especially erratic during periods of global economic or political stress'.[29] Recent market observation, however, does not support this scepticism. Today global uncertainty drives most investors away from emerging markets' assets, even though recent volatility has dropped and their stock index fell less compared with the MSCI's Europe Index, Japan's index, and the Dow Jones Industrial Average, over the last five-year period.

6.6   CONCLUSION

What fully modifies the scope of risk that the global economy faces, is precisely that it is global. Strong and lasting global growth belongs to the past, given the many risks and vulnerabilities that spill over and create volatility. As the global economy becomes an 'echo chamber' that propagates and accentuates imbalances, it is doomed to face cycles of stop-and-go. The absence of institutional stabilization mechanisms, such as 'lender of last resort' funds, makes the global economy vulnerable to shocks as never before.

Rising risks without traditional warning signals thus require the risk analysts to be more agile, broad-minded and innovative than in the past. Volatility and complexity make quantitative assessment of country risk, including ratings and rankings, at best partial tools and at worst recipes for simplistic outlooks. The shortcomings of ratings and panel-based market consensus methods had been exemplified on the eve of the Asian crisis, combined with the Russian default a year later. These pitfalls are still larger in the aftermath of 09/11. Only an array of converging analytical approaches can lead to a more rigorous examination of the economic, institutional and socio-political fabric that holds or distorts a country's development path. Today, risk aversion is accentuated by shareholder pressure for stable and predictable dividends as well as tighter capital adequacy regulations. This has a severe impact on market access for most emerging market countries. Altogether, in a global system more complex and decentralized, the combination of geopolitical turmoil and market-based forces make the world more insecure and less predictable.

NOTES

1. See Bouchet et al. (2003).
2. Spanier (1968), p. viii.
3. Kennan (1947).
4. CIA (2002b), Introduction, p. 1.
5. Alan Greenspan, 'Global finance: is it slowing?', remarks at the Banque de France International Symposium on Monetary Policy, Economic Cycle, and Financial Dynamics, Paris, 7 March (2003).
6. Huntington (1993 and 1996).
7. Ulrich Beck (2001), 'The silence of words and political dynamics in the world risk society', speech to Russian Duma, November.
8. Gupta et al. (2002).
9. 'More chips, fewer choppers', *Business Week*, 14 April 2003, pp. 36–7.
10. O'Brian (2002).
11. Barro (1998).
12. Naim (2003).
13. See among many other authors: Weston and Sorge (1972), p. 60.
14. Bram (2003).
15. Bram et al. (2002).
16. Hobjin (2002).
17. IMF (2001).
18. See McKibbin and Stoeckel (2001).
19. CIA (2002a), p. 50.
20. Camus, Albert (1966), p. 197.
21. Ganor (2002).
22. Cohen (1973), p. 93.
23. Stiglitz (2002), p. 282.
24. Calpers-Country and Market factors, in www.calpers.ca.gov/invest/emer-gingmkt/country-market.htm
25. 'War and terrorism fears hit bookings at Qantas', *Financial Times*, 21 February 2003.
26. CDC Ixis, 2003 'Asie et SRAS: une estimation des impacts sur la croissance', Marchés Emergents, 30 April.
27. Monfort and Christian Mulder (2000).
28. Net short-term debt is equal to original claims < one year minus short-term maturities coming due 'between one and two years' of year t-2, in order to obtain the 'original' net short-term liabilities.
29. Karmin (2003).

REFERENCES

Barro, Robert J. (1998), 'The IMF doesn't put out fires, it starts them', *Business Week*, **3607**, 12 July.

Bouchet, M.H., B. Groslambert and E. Clark (2003). *Country Risk Assessment: A Global Tool for Investment Strategy*, New York: Wiley.

Bram, Jason, James Orr and Carol Rapaport (2002), 'Measuring the effects of the

September 11 attack on New York City', *FRBNY Economic Policy Review*, November, 5–19.

Bram, Jason (2003), 'New York City's economy before and after September 11', *FRBNY Current Issues in Economics and Finance*, **9** (2), 81–96.

Camus, Albert (1966), 'Le terrorisme individuel', *L'Homme Révolté*, Paris: Gallimard.

CIA (2002a), 'Global Trends 2015. Terrorism-related excerpts', *The War on Terrorism*, www.cia.gov/terrorism/global_trends_2015.html

CIA (2002b), 'US national strategy for combating terrorism', Washington, DC.

Cohen, Benjamin J. (1973), 'The transition to modern imperialism', *The Question of Imperialism*, New York: Basic Books.

Ganor, Boaz (2002), 'Defining terrorism: is one man's terrorist another man's freedom fighter?', International Policy Institute for Counter-Terrorism, www.ict.org.il/articles/define.htm

Gupta, Sanjee, B. Clements, R. Bhattacharya and S. Chakravarti (2002), 'The elusive Peace Dividend', *Finance and Development*, **4** (39), 4951.

Hobjin, Bart (2002), 'What will homeland security cost?', *FRBNY Economic Policy Review*, November, 21–33.

Huntington, Samuel (1993), 'A clash of civilizations?', *Foreign Affairs*, Summer.

Huntington, Samuel (1996), *The Clash of Civilizations and the Remaking of World Order*, New York: Simon & Schuster.

IMF (2001), 'The global economy after September 11', *World Economic Outlook*, December, Washington, DC.

Karmin, Craig (2003), 'Emerging market stocks look like a safer bet', *Wall Street Journal*, Money and Investing, 21 March.

Kennan, George (1947), '"Mr X": the sources of Soviet conduct', *Foreign Affairs*, Quarterly.

McKibbin, Warwick and Andrew Stoeckel (2001), 'The aftermath of terrorist attack in the US', December, www.economicscenarios.com.

Monfort, B. and C. Christian Mulder (2000), 'Using credit ratings for capital requirements on emerging market economies: possible impact of a new Basel Accord', *IMF Working Paper*, 00/69, March.

Naim, Moses (2003), 'The five wars of globalization', *Foreign Policy*, January/February.

O'Brian, Maria (2002), 'Playing for high stakes', *Latin Finance*, **143**, December, 13.

Spanier, John (1968), *American Foreign Policy Since WWI*, 3rd revised edn, New York: Praeger.

Stiglitz, Joseph E. (2002), *Globalization and its Discontents*, New York: Norton.

Weston, V. Fred and Bart W. Sorge (1972), *International Managerial Finance*, Homewood, IL: Irwin.

7. The digital divide

Robert A. Isaak

INTRODUCTION

September 11, 2001 was a terrorist reaction to American troops in Saudi Arabia and to a US-dominated globalization of the world economy made possible by the information technology (IT) revolution. This revolution served to widen the wealth gap between the United States and Europe as well as between the developed and developing countries. The question is whether or not the 09/11 transformation of the international system had the effect of freezing these inequalities in place, given the increased theoretical access to the Internet from all places in the world due to globalization. The dot.com-led economic boom in the United States preceding 09/11 permitted the Americans to have a cheaply subsidized, learning-by-doing collective experience that spread access to the Internet to the majority of the population and taught thousands of young entrepreneurs and millions of teenagers and college students the basic technologies and e-thinking required for Internet-based business and entrepreneurship. And just as other developed countries, such as those in Europe, started to come on board, 09/11 threatened to freeze the process, drying up venture capital and slowing down the motivation and tolerance for risk-taking required to transform national economies into global e-competitors. For the latecomers, the e-transformation of their economies appeared suddenly to be more difficult both economically and psychologically. So while the e-revolution spread through globalization, the critical follow-up financing and investment in both businesses and educational institutions slowed down, giving disproportionate competitive advantages to e-businesses and cultures already established. Despite exceptions such as the Nokia phenomenon in Finland and French leadership with Minitel, the European perspective on the digital divide is usually caught between the fast revolutionary American-generated IT transformation of the service sector, on the one hand, and the religious and political efforts of deeply rooted cultures to preserve traditional ways of life and systems of belief, on the other hand.

But there was a countervailing effect to the 09/11 transformation. The official Bush administration reaction, declaring war against all potential terrorists everywhere in the world – and its subsequent military interventions in various countries – accelerated a global anti-American movement that had already been epitomized by the trashing of McDonald's restaurants as symbols of US-dominated globalization. Not only did traditional allies of the US, such as France and Germany, counter US hegemony on the diplomatic chessboard, but economic and business competition sharpened as well – from the spread of the euro to the increasing adoption to the Linux operating system at the expense of Microsoft. Thus, 09/11 could be interpreted as dampening venture capital for the development of economic growth stemming from New Economy innovation, on the one hand, while stimulating the spread of cost-cutting digital technology to less developed cities, regions and countries, on the other. On one level, the question becomes: does the digital revolution represent merely the spread of a new system of distribution via the Internet and its New Economy rules? Or does it provide a transformative democratization of opportunities in terms of communication, information and business networking that goes beyond mere evolution in the forms of speed and search capability?

On yet another level, does the existing digital divide serve to protect the integrity of traditional indigenous cultures from being bombarded by information overload and an extension of English-language hegemony beyond the radio, TV and print media? Or does it further marginalize less-advantaged peoples and let the first-movers dominate global markets until the developing regions can be educationally and technologically brought up to the digital level of the developed world?[1]

7.1 MORE INTERNET ACCESS, MORE ECONOMIC GROWTH

Research published since 09/11 has demonstrated that increased Internet access does significantly increase economic growth. A cross-country regression analysis by Antonina Espiritu comparing 20 industrialized and 16 developing countries confirmed a positive and significant relationship between Internet use and growth, as well as finding significant evidence of differential growth between developed and developing countries correlated with differences in internet access and usage (Espiritu, 2003, p. 450).

Since 99.6 per cent of the populations of Africa and South Asia did not use the Internet in 2000, there is clearly a 'digital divide' that impacts upon growth rates in these developing regions compared with more 'connected' developed economies (Kenny, 2003, p. 76–8). Nor is the digital divide limited just to certain countries: there is a marked divide within all countries, creating relative economic clustering between profitable areas and unprofitable peripheries. For example, in Mexico, in the 1990's billions of dollars were invested to develop information and communication technologies and networks, but these dollars benefited mainly central Mexico City, Guadalajara and Monterrey. With the exception of cellphones, even the medium-sized cities such as Merida, Leon, Saltillo and Ciudad Juarez missed the technological development boom (Sinclair, 2002, p. 21). The argument of the structuralist school of economics that global capitalism is structured to overdevelop rich metropoles and to underdevelop outlying periphery areas appears to apply to the digital divide as much as to any other aspect of development.

The irony, of course, is that technologically speaking the Internet has the potential to bridge the metropoles and peripheries in terms of communication and access to information. However, the reality remains that many outlying periphery areas in developing countries do not have the infrastructures to make Internet access viable. From India to Africa, Russia to Eastern Europe, the electricity infrastructure critical to bridging the digital divide is still too often absent.[2]

7.2 IT INVESTMENT: A DISTRACTION FROM HUMAN DEVELOPMENT?

September 11 signalled the end of euphoria for the 'New Economy', which coincided with the burst of the dot.com bubble of the late 1990s. Charles Kenny, an economist at the World Bank, epitomized this change in mood when he argued that global Internet access is too expensive to be a universal goal, especially because of where the costs would be highest – in the developing countries with inadequate infrastructures. Kenny points out that many people in developing countries are not lucky enough to be literate in a major world language or to have credit cards or delivery services (such as FedEx and UPS) in their neighbourhoods (Kenny, 2003, p. 78). The implication is that the issue of Internet access is overemphasized and could serve to distract financial support for more critical development needs such as basic health and education. Yet after satisfying such needs, if people acquire access and skill in the use of the Internet and the ability to search for information in a language that they understand, they are undoubtedly better positioned in terms of economic competitiveness.

What is at stake here is a shift in the perceptual map of those with the capacity to invest enough money or aid to make a difference in helping to close the gap between the overdeveloped and the underdeveloped worlds. When the New Economy was hot, perception was focused upon the great promise of the falling cost of information, the replacement of scarcity with plenitude and ubiquity, the shift of markets to 'follow the free' and the willingness of venture capital to subsidize mere ideas and speculations without the need for concrete business success (Kelly, 1998). Never mind that Federal Reserve chairman Alan Greenspan noted that the resulting increase in productivity also resulted in a productivity of decision-making errors, not to mention an irrational exuberance in funding high-technology companies. Just as the Europeans were embracing the dot.com euphoria started largely by Silicon Valley, the bubble burst, venture capital shrivelled and technological and telecommunications overcapacity became obvious. Then 09/11 hit, to further dampen expectations and shift perceptions away from risk-taking towards risk reduction.

The deflationary environment suggested that when an economic recovery appeared, it would be frustratingly jobless given the increase in productivity due to the IT revolution. More concretely, many companies concluded that they overbought computer technology in anticipation of a Y2K disaster (radical shifts in computer system needs due to the date change to 2000) which never materialized. Now they found after 09/11 that they had too much technological capacity for demand and the dot.com bubble burst further undermined business confidence.

Yet, that the world economic system had changed fundamentally, no one could deny. The Reagan–Thatcher policies of deregulation, privatization, union-busting and supply-side economics gave globalization a distinctive Anglo Saxon, if not American, coloration. And part of this globalization phenomenon was clearly fuelled by the IT New Economy revolution. So after 09/11, economic elites in the world understood that they needed to master globalization and IT economics or be left behind without innovation, investment and global competitiveness. Many continental Europeans quite naturally resisted this globalization as liberalism since it served to undermine their traditional way of life, including its leisurely pace. When 09/11 hit the United States, they expressed empathy for the Americans at that moment, while at the same time thinking with Aristotle that chance is the arrow that strikes the man standing next to you. After an initial honeymoon of support for the strong, anti-terrorist war policy of the Bush administration, the Europeans found themselves protesting on two fronts: against the impatience of the Americans, prone to military intervention to transform 'rogue states' somewhat linked to terrorism, and against the speed of American-dominated globalization in economic competitiveness. Indeed, the very survival of what it meant to be European seemed to hinge on slowing things down for the sake of peace and the traditions which made European civilization distinctive. So just as Charles de Gaulle played his own zero-sum game within the variable-sum game of European integration in order to tilt the rules towards his vision of a Europe of separate, distinctive states, Jacques Chirac played a zero-sum game of diplomacy in the Iraq crisis of 2003 at the global level, to counter the Anglo-American tilt of globalization on the one hand, and to bolster up the Franco-German axis of influence within the EU on the other. The New Economy slipped into the background as security issues and economic malaise came to the fore as priorities.

Governments began to intensify their efforts to monitor potential security threats using technology, while counter-culture protestors used the same technology to get around government scrutiny and to organize global protests. While European governments may not have gone as far as the US government in terms of monitoring student library borrowing habits, their anti-terrorist activities increased and had a dampening effect upon the motivation of students to speak out or to take creative intellectual and professional risks. A global economy of dot.com boom had become an economy of fear and of physical and economic insecurity. The creative, risk-taking, free-speaking and networking atmosphere so critical to full human development (and New Economy innovation) was systematically undermined.

While issues of war and peace and terrorism trumped IT as a distraction from human development, still the digital divide remained an appealing form of technological rationality (to use the phrase of Juergen Habermas) by which elites from industrialized states could manage the problems of developing countries. Things were getting very complicated very fast and a great technological simplifier – like universalising Internet access – seemed to be a relief to those looking for a quick fix (that is, most politicians) (Ishaq, 2001, p. 44). That 20 per cent of Zambia was infected with AIDS was inconvenient and to be responded to with humanitarian gestures (after all, AIDS travels globally much more easily than before). But most of the efforts of the G-7 elites focused upon national security issues and upon resurrecting a stagnating economy, while health and environmental issues slipped off the main agenda. The November 2001 WTO meeting at Doha, Qatar, calling for attention to be paid to the deprivation of fresh water and healthy sanitation in developing countries, was merely the exception that proved the rule. An emerging divide between world public opinion and the American administration's vision of globalization overwhelmed perceptions of the other 'digital' divide. But one digital social movement was not to be denied and quietly built up competence and a global voluntary network that was to become the definition of 'follow the free'.

7.3   THE EUROPEAN STAKE IN THE OPEN SOURCE MOVEMENT

A young Finnish programmer, Linus Torvalds, wrote Linux as an independent but compatible version of Unix for the PC without realizing it was to become the impetus of the global open source social movement against the domination of the Microsoft operating system in the digital world. This effort reinforced the impact of Richard Stallman's Free Software Foundation (Stallman having come up with the name POSIX: Linux is based on the POSIX standards), which are ISO standards.[33]

Because it is open source, Linux can be downloaded off the Web for free. And as an operating system, its flexibility permits it to run anything from an IBM supercomputer to a Motorola mobile phone. Since many Europeans have as much stake as developing countries in not paying license fees to Microsoft, the rising fashion of shifting to Linux, particularly in the corporate server market, has been one of the key global digital events since 09/11. Linux has continued to demonstrate exponential growth, accounting for about 14 per cent of the global market for server computers and forecast by market researcher IDC to possibly reach 25 per cent of the market and the number two position in the world in 2006 (Kerstetter et al., 2003, p. 48). IBM, Intel, Oracle and Dell have put their support behind Linux – not to mention China. Intel, for example, can use the flexibility and low cost of Linux to pursue its strategy of lowering the cost of its chips to keep market share while not becoming more dependent upon Microsoft. However, the movement behind adopting Linux goes well beyond anti-Microsoft sentiments: it includes the ability to operate in one's own language (Brazil's rationale), the ability to establish internal expertise in modifying, maintaining and developing this software, and the ability to control the security and privacy of the software. Since 09/11 the security business for IT has greatly expanded.

The Europeans have embraced the opportunity to counter the domination of Microsoft via Linux, using their chief antitrust investigator of the European Union, Mario Monti, to protest against the bundling of free products (such as the browser) in the Microsoft operating system, thus denying the market for those products to most would-be competitors.

The American Justice Department did not succeed in anything but half-hearted measures to restrain the monopolistic tendencies of Microsoft, any more than US antitrust efforts help to break up the power of large oil firms. One reason, of course, is that these quasi-monopolies are American 'national champions', helping to foster American economic growth in conditions of increasingly stiff international competition. Another more subtle reason is that the marketing of software operating systems is so sophisticated that neither government regulators nor anyone else has fully understood how 'standards' can effectively be used – an issue transcending intellectual property rights (J. Isaak et al., 1994). To give in to 'free' open source standards completely, of course, could set a precedent consistent with American founder and inventor Benjamin Franklin's admonition that any invention or discovery is the rightful property of all of mankind: this is not a happy principle for the existing consensus view of US competitiveness which relies upon its legal protection of commercial technological innovations, including software. And even the Europeans have reservations about intellectual property rights – compared, for example, to the inhabitants of developing countries, who have much less to lose if all software were to become 'free'. For example, although Linux has only 2 per cent of the desktop computing market in the world, in Spain the region of Extramadura gave away over 10 000 Linux-based PCs to residents and in 2003 Wal-Mart (the world's largest business) sold US$200 Linux-based PCs (Kerstetter et al., 2003, p. 50). At the very least, the Linux open source movement is softening up Microsoft's domination, and if people *en masse* begin to 'follow the free' in earnest, Microsoft could soon be in big trouble. The argument here is that transparency of American hegemony since 09/11 and the resulting global anti-Americanism make the rapid expansion of this 'anti-Microsoft' movement more likely than ever.

However, the movement among intellectual property rights protectors in the WTO and elsewhere could slow the Linux movement down. Thus the holder of the original patents upon which Linux is based, the SCO Group, is forming a licensing division and hiring legal counsel in order to threaten IBM's selling of Linux: but this is for the sake of money, not an anti-Linux position, since SCO is not only a Linux supplier but one of the major advocates of Linux. Ultimately, open source software is bigger than Linux and may well find as much resonance in the European Union as it does in China.

7.4 THE EUROPEAN CONUNDRUM: WHAT THE DIGITAL DIVIDE PROTECTS

To the extent that the information revolution speeds up economic processes and undermines traditional European cultures and lifestyles, many Europeans merely opt out of the e-revolution to hang on to their habitual way of life. Dependence upon the state for social welfare and education remains the acceptable norm, even though financial support is increasingly limited, given stalemated economic growth. In Europe such taken-for-granted state dependence may inadvertently undermine the legitimacy of becoming a risk-taking entrepreneur, out to found a New Economy e-business. While entrepreneurship has become more fashionable among the younger generations of Europeans, venture capital has become more difficult to come by for speculative start-ups since the popping of the dot.com bubble and the shock of 09/11. Overwhelmed by uncertainty and change, many Europeans understandably revert back to old rituals that bring a sense of social solidarity, and identity with a successful recent past. Unions mobilize workers to protest against cutbacks in wages, benefits and jobs partially due to the globalized open competition with low-paying developing countries like India and China. Meanwhile, unemployment rates rise and structural economic reforms falter. 'Old Europe' seems older now, after 09/11, and the people in the countries in the process of being admitted to the European Union are uncertain as to how much the established elites of the core EU countries will be willing to subsidize their agriculture, much less their development and capacity to bridge the digital divide. Some of the would-be new entrants to the EU have invested some policy chips in the United States, persuaded that after the Iraq conflict is resolved they may be more apt to have financial and technological support from that quarter than from a stodgy euro elite under financial and security pressures at home and abroad (for example, Poland).

The European dilemma is that traditional state sovereignty is being undermined from at least four fronts:

1. The need to give up individual state sovereignty for a deeper, 'supra-national' EU constitution before the EU is further expanded.
2. The domination of security and foreign policy by the United States, both within NATO and outside of it, given the reluctance of the Europeans to create a viable European army or to come to consensus on foreign policy and security issues (such as Iraq in 2003).
3. The global diffusion of state power and regulation that has come with the IT revolution, where the 'freedom of access' logic of the new digital economy directly contradicts the traditional government regulations upon which European governments have so long depended.
4. The global shift of power towards large multinational companies and away from sovereign states.

The EU used multiple strategies to cope with the impact of the IT revolution upon its effort to coordinate the 'shared sovereignty' of its members. The most significant was probably the Lisbon summit of March 2000 in which the European heads of state agreed to update the infrastructure of communication technologies, to bring the knowledge required by this infrastructure into schools, to try to unify the European patents system, to improve conditions for entrepreneurship and small businesses, and to begin to systematically benchmark competitiveness. The European Commission was asked to come up with an 'eEurope Action Plan' with results by 2002. September 11 served as a distraction of attention from this e-agenda and made consumers and venture capitalists more defensive. Moreover, the political backlash against the privatization embodied in the Thatcher–Reagan-led globalization revolution had the inadvertent effect of exaggerating the risks of applying creativity and entrepreneurship in the public sector (R. Isaak, 2002, p. 87).

As Raphael L'Hoest has noted, the only viable solutions to the challenges confronting the EU in dealing with the digital economy focus upon public–private self-regulatory mechanisms, such as the non-profit German D-21 Initiative set up in 1999 to move Germany from an industrial to an information society, which includes 200 companies from all economic sectors and the German government (L'Hoest, 2001, p. 49). While the Europeans have had long experience with peak organizations in a corporatist model of governance, whether or not they can easily develop a spontaneous form of networking between the public and private sectors that builds consumer confidence to the point of widespread on-line purchasing in Europe is another matter. E-entrepreneurship taught by the state does not have to be a contradiction in terms, but the traditional antagonism between the public and private sectors makes it appear to be so. And the defensive reactions engendered by 09/11 uncertainties on top of the end of the economic boom of the 1990s threaten to slow down progress in building confidence in such public–private initiatives. A global political economy focused upon fear, uncertainty and growing insecurity siphons off funding and collective energy that might otherwise go to social support for the innovative initiatives and creative brainstorming so critical to fruitful digital development.

Nevertheless, the potential cost savings promised by IT economic restructuring have already shown promise in moving beyond this potential defensive socio-economic stalemate in a number of pilot projects in Europe. Barcelona, Valencia, Bologna, Brussels, Amsterdam, The Hague and Stockholm have not let 09/11 stop them from pushing the boundaries in public–private partnership in order to cut the cost of service delivery and to become wired cities. In all of these cases, government sponsorship appears to be necessary at the beginning to subsidize the infrastructure costs of getting a project started, but thereafter the aim is to create a sustainable private sector business (Baines, 2002, p. 24). Government support makes the use of universal broadband financially viable, and local community and housing projects that are coordinated to make use of the technology assure social and political cooperation at the grassroots level. Thus in Sweden, fiber-based technologies have been introduced by social landlords who wire apartments or homes through local housing associations and then turn over the management of the network to a local branch of a private utility company. However, even once the technology becomes available and widespread, there is no assurance there will be widespread demand or that this new distribution system will lead to a quick economic improvement in these areas (Baines, 2002, p. 23). Informed discussion in the US argues for government provision of the 'wires' for the infrastructure just as the government provides and maintains the road system. For while 54 per cent of Americans may be using the Internet, 46 per cent are not yet on-line: large segments of the populations of the states of West Virginia, Tennessee, Kentucky, Missouri, Illinois and Ohio are digitally ignorant.

7.5   EDUCATION IS THE KEY TO OVERCOMING THE DIGITAL DIVIDE

Even if cities, pilot regions and, eventually, rural areas are 'wired' and obtain access to the Internet, without education and motivation to adapt to the digital revolution there is no assurance people will use these new technological networks. Those from older generations often resist using e-mail, preferring old habits and often the aesthetics and time spent in traditional forms of communication, both oral and written. Poetry, for example, is a slow medium of communication. Prose is fast. E-mails are superfast. Instant messaging is hyperfast. Quality defects and a lack of precision often accompany speed. Faster means of communication are not always better, and often invite a productivity of errors.

Since much of traditional European education is oriented towards the past, particularly the slow past of literature, philosophy and letters, to have all European educational systems update themselves to adapt to the digital economy is to ask for a social revolution. Many traditional academics will argue that the very integrity of Europe depends upon the slow, systematic educational system (the typical German argument in debates about modernizing the university system). But the main difficulty is that there is no necessary link between this slow educational system and employment. That is, one may slowly obtain a PhD in Heidelberg and not find a job at the end of this academic rainbow. Moreover, the absence of a BA degree in Germany (the *Vordiplom* is not quite the same thing, nor respected as such) results in many German students dropping out before they complete their *Diplom* or MA degree – leaving them officially with nothing. In short, there is a high cost in terms of human capital and employment in preserving the traditional integrity of the German university system. There is, of course, a movement to reform this system under way, and private universities are starting to sprout up in Germany. Public–private sector cooperation here is perhaps more critical than anywhere else. But the process of educational reform is painfully slow for this generation of students. The very success of the post-Second World War social market economy model in Germany has created a state bureaucracy that stifles business, blocks reform and encourages resistance to change because of its generous welfare benefits. The risk-aversion of the German culture contradicts the digital economy's demand to embrace risk-taking and uncertainty, to assume plenitude rather than scarcity, to let go at the top in terms of clinging to past success and to use ubiquity strategies in marketing rather than the old-fashioned notion of creating a perfect product and then of assuming the customers will automatically come.

Other EU countries have adapted much more quickly both in terms of offering university degrees that take less time and in offering more curricula in the English language, which makes Internet access that much easier. Again, resistance to eliminating traditional national language requirements is understandable and may or may not be worth the trade-off in terms of e-competitiveness. The emerging French two-tier model with university degrees offered in many universities in both French and English (that is, in the *grandes écoles*) may be the wave of the future, permitting prestigious posts to be filled by those trained in the French system while opening the educational system to the English and on-line expectations of foreign students and many young French students as well. Without cultural resistance, the French language could shrivel in significance and thus countries can be expected to resist the hegemonic demands of the English-speaking Internet driven by the hyperpower, the US. Behind the split on American intervention in Iraq between Germany and France, on the one hand, and the US and UK, on the other, is a deeper cultural fissure between communitarian capitalism and the individualistic, Anglo Saxon form of capitalism (Lodge, 1991, p. 15). The difficulty, of course, is that the digital revolution rewards the creative individualistic entrepreneur which statist-oriented, communitarian capitalism can suffocate. On the other hand, there are networking, trust and team aspects of IT development which are compatible with IT economic development. However, the difficulty of the communitarian economy of Japan in adapting to the global digital economy in the 1990s serves as a warning sign for Europeans in terms of the consequences of carrying communitarian capitalism too far.

Education, ultimately, is the soul of a culture. The digital divide can be interpreted as a way of protecting traditional cultures and languages from extinction (an argument, of course, which can apply to television access as well). Again, the utility of the French paradox becomes apparent: nations should encourage those who would lead the country to obtain educations that have deep cultural roots, on the one hand, while adapting to the digital revolution just enough for competitiveness without destroying these distinctive roots, on the other hand. Otherwise, as Swiss playwright Max Frisch once told me, 'Technology is the art of arranging life so that one does not have to experience it.' The cultural heritage of a society serves as a beam of light that illuminates certain kinds of things over others, that legitimates specific kinds of learning. The key to bridging the cultural divide without losing cultural integrity is to view digital technology as just one medium or mode of distribution among many – neither to be ignored, nor to be overused.

Elsewhere, I have defined collective learning as 'a social learning process of distinguishing legitimate patterns of adaptive behaviour within an organisation in order to manage environmental change without losing cultural integrity' (R. Isaak, 2000, p. 20). September 11 served to up the existential stakes of collective learning. The only viable recipe is to help others in the digital darkness to find their own light in terms of their own language, their own culture and their own speed of development: health, basic education and then Internet access seem to be the correct priorities. Without such access, life-sustaining work may become increasingly scarce (Nulens et al., 2001, pp. 182–4). But without health and a competitive education, such work in and of itself may be of little long-term value. Free Internet access to literary and scientific libraries can serve to jump-start educational programs. In the modernization process, however, the use of digital technology must be focused to capture and preserve indigenous cultures and languages for future generations rather than to dissipate them.

The digital revolution has had the effect of making the quality of human capital the most important ingredient of competitiveness and lifetime learning a prerequisite to continuous employment and welfare financing. The digital economy speeds things up and leads to information overload. Quality education sorts out the wheat from the chaff, converts information into knowledge, and then transforms uncertainty into calculable risk in an applied way that can bring economic growth, job creation and sustainable welfare benefits to a national community.

7.6 CONCLUSIONS

September 11 served to highlight the existential differences between traditional continental communitarian forms of capitalism on the one hand, and Anglo Saxon individualistic capitalism on the other. Clearly the individualistic forms of capitalism had an advantage in the digital economic revolution, as illustrated by the Thatcher–Reagan ideological domination of globalization and the Internet entrepreneurship resulting from its rules of privatization, deregulation and freeing up of flows of capital, trade, technology and information. Yet, European countries such as Finland demonstrated with Nokia that communitarian-oriented cultures could also adapt quickly to the digital revolution (and Finland, not accidentally, comes in first place in surveys of educational quality in secondary school math and science in the world).[4] So forms of collective learning which adapt to the digital revolution without a loss of cultural integrity are definitely possible. Such collective learning depends upon localizing technological infrastructures of access outside the major cities to permit citizens with basic educational literacy and learning motivation to plug into the system and benefit from the falling costs of all kinds of information in the world.

However, 09/11 and the Iraq war also indicated that Europe could no longer take the US security umbrella for granted, but would be forced to create its own security structures, which will become increasingly expensive in the twenty-first century. The relatively inexpensive security structures that permitted the commercial success of the European Community after the Second World War will have to be restructured and will lead to higher taxes as American troops continue to be withdrawn from continental Europe (Smith, 2003, A3). In addition, the costs of helping to modernize the ten new states joining the European Union will be significant, even given the trade-off of cheaper labour coming from those states in terms of EU competitiveness.

Here the digital economy may well help to reduce the costs of modernization, provided that basic health and educational infrastructures can be put in place and that consumers gain confidence in using the Internet not just for communication, but for buying and selling goods and services. Close cooperation between the public and private sectors for the sake of updating educational infrastructures and of creating incentives for entrepreneurial, small-business job creation will be the critical tasks for Europe once the new European constitution or charter is agreed upon, the euro is taken for granted as a legitimate world currency, and the first wave of EU enlargement is regulated. In this process, the digital divide will serve as a cipher indicating the speed at which local cultures should or should not adapt to largely unregulated global information and technology flows via modes of dynamic distinctiveness that enable 'Euroculture' to avoid becoming stagnant or frozen. The very integrity of what it constitutes to be a European hangs in the balance.

NOTES

1. I am grateful to Professor Roy Girasa of Pace University for this observation, and to Professor Yusaf Akbar for suggestions regarding the impact of 9/11 security concerns upon freedom of expression.

2. See, for example, Landre (2002), Treadgold (1998), Melymuka (2001), Hammons and Blyden (2000), Starobin and Belton (2000), Hammons and Bicki (2000).
3. I am grateful to James Isaak for this insight (among other suggestions he made for this chapter). See Isaak (2000), and www.jimisaak.com. Also see Ramond (1997).
4. See, for example, Finland's first-place ranking in the Readiness Subindexes in World Economic Forum *Global Information Technology Report 2002–2003*, p. 16; See also Finland's first place in the Technology Achievement Index in UNDP *Human Development Report*, 2001, p. 48.

REFERENCES

Baines, Steward (2002), 'Wired Cities', *Communications International*, 20–24 April.
Espiritu, Antonina (2003), 'Digital Divide and Implications on Growth: Cross-country Analysis', *Journal of American Academy of Business*, **2** (2), 450–55.
Hammons, Thomas and Z. Bicki (2000), 'Eastern and Western European policy on electricity, infrastructure, connection', *IEEE Transactions on Energy Conversion*, September, **15** (3), 328.
Hammons, T.J. and Bai K. Blyden (2000), 'African electricity infrastructure interconnections and electricity exchanges', *IEEE Transactions on Energy Conversion*, December, **15** (4), 471.
Isaak, James (2000), 'Towards equal Web access for all', *ITPro*, November/December and www.jimisaak.com
Isaak, James, Kevin Lewis, Kate Thompson and Richard Straub (1994), *Open Systems Handbook, A Guide to Building Open Systems*, IEEE Standards Press.
Isaak, R. (2000), *Managing World Economic Change*, 3rd edition, Upper Saddle River, NJ: Prentice-Hall.
Isaak, R. (2002), 'Building creativity and entrepreneurship into standards for public sector management', in D. Braunig and P. Eichhorn (eds), *Evaluation and Accounting Standards in Public Management*, Baden-Baden, Germany: Nomos Verlagsgesellschaft, pp. 86–93.
Ishaq, Ashfaq (2001), 'On the global digital divide', *Finance and Development*, September, **38** (3), 44–50.
Kelly, Kevin (1998), *New Rules for the New Economy*, New York: Penguin Putnam.
Kenny, Charles (2003), 'Development's false divide', *Foreign Policy*, January/February, **134**, 76–8.
Kerstetter, Jim, Steve Hamm, Spencer Ante and Jay Greene (2003) 'The Linus uprising', *Business Week*, March 3, p. 48–50.
Landre, Martin (2002), 'The utilization of engineering services bulk infrastructure components in integrated development planning', *Development Southern Africa*, **18** (2), 329–56.
L'Hoest, Raphael (2001), 'The European dimension of the digital economy', *Intereconomist*, January/February, 44–50.
Lodge, George C. (1991), *Perestroika for America*, Boston, MA: Harvard Business School Press.
Melymuka, Kathleen (2001), 'Africa 1.0', *Computerworld*, 7 February, **35** (27), 35.
Nulens, Gert, N. Hafkin, Leo Van Audenhove and B. Cammaerts (eds) (2001), *The Digital Divide In Developing Countries: Towards An Information Society In Africa*, Brussels: Brussels University Press.
Ramond, Eric (1997), 'The cathedral and the bazaar', www.gnu.org

Schreyer, P. (2000), 'The contribution of information and communication technology to output growth: a study of the G7 countries', *OECD, Directorate for Science, Technology and Industry, Working Paper 2000/2*, Paris, p. 5.

Sinclair, Bruce (2002), 'The Great Digital Divide', *Business Mexico*, Spring, **13** (2), 21–22.

Smith, Craig (2003), 'Germany's military sinking to "basket case" status', *New York Times*, 18 March, p. A3.

Starobin, Paul and Catherine Belton (2000), 'The crumbling of Russia', *Business Week*, 9 November, **3698**, 60.

Treadgold, Tim (1998), 'India's promise falters on basic infrastructure', *BRW*, 11 February, **20** (42), 58.

8. Global investment and trade flows: a framework for understanding

John McIntyre and Eric Ford Travis

'. . . quand on cède à la peur du mal, on resseut déja le mal de la peur.' Pierre Augustin Carol de Beaumarchais (*Barbier*, Acte II, Scène 2)

INTRODUCTION

This chapter focuses on the large-scale impacts of terrorism on the international business environment and globalization. It will attempt to determine the more specific effects on international trade or the physical movement of goods across boundaries, and foreign direct investment (FDI), covering regional aspects and seeking to distinguish differential impacts on developed and developing countries. Additional attention is paid to reactive and proactive government policies enacted and how they too can equally affect the global economy. Time is utilized as a central guiding concept to consider the variegated impacts. Portfolio investment is mentioned in passing, as it is best left to specialists able to deal with the intricacies it entails. Nor does the chapter attempt to correlate an exhaustive taxonomy of the various forms of terrorisms with transnational corporate strategies nor does it delve to any depth to the international firm's choice of market entry strategy, or various configurations of the global supply chain as a function of a global environment increasingly concerned with potential terrorist threats on the firms' activities in home or host country settings.

8.1 SHOCK WAVES

The terrorist attacks directed at the United States and the symbols of globalization on September 11, 2001 did more than destroy thousands of lives and cause billions of dollars in direct damage. They also served as a catalyst for change in the global political, business and economic environments. It is paradoxically easier to impute causality in the political arenas than it is in business and economics. The attacks surely had a greater economic resonance due to the coinciding global economic downturn. The vagaries of the global economy's synchronized cyclical movements were intertwined with full-blown terrorism. Disentangling, conceptually, at a specific point in time, the differential economic effects is evidently problematic. Econometric studies may at a later point, with more data sets, shed beneficial light.

In the third quarter of 2001, economists acknowledged that the world's economies were in recession, using IMF annual growth rates as a measuring standard. The terrorist actions and dynamics of the recession displayed the extent of economic integration existing in the world today and what globalization in reverse, as some termed it, might mean. The chief global economist at Morgan Stanley, Stephen Roach, remarked: 'One by one, every major country is tipping into a rare and possibly lethal recession. It is far reaching and deep, and much of that has to do with the fact that we've become much more interconnected' (*New York Times*, Nov. 22, 2001)

The pre-09/11 IMF projections in the *World Economic Outlook* of April 2001 already showed evidence of economic stagnation in most regions of the world. Much of this stemmed from the collapse of the 'dot com' industry, the financial crisis in Japan and its spread to Asia, mirrored by similar problems in Latin America, and fuelled by the general insolvency of several developing nations. Earnings and profits from the United States' computer and information technology sector began declining in 1998 as a result of overinvestment. In the last three years of the 1990s, the investment share of the United States' GDP growth rose from a normal level of one-sixth to one-third. ('Of shocks and horrors', *The Economist*, 26 September 2002) By 2001, investment was at a low point, with a 15 per cent drop during the second quarter alone (Baily, 2001)

Some theorists argued that the recession was merely another aspect of the business cycle, not much different from those preceding it. The domestic and global markets do to some extent have self-perpetuating and self-regulating mechanisms which create predictable business cycles, even more pronounced with greater economic integration. 'As economic and financial interdependence continue to increase, developments in one economic area will affect other economies more than in the past. As a result, global business cycles are likely to become self-reinforcing, which could make booms and recessions in developed economies more severe' ('United we fall', *The Economist*, 26 September 2002).

The point in contention is the degree to which other factors influence these cycles. An exogenous shock such as a terrorist attack of some magnitude, in an age of instantaneous mass mediatization, can obviously have a direct impact, but how is this further magnified in the loss of consumer confidence and the perception of increased risk by decision-makers, investors and financial authorities? While we know that security measures properly targeted and timed are essential to stem terrorism, we wonder how economic policy responses addressing the problem alleviate or exacerbate the situation in times of heightened uncertainty. Even if this question is answered, economic impacts of non-economic phenomena are virtually impossible to quantify. In addition, even if a terrorist act does not have a large, direct and immediate impact, governments, institutions and companies still suffer additional transaction costs from needed preventive and protective steps in the ensuing period.

Historically, terrorism has been focused against nation-states, directed at either their governmental institutions or civilian populations. The 09/11 attacks could signify a shift in terrorist thrust, targeting instead capitalism and commerce, unintended or not. Excluding, 'human victims of the World Trade Center event, the great majority of the casualties of terrorist attacks in 2001 were civilians; aside from the World Trade Center, only five business-related casualties were reported in 2001. While the incidence of terrorism grew steadily in the 1960s and 1970s, it has actually declined since the 1980s' (Knight et al., 2003). If terrorist groups perceive a greater overall destabilizing impact against nation-states they target through business operations and hubs, then it could be deduced that more attacks against commercial targets will ensue. The states being targeted must assess the extent of the impact to prepare for future contingencies. Seeking to evolve an analytical framework to think through impacts and strategies is part of the essential series of first steps.

Peter Enderwick has attempted to develop a worthy initial conceptual framework to discern the multiple impacts of the 09/11 terrorist attacks (Enderwick, 2001). His view consisted of a series of concentric circles, with 'primary impacts' at the centre, surrounded by 'secondary impacts', 'response-generated impacts' and 'longer-term issues'. The airline industry and tourism are the two obvious 'primary impacts'. As the rings move outwards, they become less directly affected, more distant temporally, and also less concretely linked in causality. The other impacts range from investment and security (secondary impacts) through government spending and growth rates (response-generated) and, finally, to concepts such as sources of resentment and geopolitical alliances. An alternative, simplified version to Enderwick's proposal is presented in Figure 8.1, and is modified to coordinate with this chapter.

The notion of time as quantified through traditional economic, financial and risk measures is a key international business environment factor influencing trade and investment decisions. Closer to the centre of the diagram are immediate impacts. Again, predictably they are the easiest to determine. Those further away from the centre are more distant in time

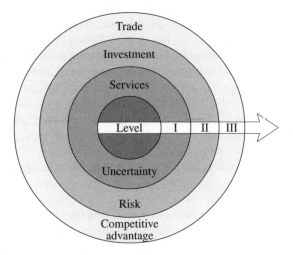

Figure 8.1 Adapted circular framework

and effect and also more difficult to define. In this diagram, there are two groupings, one extending upwards and the other downwards. They are all intertwined in a complex manner and difficult to isolate. For example, uncertainty in the wake of a terrorist act leads to a perception of increased risk, which can repel direct manufacturing and facilities investment and possibly lead to more merchandise exports and imports to compensate or substitute for reduced foreign direct equity investment. Some countries might also be able to convert a low risk level of terrorism into a competitive advantage, compared to other regions, thereby attracting more investment, increasing domestic production and possibly reducing the levels of trade in merchandise.

8.2 IMPACTS OF TERRORISM ON THE INTERNATIONAL BUSINESS ENVIRONMENT

8.2.1 The Uncertainty of Risk and Risk of Uncertainty

The difference between risk and uncertainty is central to this analysis. Risk is quantifiable and determined through historical precedent. It is measured as a probability and included in the determinations not only of insurance, but also is used to weigh calculated return on investment. There are different types of international business risk: political, competitive, monetary, foreign exchange-related, transactional and so on. Businesses determine their courses of action based upon risk assessment. With equal levels of risk, a company will choose the course of action with the greater return.

Many factors can be accounted for, through careful research and due diligence, but not all as we move farther out along the time spectrum, from an area of probabilistic risk to an area of uncertainty. Experienced companies are naturally better able to assess risk accurately and, often, reduce it through risk management measures. This is true of multinationals, which deal with multiple risks in every venture, such as the possible occurrence of natural disasters. In addition, insurance and reinsurance companies can also assist in the reduction of risk, but at a cost. Most business-to-business transactions today are payable in the short term, and individual countries are rated based upon corporate default rates as an indicator of local business, financial and political outlooks. One of the first indicator subsets used by insurers is 'political factors likely to interrupt payment or performance of contracts in progress', or interruption in the global supply chain and logistical flows (COFACE, 2002).

Terrorist actions are not as easily categorized, analysed or predicted. 'The increased proliferation of dangerous technologies and the existence of terrorist groups such as Al Qaeda that would not hesitate to use weapons of mass destruction raise the spectre of a potentially worse mass-casualty attack in the future. There has been a chilling new conjunction of capabilities and intentions' (Litwak, 2002). Insurance companies more easily factor in even hurricanes than terrorist actions. This is due to the fact that terrorists are not random in their targets or timing; they are for the most part highly calculated. Even with a surprisingly voluminous history of terrorist actions in the past century, there is no mathematical formula for predicting the next attack. In the United States, there are areas at high risk of tornadoes. Hurricanes follow more or less the same corridor across the Atlantic. As the world has learned, terrorists can attack at any time and anywhere in the world, from Bali, Indonesia, to the capital of the capitalist world, New York City. Their actions can range from individual kidnappings in Colombia to the possibility of releasing a biological weapon with global consequences.

What is unique about the terrorist threats is that they are not unified. Each group has goals that might align with others on a regional or cultural basis, but overall, terrorists are fragmented in terms of goals, methods and location. Even the individual groups are liable to be comprised of 'sleeper cells' that are not even aware of the other members of their organization. What this means is that the only way to attempt a risk evaluation is to gather as much information as possible. This has proven difficult even for the most powerful and adept governments, much less businesses. In addition, most knowledge of possible risk factors is made apparent within days, if not hours, of potential terrorist threat and is too late for businesses to anticipate and mitigate effects. What the business environment is left with is a great deal of uncertainty and the high cost of building information, distribution and production systems that are 'redundant' and therefore shock-proof. The additional costs and the ensuing reduction in global competitiveness are incalculable, if such a failsafe approach is pursued *in extenso*.

Uncertainty is a consequence of the lack of historical knowledge on the manifestations of terrorism and their multiple consequences. Media reporting compounds the situation:

> Terrorism's main impact is the fear and generalised stress that it engenders among the peoples of individual nations and the world. It is this same psychological response that in turn impacts the macro-economy, affects consumption, and may lead to widespread panic or obsessions that can have harmful long-term societal effects. The media are a key institution that both inform about terrorist activity and amplify its effect. (Knight et al., 2003)

Terrorists count on media coverage to spread fear and widen the impact. A direct attack on a bus might harm only a few individuals, but once it is covered in the media, it reaches a vast audience. Citizens who see news of a bus bombing on the television might decide to stop riding the buses, which could disrupt flows of labour. Considering the extent and technological advancement of media today, a story reaches virtually all parts of the globe virtually instantaneously. Television media coverage of the 09/11 attacks began literally within minutes, and were picked up worldwide. Viewers around the globe witnessed the events as they occurred, showing the entire world what a terrorist group was capable of doing to the United States. This was undoubtedly one of the terrorists' desires.

The situation has definitely had some effect on both globalization and the business environment, but economists and politicians have difficulty agreeing on how or what:

> Unquestionably, the events of September 11 have reshaped the debate over globalisation. A trend that many economists characterised as irresistible suddenly appears less so. Foreign assembly operations have become less attractive to US corporations now that there is the fact, or even the danger, that their trucks will be stuck in mile-long queues at the US–Canada or US–Mexico border. Companies like McDonald's and Starbucks, whose main opportunities for market growth are outside the United States, now must factor in extra costs of security when contemplating opening another outlet abroad. Computer programmers from India and graduate students from Pakistan will face additional hurdles when attempting to obtain temporary residency in the United States, and American companies will think twice about posting their executives abroad. Foreign trade, foreign direct investment, and international migration all will grow less quickly than they did before the terrorist attacks. (Eichengreen, 2001)

Uncertainty is always present in the global environment. Businesses obviously prefer certainty to risk, and risk to uncertainty. Some economists believe there should be an economics of terrorism: 'terrorists have inflicted enough damage in enough places during the past 30 years for economists to credibly evaluate how terrorism affects economic activity' (Shapiro, 2003). Shapiro cites evidence of economic development and growth in areas suffering from long-term terrorist action and threat such as Colombia, Northern Ireland, Israel and the Basque region of Spain. 'Where terrorism has been more occasional and local, the economic impact is modest, resembling ordinary crime. So long as al-Qaida or its counterparts are unable (or unwilling) to use weapons much more powerful than airliners, especially nuclear weapons, any ambition to derail a large, advanced economy like ours will fail.'

The problem is that terrorism is definitely not isolated or local any more. Also, terrorists will in all likelihood use whatever means are at their disposal. Furthermore, as the full impact of a major terrorist act cannot be legitimately measured, the validity that a 'huge terror strike is a blip in a vast economy like the United States' must come into question (Shapiro, 2003). As mentioned previously, such an action could have more long-term implications, especially if it leads directly to a change in the economic or defence policies of governments. In addition, Shapiro does not take into account, or underestimates, the intrinsic power of ideas in the political and economic realms. Governments and businesses will be more conservative and defensive in their actions if they sense a threat, even without actual substantial risk. For some specific markets, terrorism can be accounted for as a defined risk factor, and could possibly be factored in the sense of an *ad valorem* tariff. The rest of the world will be a domain of uncertainty, which will carry the highest tax rate of all.

8.2.2 Business Sectors

The dynamics of the international business environment will change with rising levels of perceived or actual threat of terrorist activity. They will also evolve over different time and spatial horizons. One instance of this is the institution of a terrorist threat level warning code in the United States. The United States government uses four different colour codes – green, yellow, orange and red – as official indicators of the probability of imminent terrorist activity. Government personnel are expected to increase their vigilance accordingly to match the level of threat. This warning system has been adopted by the media sector of the United States as well.

What the warning system signifies is an attempt by a government to convert the uncertainty inherent in terrorism into a usable representation of risk, even if it is targeted more at public information than at traditional national security. The distinction helps reduce the anxiety of both individuals and businesses, contributing to a more tranquil and alert society. Even if the intelligence from which the terrorist threat level system distilled is vague, the end result is simple in concept and easy to disseminate. For example, the intelligence data that there is a heightened chance of terrorist activity on the East Coast of the United States helps no one except directly involved security personnel. However, elevate the visual code to 'orange', put it on television, and the nation feels empowered.

As with all actions and systems, there are transaction costs. One is that the code is overly general and a relatively blunt instrument. While this makes it easy to understand and implement, it also prevents specificity. A localized terrorist threat can elevate the warning level and be applied to the entire country, and a marginally elevated level of terrorist activity could easily translate into a higher colour, as there are only the four to choose from. Elevated levels signify additional risk, which directly affects both individual consumer and business behaviour. Consumer confidence is strained, spending may be reduced, and general business activity slowed. No study on the macroeconomic effects of code shifting exists, although good preliminary assessments of the consequences on the travel, tourism and entertainment industries are available.

Further response by the US government to 09/11 focused on bio-terrorist activity. On 12 June 2002, President Bush signed into law the Public Health Security and Bio-terrorism Preparedness and Response Act of 2002, also known as the Bio-terrorism Act (BTA), under the Food and Drug Administration. The Act seeks to prevent bio-terrorist threats to national food supplies, including food imported from foreign sources. The law was due to be implemented on 12 December 2003, and has four major provisions: registration, prior notice, administrative detention and record keeping. The first two provisions have the most direct impact on trade. Registration requires that domestic and foreign facilities that manufacture, process, pack or hold food for human or animal consumption in the United States register with the FDA by 12 December 2003. Prior notice requires that US purchasers, importers or their agents submit prior notice on the importation of food starting no later than that date (US Customs).

Another system change is the Advance Manifest Rules enacted by the United States Customs and Border Protection, related to the Container Security Initiative (CSI). Over 90 per cent of world cargo moves via containers and many nations trade primarily by sea. The United Kingdom, Japan and South Korea each depend on sea cargo for over 90 per cent of trade and in the United States over 50 per cent of imports by value arrive

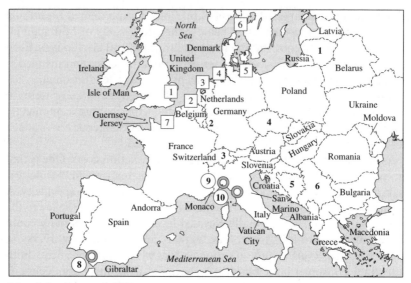

Map 8.1   Ports of CSI

on ships. CSI was announced on 17 January 2002, and the first 18 participating ports from around the world were committed one year later to the
day, with the ports in Asia and Europe shown on Map 8.1. The primary
intent is to screen shipments at ports before loading to prevent dangerous
cargo from entering the United States. The foreign governments assist in
targeting high-risk shipments and perform the screening under observation
of the CSI, while low-risk and CSI pre-screened shipments are given more
rapid entry. Targeting, of necessity, is based upon national security data,
which has raised some questions about bias and possible disparate impact
on certain regions or countries of the world (US Customs).

The map is from www.maps.com. Ports 1–7 are those that are already part
of CSI, and are represented by a square. These ports are: 1) Felixstowe, 2)
Antwerp, 3) Rotterdam, 4) Bremerhaven, 5) Hamburg, 6) Goteborg, 7) Le
Havre. Ports 8–10 (represented by a circle) will be added soon: 8) Algeciras,
9) Genoa, 10) La Spezia. Ports in Asia that are currently involved are:
Singapore, Yokohama and Hong Kong. In addition, ports in Asia that will
be included are: Shanghai, Kaohsiung in Taiwan; Pusan, Korea; Tokyo,
Nagoya, and Kobe, Japan; and Laem Chabang, Thailand. Canadian ports
of Montreal, Vancouver and Halifax are currently members.

The 24-Hour Sea Advance Vessel Manifest Rule requires electronic submission of manifests to US Customs for all vessels calling on US ports at
least 24 hours prior to loading from an overseas port. This is considered a
matter of national security by the United States, and failure to comply will

result in 'Do Not Load' messages on containers. The final stage of this rule was enabled by 1 October 2003. There are similar rules for air, truck and rail freight as well. Advance Manifest for air must be submitted a minimum of eight hours before loading for couriers and 12 for other shipments; for trucks it is four hours, for rail eight hours (US Customs).

Another alteration to the United States Customs regulatory framework directly resulting from terrorist threat is the Automated Commercial Environment (ACE). This new system began its development in August 2001, prior to the 09/11 attacks. The US government believes ACE will revolutionize how Customs processes goods imported into the United States by providing an integrated, fully automated information system to enable the efficient collection, processing and analysis of commercial import and export data. This automated system facilitates transactions between US Customs and the business community by reducing labour and time. Implementation is the primary obstacle, as initially only a few Customs trade account managers and 40 selected importers were targeted for inclusion. Expansion to the business community as a whole is a much more lengthy and involved process.

Initially, a country instituting additional customs regulations such as electronic submission of manifests on merchandise imports and exports, all in the name of security, is being seen as an additional trade barrier by other countries. Companies from other countries are forced to alter their manner of doing business to comply with the new laws. This raises transaction costs, initially reduces trade and has the possibility of igniting retaliatory measures from foreign governments. However, over a longer period of time, harmonization of trade practices will streamline the customs process, saving time, enhancing productivity and increasing profits. Eventually such a change could have the potential to increase overall international trade in merchandise. 'There will be a strong incentive to invest in new technologies that will minimise disruptions to international business. More investment in such equipment will allow international traffic to move more quickly, whether that traffic takes the form of trucks, container ships, or passenger airlines' (Eichengreen, 2001).

The hardest-hit sector has been the service sector. In most developed countries, this sector makes up a majority of the economy, so even a minute effect on the sector can have severe impacts. 'The United States generates roughly 70% of its GDP in the form of services, and services accounted for 30% of U.S. exports' (Bernal, 2002). Other problems could manifest themselves from less tourism and international travel, as receipts from tourism and the service sector are often critical to many developing economies. 'Narco-trafficking' could increase as an alternative source of income in these areas. In addition, migration to developed countries in search of employment could increase and cause potential security and political problems, with possible labour displacement.

The airline industries worldwide have suffered immensely. Not only do airlines around the world code-share flights with airlines from other countries, but also many own substantial shares of foreign airlines. World Bank estimates are that air freight costs rose 15 per cent after September 11. ('Is it at risk?', *The Economist*, 31 January 2002) Some argument has been made that capacity has merely shifted to private air services or other means of transportation, but the damage to the industry as a whole has not been ascertained in other areas of the economy. Tourism has also been closely connected to the fate of the airline industry. Consumer confidence levels have affected tourism such that even domestic hotels have trouble filling their rooms, much less those located in resort areas. Again, the multinational hotels cross many borders and are closely intertwined in numerous economies.

While the short-term effect on tourism and travel has been devastating, in the medium term relief will come regionally. Tourists and companies alike will return initially to the markets with the least amount of uncertainty concerning terrorist action. The Caribbean islands are being viewed as a relative safe location for many Americans and Europeans, while the Pacific countries will still suffer from higher levels of uncertainty and proximity to terrorist areas (Bernal, 2002). Trading relationships will not suffer as much as tourism, with the exception of course of political conflicts. This is especially true of both regional and multinational corporations. Multinational corporations now account for about one-third of world output and two-thirds of world trade, but most of it is concentrated within the economic triad of the United States, Europe and Japan (Bernal, 2002).

Multinational corporations, and in some instances regional corporations, have a decided advantage over domestic exporters or international companies when it comes to dealing with uncertainty and terrorism. Multinationals have the experience to successfully manoeuvre in troubled environments. In many cases, they are even seen as a local company. For example, an American or European multinational that acts locally and employs mostly local workers and managers is much less a target of terrorism than an international company that employs many expatriates and does not adapt to local culture and society. Thus, for medium-risk countries, companies might shift away from using expatriates if they have the ability to do so, and shift towards employing more local workers. This can be a source of numerous problems for the home corporation and the assessment will be determined by which transaction cost is lower, the terrorist threat or conflicts in management.

Inherent in the multinational firm is a sense of flexibility, which may lower overall risk. When operating in many different economic and political environments, the company must be able withstand difficult times in one location by being profitable in another. In this sense, a multinational is similar to diversifying a portfolio: the more non-correlated (or negatively correlated) locations a firm invests in, the lower the risk:

> Flexibility is achieved via networks of dispersed, agile business units. Indeed, the international firm that operates via a network of decentralised regional headquarters, each located in its key markets around the world, instead of via a single 'world' headquarters at one central location, enjoys greater flexibility. Moreover, the globally dispersed international firm is likely to possess a deeper understanding of evolving events in the markets where its subsidiaries are located. Establishing local operations also facilitates the cultivation of key, local contacts. The 'insider information' and contacts that derive from locally-based positioning is likely to be superior to that of the firm that concentrates its operations in a single location far removed from the market. (Knight et al., 2003)

Some multinationals are truly global and see foreign direct investment as a cost effective alternative to exporting. These firms would have extreme difficulty withdrawing from all of the markets that are deemed threatened by terrorism. For example, Toyota Motor Company sold 2.343 million vehicles outside of Japan and of these, 1.379 million were manufactured in the local markets. Nestlé, of Switzerland, only sells 2 per cent of its total production in its home market. There are almost 500 Nestlé factories located around the world, lowering the need for exports to a minimum. Nestlé endows each region with its own strategy and management organizations (Jeannet, 1998). 'I do not know how a global firm could not be decentralised,' says Jack Greenberg, head of McDonald's (Micklethwait and Woolridge, 2000). Again, if exporting becomes more difficult due to increased trade barriers or threat of terrorist action, then companies will consider the other alternatives available to them, such as FDI, which will change the relative levels of activity in business sectors.

8.2.3 Comparative and Competitive Advantages

Comparative advantage is based on the theory that a country, and global trade in general, will benefit if each country specializes its production on the product or products that it is able to produce more efficiently than other products. It is based on the advantages that accrue to a country's economy: natural, acquired, informational and government-induced, among other sources. Governments can attempt to influence the general perception of terrorist threat in their country in order to influence the terms of trade and the willingness to engage in trade. Similarly, burdensome regulation to overcome real or perceptual threats may shift the nature of the terms of trade in a comparative advantage as opposed to other countries that have fewer comparable trade barriers.

Another important concept regarding terrorist threats is the idea of competitive advantage. Competitive advantage is the concept that a country can offer a more suitable environment for businesses than another country, thereby benefiting the firms which choose the right location. The traditional view consists of the 'Porter Diamond': factor conditions, demand conditions, related and supporting industries, and firm strategy, structure and rivalry. It is not difficult to imagine how terrorism or its absence can be included in such a framework.

Factor conditions can range from the level of skilled labour to political stability. If a country can offer safety in addition to other production factors needed, it will have an advantage during times when terrorism is occurring. This will benefit the domestic companies that are located within such countries, and they will have a competitive advantage against those from countries that suffer from terrorist threat. Likewise, such conditions will appear attractive to multinationals that either desire multi-domestic production, or desire new production for export. The end result could be a substantial shift in foreign direct investment away from countries with high threat levels to countries with lower levels of threat. Such scenarios also entangle with political actions, as foreign investment, trade benefits and economic incentives can be reserved for countries that are willing to comply and coordinate efforts with either unilateral or multilateral efforts against terrorism.

8.2.4 Globalization

> Globalisation today is not working for many of the world's poor. It is not working for much of the environment. It is not working for the stability of the global economy. The transition from Communism to a market economy has been so badly managed that, with the exception of China, Vietnam and a few Eastern European countries, poverty has soared as incomes have plummeted . . . Part of the problem lies with the international economic institutions, with the IMF, World Bank, WTO, which help set the rules of the game. They have done so in ways that, all too often, have served the interests of the more advanced industrialised countries . . . rather than those of the developing world.

So runs the famous argument by former World Bank Senior Economist and Nobel Prize winner Joseph Stiglitz (Stiglitz, 2002, p. 214).

Globalization remains a highly contentious topic. Globalization itself has been suggested as one of the targets of the September 11 attacks (Bernal 2002). While it is viewed as progressive, modernizing and inevitable by many, particularly in the developed world, others, generally from the developing world, see it to be limiting, exploitative and imperialistic. Any single issue of globalization can result in polar opposites; for example, modern infrastructure can be viewed as economic opportunity or destruction of the environment and Internet access can be seen as opening new horizons or introducing ideas that destroy cultures. 'Contradictions abound. American leadership seems strong – and countries everywhere assail it. Economic pressures draw nations together – and cultural and political differences pull them apart. Some technologies favour global commerce – and others abet terrorism' (Samuelson, 2003).

Globalization is fraught with issues that can be exploited dialectically and ideologically by non-state terrorist actors. There has been overdependence on the United States economy, accounting for 64 per cent of the growth from 1995–2003. The economies of Europe and Japan have become stagnant. Developing countries suffer from high levels of indebtedness. Globalization has not adequately filled in the chasm between the developed and developing countries. Indeed, in some ways, there may well be more separation than ever, in terms of income, with the heaviest concentrations in wealth, productivity growth and export levels located largely in the United States, Japan and the EU. Money and wealth, the argument runs, are held by multinational corporations and, in turn, they individually wield the economic might of nation-states. Some – Texaco, Chevron and DeBeers, for example – have even been accused of possessing private mercenary armies (CNN Italia, 2000). Globalization has heightened the centrality of multinational corporate actors while making the market more difficult to enter and survive for companies from emerging countries.

> Already the total revenue of Mitsubishi, a giant corporate *keiretsu* of Japan, exceeds the gross domestic product (GDP) of South Korea and Citi Group's revenue exceeds the total output of India. Microsoft is bigger than the Netherlands, GM is bigger than Turkey, Philip Morris is larger than New Zealand, and Wal-Mart is bigger than Israel. The combined revenues of GM and Ford exceed the combined GDP for all of sub-Saharan Africa. In fact, 51 of the 100 largest economies in the world are corporations. Top 500 corporations account for nearly 30 percent of the world's total economic output and 70 percent of the world-wide trade. Between 1950 and 1997 the global economy expanded, thanks largely to corporations, from an annual output of $5 trillion to $29 trillion, an increase of nearly six-fold. Growth during the last decade exceeds that during the 10 000 years from the beginning of agriculture until 1950. (Chang, 1999)

Not only has the 'Triad' generated the greatest rate of economic growth and spurred on globalization, but it has stretched the underlying political theory at the seams.

'Modernization theory', as it is often termed, views globalization as stability-inducing, beneficial and in positive-sum terms. The more that capitalist, Western European democratic ideals are spread, the faster countries will develop. At the other end of the spectrum is 'dependency theory', a theoretical construct penned in Latin America at a time of social ferment and given an audience outside of the region where it might provide a supporting rationale or veil for extremist actions. It considers the developed world as protectionist and exploitative, using the developing world for cheap labour and raw materials and actually limiting its development. Many *dependencia* theorists who held sway in the 1960s argued that developed countries have a limited concept of democracy, coupled with a largely capitalistic and paternalistic frame of reference. Dennis Ross, a peace envoy to the Middle East under President Clinton, said the United States' choice of friends in the region possibly contributed to the anger and resentment reputed to have propelled al-Qaida's terrorist enterprise. 'We are resented in no small part because we are seen as using democracy as a tool or weapon against those we don't like, but never against those we do like', argued Ross, now director at the Washington Institute for Near East Policy. Such perceptions, grounded or not, seem to have survived, often side by side, with the analysis popular in the 1960s and 1970s, in some quarters (NCTAUUS, 2003). They are most probably fertile ground to plant the seeds of terrorist ideology.

Moral judgements aside, what is important is understanding how globalization interacting with underdevelopment can either directly stimulate terrorist activity or provide a corrupted rationale for terrorist groups. Just as critical is determining how terrorist activity can influence globalization. If certain terrorist organizations include globalization itself as one of their targets, then any perception of success in stemming the process of globalization could well heighten the level of terrorist activity. The need to reduce environments hospitable to terrorists provides an impetus not only for economic and social development worldwide, but also for political or regime change among the developed countries. Alan Greenspan, in Congressional testimony, has argued:

> contrary to current opinion, developing countries need more globalization, not less. Such a course would likely bring with it greater economic stability and political freedom. Indeed, probably the single most effective action that the industrial countries could implement to alleviate the terrible problem of poverty in many developing countries would be to open, unilaterally, markets to imports from those countries. (Greenspan, 2001)

It is widely believed that withdrawing from the global economy into a state of isolationism to establish a *cordon sanitaire*, maximizing security, perhaps at the expense of competitive advantages, will not stop terrorism.

Similarly, forced isolation of 'rogue' countries suspected of harbouring or abetting terrorists will not make them disappear. The roots of the problems causing risk and uncertainty will still exist as US Special Trade Representative Zoellick observed insightfully:

> Erecting new barriers and closing old borders will not help the impoverished. It will not feed hundreds of millions struggling for subsistence. It will not liberate the persecuted. It will not improve the environment in developing nations or reverse the spread of AIDS. It will not help the railway orphans I visited in India. It will not improve the livelihoods of the union members I met in Latin America. It will not aid the committed Indonesians I visited who are trying to build a functioning, tolerant democracy in the largest Muslim nation in the world. And it certainly will not placate terrorists. (Zoellick, 2001)

A paradoxical idea is that if Osama bin Laden and his associates behind the 09/11 attacks were targeting globalization, they may have produced an effect opposite to their intent. The US and other globalized economies were in a downturn prior to the attacks. The wave of terrorism spurred further international cooperation, yielding a more globally integrated environment in the face of a common threat as noted by Stephan Richter, President of the Washington-based the *Globalist*:

> Even before the terrorist attacks, the fall in US demand ripped holes in the economies of its trading partners from Mexico to Taiwan. Countries in Latin America and Asia especially felt that they were on the short end of the stick. It was Osama bin Laden's attack on the United States which has changed all of the dynamics of that blame game. Much of the pointed criticism of the United States and globalisation has now either been toned down considerably – or come to a halt . . . Prior to September 11, the United States was indeed embarking on a unilateralist course in foreign economic policy. It was a course that was essentially anti-co-operation placing US interests before attempts at prolonged and often frustrating dialogue or compromise with others. But the need for co-operation in the fight against terrorism has trumped the Bush Administration's economic isolationists. As a result, globalisation – and not just economic globalisation, but globalisation in all its facets – is the emerging order of the day. (Richter, 2001)

A crisis whose geographical dimensions are uncertain and uneasily contained in one country or region can reverberate with momentum through the entire global economic system. Examples abound from finance to public health crises. Just as 09/11 had far-reaching implications, so does the SARS epidemic, which issues a dire warning about the global nature of a bio-terrorist catastrophe. SARS began in a region of China which, in the past 20 years, has become a point of fulcrum in the global sourcing of parts and manufactured products:

> Although public health authorities may finally be stemming the pace of the out-
> breaks in some countries, even as new cases are reported in others, SARS con-
> tinues to pose a serious danger to the world economy. Analysts are already trying
> to measure how many tens of billions of dollars of GDP have been lost – and
> how much higher costs may go. Both the 1997 Asian financial crisis and SARS
> reveal a common threat – how globalisation, despite its considerable benefits,
> also brings with it unanticipated risks . . . The movement of the great flu epi-
> demic after World War I was measured in many months. Now a SARS virus,
> aboard an infected person, can get half way around the world in a matter of
> hours. (Yergin, 2003)

Terrorist activity might either impede the more visible and tangible
aspects of globalization, or enhance further integration, or a combination
of both. While it has definitely reduced international travel, it has also been
somewhat compensated through enhanced communications infrastructures.
'Your threats and opportunities increasingly derive from your points of
contact. Globalism is the triumph of free-market capitalism. The technologies driving globalism are computerisation, miniaturisation, digitisation,
satellite communications, fiber optics and the Internet, which reinforces its
defining perspective of integration' (Frieden, 1999). Terrorism, or even the
idea of it, definitely has the potential both to utilize and then hinder or even
reverse globalization. 'Fear of terrorist acts, however, has the potential to
induce disengagement from activities, both domestic and cross-border. If we
allow terrorism to undermine our freedom of action, we could reverse at
least part of the palpable gains achieved by post-war globalisation', noted
Alan Greenspan, President of the Federal Reserve Bank system of the
United States (Greenspan, 2001).

8.2.5   Regional Development and Underdevelopment

Globalization does not have the same effect everywhere. The developed countries have always benefited disproportionately from the terms of trade and
equity and portfolio direct investment. Out of the developing countries, few
receive substantial trade and investment advantages. Some argue that regionalism is a stage in the progression to globalism, increasing intra-regional trade
and enabling regional companies to compete on the global market. Others
believe that it is a regression from and hindrance to the globalization process,
and that intra-regional alliances are self-replicating and increase trade barriers:

> In any case, regional and bilateral deals are a poor second-best to global free
> trade. By definition, preferences granted to some are handicaps imposed on
> others. Countries that are excluded from such agreements suffer. Yet, the deals
> create their own logic, where those who are discriminated against, seek their own
> preferential deal. (Ruggiero, 2003)

Whatever the point of view, regionalism is a definite and measurable reality. It has a substantial economic impact, both for those included in regional alliances and for those excluded, as by definition, only those in the region are invited to the party:

At the economic level, globalisation is creating larger units, as in forms of corporate entities such as multinational corporations, and the coalescing of national economies through regional integration, forming regional trade blocs. Trade blocs are a fundamental aspect of the world economy, in terms of share of world trade they encompass and the number of countries that participate in them. In 1995, 51 reciprocal, GATT- notified regional trade agreements were in force and accounted for 50% of world trade. A 1992 survey listed 23 preferential trade arrangements, encompassing 119 countries and accounting for approximately 82 % of international trade in goods . . . Intra-regional trade has grown rapidly throughout the world since the late 1940s, including accounting for almost 70 % of trade in Western Europe. (Bernal, 2002)

Some regional formations are intended for protection and others for competitive advantage, but the losers in both always seem to come from the same regions:

Measured either in terms of trade or direct investment, integration has been highly uneven. A few developing countries have managed to increase their trade a lot. They are the same countries that have attracted the lion's share of foreign direct investment. A recent World Bank study noted that 24 countries, home to 3 billion people, and including China, Argentina, Brazil, India and the Philippines, have substantially increased their trade-to-GDP ratios over the past 20 years . . . another 2 billion people live in countries that have become less rather than more globalized. In these countries, including Pakistan and much of Africa, trade has diminished in relation to national income, economic growth has been stagnant, and poverty has risen . . . income per head in the 'non-globalising' countries fell on average by 1% a year in the 1990s. (*The Economist*, 31 January 2002)

Most of the developing countries have not been able to compete effectively on the global market. 'The terms of trade for the least developed countries have declined a cumulative 50% over the past 25 years' (Bernal, 2002). Poverty and income disparities remain a fierce enemy in reaping the trade and investment benefits of an interdependent world economy. Alleviating poverty, as broadly defined by the World Bank, can be one of the several keys in combating terrorism. Countries with limited competitive capabilities are often disenfranchised as global actors, furthering regional fragmentation.

There were 51 countries present at the founding of the United Nations whose structure now encompasses over 190 member countries. When the

IMF and World Bank were formed in the 1940s, fewer than a quarter of the current members were present. As new countries have joined over the years, they have become bound by their pre-existing organizations rules. 'The advent of regional alliances and unions has prompted a realignment of positions and interests across the globe' (Kapur, 2003).

Terrorism impacts differentially across regions of the world, along the fault lines of economic development, when allied with extremist and fundamentalist ideologies inimical to the core values of democracy and market economics. Not unexpectedly, the uncertainty impacts of this global scale phenomenon have been felt, in traditional trade and foreign investment terms, more acutely in the developing countries. This essential observation is grounded in the logic of economic development rather than the controversial 'clash of civilisations' thesis in which culture, religion and ethnicity are the controlling variables (Huntington, 1993).

8.2.6 Muslim Countries: Least Globalized, Most Affected

Countries and regions seen as being associated with terrorism are not only poor, but stand to be more affected by the terrorist attacks than open, tolerant and developed countries. 'In short, globalisation is not, and never was, global. Much of the world, home to one-third of its people and including large tracts of Africa and many Muslim countries, has simply failed to participate. The shocks of 2001 risk worsening this long-standing marginalisation' (Bernal, 2002). The Middle East and Africa, in particular, are cited often as being left out of trade and investment. 'Iran is rated the least globalized of the 62 countries surveyed, a symptom of the continuing marginalisation of much of the Middle East reflected in the region's stagnant growth, falling share of world trade, and poor record in attracting investment' (*Daily Policy Digest*, 2003)

Investment in Islamic countries has dropped since the events of 09/11. Growth has taken a similar nosedive. Indonesia during the year 2002 showed drastic differences from 2001 as regards its economy. 'Growth during the first quarter only reached 2.47%. Foreign Direct Investment approval dropped 88% in the first quarter of 2002 to $291.5 million from $2.44 billion in the same period of 2001. Indonesia is still in the dumps economically, a fact that will not change in the near term' (Global Policy Forum, 2002) Indonesia is the largest Muslim country in the world and is considered by many to be a hot spot for terrorist activity.

Egypt suffered similarly, if not as dramatically, due to 09/11:

> Over two thirds of Egypt's trade is with the US and the EU, the two regions most directly affected by the attacks. Hence there was a direct and considerable negative impact on the economy . . . The GDP growth rate was estimated at 4.9% for

FY2000/01 was revised down to 1.5%–2% for FY2001/02 . . . Annual inflows of FDI into Egypt had reached their height in 2000 at $2 billion. In 2001, by contrast, FDI flows dropped to $509 million by the end of FY2000/01 and around $390 million through the first three quarters of FY2001/02 . . . the decline in FDI is expected to continue in the future due to increasing global uncertainty. However, there has been a fairly stable influx of Arab money into Egypt in the wake of September 11, dampening the negative decline in FDI. (ACC Egypt, 2002)

Economic backlash is most apparent where there are Islamic fundamentalist movements fighting for a religious state, including areas in Indonesia and the Philippines. The image projected hinders economic progress in the country and reduces the attractiveness of such host environments. Even countries little affected by fundamentalist unrest or separatist activity are bracing for the worst, as they fear they will be found guilty by association:

> Foreign investment means bringing in foreign expatriates to manage, and it may become harder to bring people in . . . Now they want to know whether Islamic radicals are going to take over Malaysia, Indonesia, the Philippines and Thailand, and how safe is Singapore? There's no question that the two major kidnappings by the Abu Sayyaf have deterred new business interests in the Philippines . . . There will be some effect on foreign investors coming to Muslim countries, because of the way Islam has been portrayed – even though there have been desperate attempts to say Muslims and terrorists are separate. Most people still think Islam has the potential to be destructive. (*Dateline*, 2001)

The image of Islamic radicals operating in these countries has complicated existing trading relationships. An executive at a large Kelantan (Malaysia) textile plant, 85 per cent of whose output is exported to America, reports encountering difficulties dealing with US buyers in the aftermath of September 11. 'The buyers in the US have suddenly become more stringent. We don't know if this is because of the incident or just that they are raising standards, but they tend to reject products for small mistakes that last time were acceptable to them' (*Dateline*, 2001). Another side effect of the fear of investing in countries with large Muslim populations is that the money will instead be diverted to China and India at South-East Asia's expense, compelling evidence supporting the ability of terrorists to alter the global business environment. Integrating such countries into the global economy remains the challenge of what some observers have called the 'crescent of crisis'.

Various economic studies, indicators and rankings also mark Islamic countries as inhospitable. Some of the studies and rankings are argued to be biased against developing countries not heeding the demands of open markets and free trade principles. There are also charges of political motive by those creating and conducting the studies. Nevertheless, the rankings and indicators are widely used in the business community. More often than not, Muslim countries cluster in the lower half of any such rankings, usually at the very bottom. Western European and other developed countries dominate the upper range of these rankings.

The 'Index of Economic Freedom', sponsored by the Hoover Foundation, is one such ranking. It takes into account issues such as trade, fiscal burden of government, government intervention, monetary policy, foreign investment, banking and finance, wages, prices, property rights, regulation, and black market activity. If a country is ranked low, it is theoretically hurt in its ability to increase investment and trade and subsequently increase wages due to global public perception based upon the rank. The 2001 'Index' listed Turkey at 63, Malaysia and Saudi Arabia tied at 75, Philippines at 81, Qatar at 87, Pakistan at 106, Indonesia at 114, Egypt at 120, Syria at 141, Iran at 151, Cuba at 152, Iraq and Libya tied at 153, and North Korea at 155. If a company used the 2001 ranking as part of the investment decision-making process, many of the Muslim countries in the world would be stricken from the list.

Another example of a ranking is the 'Wealth of Nations Index', produced by World Times Inc., which is intended to measure the sustainable economic and social development potential of a nation and related risks against those of other nations. It is a list comprised of 70 nations that are considered to be emerging economies by the international investment community, outside of the developed world. The three primary categories used are economic environment, information exchange and social environment. As of the 2002 list, Ireland and Israel were ranked 1 and 2 respectively. Malaysia came in at 7 and the Philippines at 21. Egypt was listed at 37, Indonesia 41, Pakistan 62 and Iran at 69.

As noted previously, isolating and ignoring terrorism in these least developed of countries may be relatively ineffective and this is so particularly in the countries suspected of harbouring, sponsoring, facilitating or tolerating terrorist activity. The more depressed these economies become, the more resentment will grow against the developed world as represented by the countries of the Triad. However, nothing can ever be completely reduced to an economic gap or underdevelopment cause and solution. Politics and culture play a determining role.

8.3   ECONOMIC DIPLOMACY: NO RSVP REQUIRED

Global integration is a highly selective process, often by invitation only, and the economic leaders address the invitations. Regional integration and growth trends can be fostered in developing economies through the trade and investment policies of advanced industrialized countries. Economic ties that bind have been severed, weakened and created in the aftermath of September 11. A system of 'rewards' for countries assisting in the war on terror has already been developed and implemented. Economic warfare has also been used to some extent, and arguably with some success, in the war on terrorism. In addition, the war on terror has given some weaker countries more leverage in financial and economic negotiations.

The struggle against all manners of terrorism utilizes the full spectrum of economic tools, including development assistance:

> The Bush Administration has made it clear that it will use every weapon at its disposal in the fight against terrorism. The IMF is one such instrument, like it or not, since the United States is the Fund's largest single shareholder. This clearly enhances the prospects for front-line countries like Turkey, who are now too geopolitically important to be allowed to default on their debts . . . On the other hand, the legitimacy of the IMF and its economic advice will not be enhanced if it is viewed by other countries, even more than before, as an instrument of US foreign policy. (Eichengreen, 2001)

It will also be easier for the current US Administration to reward friendly countries with enhanced and more rapid access to the United States market, no RSVP needed in such an understanding. Some examples concerning Pakistan include, *inter alia*, the waiver of sanctions (worth US$405 million) emplaced for nuclear weapon testing, the release of US$50 million in emergency aid, and the rescheduling of payments for US$379 million of US$34.6 billion total debt. Other countries receiving preferential treatment are India, Sudan, China, Iran, Turkey, Azerbaijan and Jordan.

Secretary of State Colin Powell said that the war on terror sets a 'new benchmark' for American diplomacy, a new measure of friends and foe ('Seeing the world anew', *The Economist*, 27 October 2001). Attention will therefore be focused on relatively fewer countries. This might conceivably come at the expense of global development and integration. 'Just as important, the attention that top officials will be able to give to facilitating a more open global economy is bound to diminish while the war on terrorism is in its military stages' (Garten, 2003).

Former allies and accompanying priorities have been discarded in the wake of the terrorist attacks of 09/11 and the subsequent war on terrorism.

> 09/11 changed how the US thinks in terms of investment, trade, and immigration – all of which are key concerns for Latin America . . . On September 5, 2001, President Bush stated 'the United States has no more important relationship in the world than our relationship with Mexico.' So then just one week later, why didn't Vicente Fox fly to Washington immediately, as Tony Blair did? It was a missed opportunity . . . one Fox most likely wishes he had taken. Britain has now

assumed the role of favoured friend for its staunch military and intelligence co-operation in the war on terrorism. It was Blair, not Fox, who were present at the State of the Union address, receiving a standing ovation from the House. (Arria, 2003)

The Bush Administration has publicly acknowledged its belief that economic and financial efforts are critical in combating terrorism.

Determined to bring US economic as well as military power to bear in the fight against terrorism, the Bush Administration has deployed a variety of economic tools such as preferential trade measures, the removal of existing sanctions coupled with loans to reward allies, and new sanctions to intimidate adversaries. In this war (on terrorism) sanctions policy is being used both as a stick and carrot. (Hufbauer et al., 2001)

The United States has been listing countries as sponsors of terrorism for 30 years now. Naming a country as a state sponsor of terrorism has been associated with comprehensive trade and financial sanctions under the International Emergency Economic Powers Act. It is argued that there are varying political agendas in the enforcement of the Act, beyond the war on terrorism. There are detractors to this approach, citing evidence that it has little of the anticipated effects, and comparing it to the less than effective Carter Administration's use of a 'zigzag linkage' foreign and trade policy in the 1970s. 'According to the State Department's annual report . . . Iran remained the most active state sponsor of international terrorism in 2000. In other words, two decades of US economic sanctions failed to reduce Iran's willingness to sponsor terrorism' (Hufbauer et al., 2001).

Such evidence supports the need for multilateral action on the trade sanction front. Between 1960 and 1970 the success rate of unilateral US sanctions dropped from 62 per cent to 17 per cent. The United States has occasionally approached the problem in policies running opposite to its long-standing allies. The United States tends to focus on isolation and sanction, while its allies (the EU) support what is often termed more constructive engagement, whose efficacy, it must be observed also, has been doubted in the post-09/11 period. In 1996, the Helms-Burton law was enacted to impose secondary sanctions on foreign firms located in Cuba. Soon after, the Iran–Libya Sanctions Act was also passed in an attempt to prevent European companies from investing in Iran and Libya (Hufbauer et al., 2001)

Along these same lines was an amendment to the Foreign Assistance Act of 1961 prohibiting US government assistance to any country that provides economic assistance or lethal military aid to a country designated as a state sponsor of terrorism. As expected, these methods have not always elicited the hoped for cooperation among the United States allies. On the contrary, they have resulted, in some cases, in more conflict with charges of extraterritoriality. Unilateralism has the advantage of decisiveness but it also has the effect of widening existing gaps between the United States and some of its allies. Joseph Nye of the Kennedy School of Government at Harvard University has concluded:

> if . . . the new unilateralists succeed in elevating unilateralism from an occasional tactic to a full fledged strategy, they are likely to fail for three reasons: the intrinsically multilateral nature of a number of important transnational issues in a global age; the costly effects on our soft power; and the changing nature of sovereignty. The September 11 attacks dramatically illustrated the importance of all three of these factors. How well the lessons will take remains to be seen. (Nye, 2001/2002)

8.4   TERRORISM AND TRADE: TIME IS A TERROR

Time has been an enemy of business far longer than terrorism. Every aspect of business is time-sensitive in the world of a globally managed supply chain. Logistics, warehousing, operations, manufacturing, linking point of sales with marketing and manufacturing all depend upon streamlining to reach continuously improving levels of quality on which to base competitive policies. Some countries are more focused on time than others, as much a cultural factor as a business practice one, as is made amply evident by comparing, say, the Mexican or Brazilian cultures with those of Germany or Japan. If assembly components or critical parts are not delivered on time, an entire manufacturing process is put on hold, raising costs substantially and challenging the survival of these firms.

The past two decades saw a shift towards 'just in time' manufacturing, where only the bare minimum inventory was kept in order to reduce costs. The risk of terrorist activity may not have directly affected time, but has definitely created additional trade barriers that inhibit maximum efficiency. Higher levels of inventory entail capital costs of both goods in transit and buffer stock. 'Recent estimates (UBS Warburg, 2001) indicate that if the United States has to carry 10% more in inventories and pay 20% more for commercial insurance premiums (and) as a result of the increased terrorism threat it would cost 0.1% and 0.3% of GDP, respectively, or US $7.5 billion and US $30 billion, respectively' (Raby, 2003). As pointed out earlier, security measures that increase the time and effort needed to pass through customs in any country inhibit trade. Eventually, the hope is that newer technologies will increase efficiency and offset the current time loss, but for the near future companies must be willing to comply.

However, it seems that security has currently reordered the priorities placed on efficiency, at least in some areas. For example, in the United States, the Mexican border has long been a concern when dealing with illegal aliens, illegal drug traffic and possibly entry of terrorist elements. It is now viewed as a porous line where terrorists could enter the country. This has resulted in some draconian changes, with economically paradoxical effects:

> Eventually, the border could be converted into a federal security area. President Bush has ordered US soldiers to help patrol the border. Now a cabinet level super-agency is on the agenda. Meanwhile, the waiting times for crossing the border back into California have doubled, tripled and at times quadrupled from the average waits before September 11. Californians are wondering out loud: How much security do they need at the border – and at what cost to the local economy and quality of life? implying a significant shift in philosophy in Washington, DC: a partial return to the 19th century view of the border as a place for military facilities and fences that defend national sovereignty. (Herzog, 2002)

The shift towards air freight and away from land and sea shipping exemplifies the extent companies are willing to go through to reduce time associated transaction costs.

> For US trade in 1998, air freight commands a typical premium equal to 25% of the transported good's value. Despite the expense, a large and growing fraction is air shipped . . . Excluding Canada and Mexico, over half of US exports are air shipped. These facts suggest two inferences: lengthy shipping times impose costs that impede trade, and importers exhibit significant willingness-to-pay to avoid these costs. (Hummels, 2000)

In many industries, spoilage represents a significant danger to commerce. Shipments of food products, cut flowers, and live animals depend upon extremely rapid delivery. Time sensitive materials are also in danger of losing value or becoming completely worthless. Newspapers, magazines, and seasonal items are all included in this. It all has a very real monetary impact. If even one link in a logistics chain is brittle, or even worse, broken, the others are rendered ineffective:

> The two-week lockout at 29 US West Coast ports in late 2002 delayed the unloading at port of more than 200 ships, carrying 300000 containers. Railcars and inter-modal shipments were parked all over the country as US and Asian exports filled warehouses, freezers and grain elevators. Costly diversions were made to other ports and many businesses laid off workers or cut back production. (Raby, 2003)

The month-long disruption at US West Coast ports was estimated to have cost Asian economies 0.4 per cent of nominal GDP. The negative impact on Hong Kong, Singapore and Malaysia was estimated to be as high as 1.1 per cent of nominal GDP (Saywell, 17 October 2002).

A terrorist strike crippling even one segment of the global logistic chain could have widespread and severe economic repercussions. Just as perception of risk reduces trade, perception of increased time factors also reduces international trade.

> For manufactured goods I find each day in travel is worth an average of 0.8% of the value of the good per day, equivalent to a 16% tariff for the average length ocean shipment . . . Estimates indicate that each additional day in ocean transit reduces the probability that a country will export to the US by 1% (all goods) to 1.5% (manufactured goods). (Hummels, 2000)

Increased, non-tariff, barriers themselves could reduce trade significantly based upon these calculations, even if the delay is only one day.

Additionally, higher regulatory hurdles, due to heightened security, may reduce the number of registered intermediary agents authorized to offer services. This also diminishes the effectiveness of competitive bidding, as there are fewer companies competing for business. If a government declares that companies must register through authorised carriers, then that is their only option. The more complex and stringent the requirements are for carriers to become registered, the more uncertain the time impacts for the business environment, possibly reducing overall trade. The advice of professionals is to 'maximise the bid process to get a good price and the best value for your transportation dollar' (Cook, 2002). Government non-tariff barriers in response to terrorist threat can reduce the value of logistics, intermediation services and shipping industry efficiency to the global business community.

Terrorism has a direct influence on bilateral trade flows, patterns and composition. A study of over 200 countries between 1968 to 1979 found a doubling of the number of terrorist incidents decreased bilateral trade between targeted economies by about 6 per cent (Raby, 2003). Interesting comparisons have been made between piracy on the high seas during the 1800s and modern terrorists. 'Between 1814 to 1860, mainly due to European powers eliminating piracy, international shipping costs fell by over 80% and the industry's total factor productivity rose by about 500%' (North, as quoted in Raby).

8.5 TRADE AND INVESTMENT: INVESTMENT IN SECURITY, INVESTMENT IN SECURITIES

Investment has always been primarily concerned with return on investment and the time value of capital. Calculating return on investment depends upon an assessment of risk. Terrorism is more about uncertainty than risk. The conundrum for international investment is patent. Imagine a financial officer in a large company attempting to plug in the colour 'orange' (using the current threat-level code) into a financial formula through an appropriate discount. Risk assessment and international credit rating services such as Coface have noted that 'the wanton destruction of the World Trade Center in New York shattered investor confidence and caused Americans to re-evaluate their sense of national security as well as the role of the United States internationally'. They have not, however, translated such considerations into a numerical upgrading of risk, while many firms increasingly analyse the United States, a traditional safe haven destination for trade and investment, using the logic of country risk analysis (COFACE, 2002).

An increase in risk level for the investor must also be accompanied and offset by an equivalent increase in return. It would be virtually impossible for countries to offer interest rates high enough to attract investment and still maintain fiscal and economic stability if there was constant escalation in terrorist threat or uncertainty. The net result will be an even narrower geographical focus of foreign direct investment (FDI) than in previous periods. Investors will turn even more to the safe havens of the Triad (Japan, the US and the EU), big emerging market countries (Brazil, India and China) and closely associated countries (Eastern Europe). Africa will become more marginalized than ever, and countries with large Muslim populations will suffer as well.

There is a definite 'push–pull' dynamic to foreign direct investment. The push comes from domestic market situations and domestic guarantees by home governments. The pull comes from foreign market attractiveness, though appearances can be deceiving:

> But attributing the sharp moves in financial flows to the erratic 'push' of capital from the centre doesn't fit the facts. The thesis fails to explain why in the 1990s huge capital flows went into East Asia while little went to Latin America and nothing to Africa . . . A better explanation for the crisis is the 'pull' thesis . . . big domestic firms [had] rosy expectations about the future returns on their investments and the future interest rates on their loans. (Phelps, 1999)

It will prove an arduous and frustrating task to persuade investors to have expectations akin to these for developing countries tainted by the precursor signs, affiliations and symptoms of terrorism.

A self-fulfilling prophecy or, some say, a vicious cycle in foreign direct investment, seems to confirm itself further in the new century. In order to attract investment, a country must have something substantial to offer. To be able to catch the eye of locational experts, corporate task force executives and investment consultants, a country must have the capital to build infrastructure, regulate and sponsor business, and maintain domestic tranquillity.

> Any new tendency for capital to flow more disproportionately to countries that have built relatively strong financial systems, political institutions, and international alliances can only be a good thing from the point of view of financial stability. This will also sharpen the rewards for countries that build strong democratic institutions that deal with minorities in ways that minimise ethnic strife, and that build bridges to their neighbours. Of course, this also means that the gap between the haves and have-nots will widen . . . Investment in sub-Saharan Africa, in contrast, is likely to be seen as even less attractive than before. (Eichengreen, 2001)

> A first qualification is that most outward FDI from rich countries goes not to poor countries at all but to other rich countries. In the late 1990s, roughly 80% of the stock of America's outward FDI was in Canada, Japan, and Western Europe, and nearly all of the rest was in middle-income developing countries such as Brazil, Mexico, Indonesia, and Thailand. The poorest developing countries accounted for 1% of America's outward FDI. ('Profits over people', *The Economist*, 27 September 2001.)

As long as this trend persists, development will stagnate in regions of the world needing it the most. 'By 1998, foreign direct investment comprised 90% of total capital flows to developing countries' (Globalisation.org, 2002) Even though there is not much FDI going to impoverished countries, their economies are so depressed that the small amounts represent a significant percentage of their GDP.

Table 8.1 displays the annual change FDI inflows from 1995 to 2002. Developed countries were the destination for a minimum of 56.1 per cent of total FDI inflows (1997) and a maximum of 82 per cent (2000). Developing countries received the rest, with the majority of this going to a handful of dominant countries, such as Brazil and China. Also shown in the table is the peak of investment flows in 2000 after rapid growth between 1997 and 1999. The years 1999 and 2000 were extremely active, with 2000 having US$1492 billion in FDI inflow, literally twice as high as any other year. This is due in part to mergers and acquisitions. Additionally, there was a dramatic decline in 2001 and 2002, losing over 50 per cent of total value in 2001.

It must be noted that statistical data from the late 1990s on FDI needs to be tempered with the fact that there were extremely high levels of mergers and acquisitions (M&A) during this time period, primarily focused on the Triad economies and less concerned with longer-term development than financial return. 'The value of cross border M&A rose from less than US$75 billion in 1987 to US$1.14 trillion in 2000. In 2001 however, cross-border M&A activity was estimated at around $600 billion'

Table 8.1   Global FDI inflows (billions US$)

	1995	1996	1997	1998	1999	2000	2001	2002
World Total	331	386	478	694	1,088	1,492	735	534
Annual % Change	28.8	16.6	23.8	45.2	56.8	37.1	−50.7	−27.3
Developed Countries	203	220	268	484	838	1,227	503	340
Annual % Change	40	8.4	21.8	80.6	73.1	46.4	−59	−32.4
Share of Total (%)	61.5	57	56.1	69.8	77	82	68.4	63.7
Developing Countries	127	166	210	209	250	265	232	194
Annual % Change	13.4	30.7	26.5	−0.5	19.6	6	−12.5	−16.4
Share of Total (%)	38.5	43	43.9	30.1	23	17.8	31.6	36.3

Source: Evans (2003).

(Evans, 2002). Mergers and acquisitions affect primarily the more mature markets in the developed countries, though investment is more common in greenfield than brownfield form in developing countries. As can be seen in Table 8.1, the dramatic drop after 2000 affected mostly the developed countries, while investment in developing countries remained relatively level year to year.

Overall international investment was declining prior to the terrorist attacks of 09/11, which reduced it further. 'Foreign direct investment flows into Latin America plunged by 33%, from $84 billion in 2001 to $56.7 billion in 2002 . . . the 33% drop of 2002 is more sharply felt than even two previous years of falling numbers. In 2001, foreign investment fell 11% and in 2000, 13%.' (*Pravda*, 2003). The OECD/UNCTAD 2002 report on world investment showed a 56 per cent decline in FDI during 2001. Levels of FDI in 2000 were at an all-time high, totalling US$1.27 trillion, but during 2001, FDI fell by over half to US$566 billion. FDI in the United States suffered as well, from US$308 billion in 2000 to US$131 billion in 2001, a drop of 57 per cent (OECD, September 2002). Further reduction was noticed in 2003 estimates. 'Global FDI inflows fell by an estimated 27% in 2002 to US $534 billion, following a 51% decline in 2001. The drop in FDI flows during 2001 and 2002 are the first decline since 1991' (Evans, 2003).

Such trends were confirmed by French Trade Minister François Loos who stated that 2002 was characterized by a notable decrease in international investments and that the once upward international investment growth trend of the 1990s was now one of stagnation (*Le Nouvel Observateur*, 23 August 2003). It would appear, given available data, that the 09/11 terrorist attacks did not cause the decline, but merely accelerated the rate of reduction in FDI through elevated risk and uncertainty. We are witnessing the redefinition of the trade and investment environment with rapidly evolving new features.

8.6 CONCLUSIONS: PREDICTIONS WANTED

The terrorist threat is not new, but history has not been a reliable guide in providing needed prediction and prevention, thereby reducing uncertainty and restoring equilibrium in the security equation. What has changed most distinctly in the post-Cold War era is the demise of an international system equilibrium correlated with the emergence of qualitatively and quantitatively distinct national security threats, heightened by their unforeseeable potential for catastrophic effects. Never before have terrorist non-state actors had the possibility of using weapons of mass destruction.

Various models have been used to forecast probabilities of terroristic events. Traditional intelligence analysis has relied on disparate data points and their creative integration to yield insights, patterns, and track leads, and has often fallen prey to the Heisenberg Principle. Code-based alarm systems, at the national or international levels, have also set in motion a range of precautionary security and general awareness measures, but their actual effectiveness is not yet fully understood.

In the post-09/11 climate, an effort was also made to ground prediction of terrorist threats and outcomes in a market-based approach, as markets tend to be efficient at aggregating a wide variety of actors' opinions on the future and express the confidence level of investors in certain outcomes.

Such an approach is unorthodox, based as it is on futures markets, and highly controversial. It allows the placing of bets, distasteful as it may appear on first blush, on catastrophic propositions ranging from the capture of a certain leader or the fall of a particular government, to the likelihood of a bioterrorist incident. The approach can be further extended through the Internet and websites patterned after the likes of NewsFutures or TradeSports in which punters may place bets on all types of occurrences.

Such a market approach to reducing uncertainty and linking it to a market model generates its own moral hazard, as financial and risk assurance analysts term it: the possibility that terrorists may indeed manipulate such a market for predictions and fulfil its own prophecies. Moreover, the full range of political and economic actors may seek to influence the forecasting process through disinformation.

Markets may in fact be no better at reducing uncertainty and predicting the future than traditional intelligence. In the absence of uncertainty-reducing techniques, firms and governments have no choice but to fall back on fail-safe approaches in boosting security and setting in motion the *cordon sanitaire* mindset, with all the regulatory overshoot consequences this may engender for trade and investment flows.

Could this be the end of an era? A turning point in regimes? In the future, will 10 September 2001, be cited as the pinnacle of United States ascendancy and end of the Washington Consensus? And September 11, 2001, as the beginning of the decline of *Pax Americana*, as historians such as Todd have argued? (Todd, 2002). As the focal point for reversal of economic globalization? There is some historical precedent to look more closely, namely the early 1900s leading up to the Depression of 1929, but the allusions are not perfect. 'Globalisation cannot be taken for granted: it may slow down, or even retreat, as it did with such calamitous results in the 1930s. And it may do so again now' ('All too familiar', *The Economist*, 29 September, 2001).

Corporate leaders do not know what to expect and consequently are vulnerable to erring on the side of cautionary principles:

> When it comes to terrorism, they are of course anxious to improve security for their firms and their employees, but they do not think enough about the systematic implications of societies' rapidly escalating preoccupation with national security. In the same vein, they find it highly improbable that the kind of globalisation they have enjoyed for decades could slow to a crawl or even come to an end. (Garten, 2003)

Political leaders often seem less certain or unanimous than business leaders, as their enemy now is uncertainty itself. While corporate coordination and cooperation, on a global scale, depend upon many factors:

> the difficulty posed by this threat is, however, precisely that it is widely dispersed. Unlike a threat from a state, such as the Soviet Union, it will always be hard to know whether the threat has increased or diminished, whether efforts to combat it have been successful or not. The result is that the alliance-creating virtue is likely to wax and wane, along with varying perceptions of threat. (Emmot, 2003, p. 43)

The current world order depends upon such alliances. Yet the vagaries of alliances may be inimical terrain for fostering cross-border cooperation. Looking both to the past and to the future, some have been emboldened to draw tempting but brash comparisons: 'The 1930s smashed the Geneva consensus, will this decade destroy its not-so-distant descendant, the Washington consensus, and with it the idea of international economic cooperation?' (*The Economist*, 'All too familiar', 29 September 2001)

International cooperation itself is being challenged. Unilateral actions have short-term goals in focus, yet their long-term consequences are difficult to assess. They can deal more rapidly than multilateral cooperation with an immediate threat, which in some cases is crucial, but erode the tissue of alliances, slowly built in the post-Second World War period. Former Mexican President Zedillo, now running a centre on globalization at Yale University, noted:

> The marginalisation of the United Nations, the transatlantic rift, the division in NATO and the European Union, and the current resentment among old friends, neighbours and partners, are all harmful to the foundations of the international system ... Now the international system and its institutions are under unprecedented stress. Deep disagreements have emerged about the best way to combat new threats to international peace and security and on how to preserve and extend prosperity. (Zedillo, 2003)

If terrorists can alter the nature of the global economy, even if only marginally so, and corner states into retrenching into traditional isolationist behaviour patterns, for whatever reason, then they have achieved success beyond their fondest dreams. By damaging political and trading relationships, they can indirectly impede globalization and development while striking directly at those they see as enemies. September 11 was indeed more than a blip on the radar of the entire world order. 'September 11 was a turning point in world affairs: its effects have been and are being felt worldwide in economic, political, social and psychological terms, and they will certainly have a profound impact on the contours, character, and pace of the process of globalisation' (Bernal, 2002).

The lesson of the early twentieth century, easily forgotten during the boom years of the late 1990s, is that globalization is reversible. 'It was derailed by war (in 1914) and by economic policy during recession (in the 1930s). This time, global integration might stall if the benefits or profit margins decrease and the costs of doing business internationally rise while governments, in a post-Doha multilateral trade negotiation, turn their backs on open trade and capital flows' (*The Economist*, 'Is it at Risk?', 31 January 2002). Terrorism is not the only source of uncertainty challenging the world today: how political leaderships respond to this challenge, handle its perception in public opinion as well as among economic elites, and use statecraft in containing it while preserving the essential beneficial traits of the post-Cold War order, are perhaps the greater uncertainties of this new international environment.

REFERENCES

ACC Egypt – American Chamber of Commerce in Egypt (2002) *Impact of September 11 on the Egyptian Economy*, August, Cairo.
Arria, Diego (2003), *Terrorism, Globalisation and the post 09/11 period: A Latin American Perspective*, analitica.com, Caracas, Venezuela, 9 February.

Baily, Martin Neil (2001), 'Economic policy following the terrorist attacks', Testimony before the Committee on the Budget, Washington, DC: US Senate, October 2.

BBC News (2002), 'Global investment almost halves', London, 22 January.

BBC News (2003), 'Mexico, Chile press debates Iraq', London, 12 March.

Bernal, Richard (2002), *The Aftershock of 09/11: Implications for Globalisation and World Politics*, Miami: North-South Center, University of Miami, September (unpublished).

Bernstein, Aaron (2002), 'Backlash: behind the anxiety over globalisation', *International Business: Annual Editions 01/02*, Guilford, CT: McGraw-Hill/Dushkin.

Chang, Sukjung John (1999), *Corporate Governance in the Twenty-First Century: New Managerial Concepts for Supranational Corporations*, Normal, IL: Illinois State University.

CNN Italia (2000), 'Belli da morire: la vera storia dei diamanti africani', CNNItalia.it, 1 July.

COFACE (2002), *The Handbook of Country Risk*, London: Kogan Page.

Cook, Thomas A. (2002), *The Ultimate Guide to Export Management*, New York, AMACOM.

Courrier International (2002), 'Un an après le 11 Septembre: "L'Empreinte du Terrorisme"', Paris, 5 September.

Daily Policy Digest (ed.) (2003), 'Globalisation not slowed by terrorists', 9 January.

Dateline: Cover Story (ed.) (2001), 'The price of anger', 12 October.

Dunn, Robert (2002), 'Reforming globalisation: the misguided attractions of foreign exchange controls', *Challenge: The Magazine of Economic Affairs*, September, Armonk, New York .

Economist, The, 'A crisis of legitimacy', 27 September 2001; 'A plague of finance', 27 September 2001; 'Grinding the poor', 27 September 2001; 'Profits over people', 27 September 2001; 'All too familiar', 29 September 2001; 'Seeing the world anew', 27 October 2001; 'Is it at risk?', 31 January 2002; 'New world ahead', 27 June 2002; 'Of shocks and horrors', 26 September 2002; 'United we fall', 26 September 2002; 'A new year; a new agenda', 4 January 2003.

Eichengreen, Barry (2001), *US Foreign Policy After September 11*, Social Science Research Council, New York, 1 November.

Emmott, Bill (2003), *20:21 Vision: Twentieth Century Lessons for the Twenty-first Century*, New York: Farrar, Straus and Giroux.

Enderwick, Peter (2001), 'Terrorism and the international business environment', *AIB Newsletter*, 4th Quarter.

Evans, Todd (2002), *Export Development Canada: FDI Monitor 2002*, June.

Evans, Todd (2003), *Export Development Canada: FDI Monitor 2003,* June.

Frieden, Jeffry A. (1999), 'Actors and preferences in international relations', in David A. Lake and Robert Powell (eds), *Strategic Choice and International Relations*, New Jersey: Princeton University Press.

Garten, Jeffrey (2003), 'A new year, a new agenda', *The Economist*, 4 January.

Global Policy Forum (2002), *Indonesia: Anti-IMF Rhetoric Tailored for Muslims*, New York, 5 June.

Globalisation.org (2002), 'OECD reports drop in foreign direct investment affecting developed and developing nations', Center for Strategic and International Studies, Washington, DC, 5 August.

Greenspan, Alan (2001), 'Globalisation', (Speech), Institute for International Economics, Washington, DC, 24 October.

Herzog, Lawrence (2002), 'California's Mexico connection: from global market to homeland security', *The Globalist*, 17 June.

Hufbauer, Gary, J.J. Schott and B. Oegg (2001), 'Using sanctions to fight terrorism', Institute for International Economics, Washington, DC, November.

Hummels, David (2000), *Time as a Trade Barrier*, West Lafayette, IN: CIBER Purdue University.

Huntington, S. (1993), 'The Clash of Civilizations?', *Foreign Affairs*, Summer.

Jeannet, Jean-Pierre (1998), *Managing with a Global Mindset*, London: Financial Times/ Prentice Hall.

Kapur, Devesh (2003), 'Who gets to run the world?', *International Business: Annual Editions 02/03*, Guilford, CT: McGraw-Hill/Dushkin.

Knight, Gary, Michael Czinkota and Peter Liesch (2003), 'Terrorism and the international firm', Florida State University, Tallahassee, FL, AIB conference presentation paper.

Lavelle, Marianne, Noam Neusner and J.M. Pethokoukis (2003), *End of an Era*, *International Business: Annual Editions 02/03*, Guilford, CT: McGraw-Hill/Dushkin.

Litwak, Robert S. (2002), 'The imperial republic after 09/11', *Wilson Quarterly*, Washington, DC, Summer.

Markuse, James and James Melvin (1988), *The Theory of International Trade*, New York: Harper and Row.

Micklethwait, John and Adrian Woolridge (2000), *A Future Perfect: The Essentials of Globalisation*, London: William Heinemann.

Monde, Le (2003), *Bilan du Monde*, Paris.

Money Matters (2002), *Wealth of Nations Triangle Index*, Boston, MA: Money Matters Institute, March.

NCTAUUS (2003), National Commission on Terrorist Attacks Upon the United States, www.9-11commission.gov, 9 July.

New York Times (2003), 'True cost of hegemony: huge debt', 20 April.

Nouvel Observateur, Le (2003), 23 August.

Nye, Joseph (2001/2002), 'Seven tests between concert and unilateralism', *The National Interest*, Winter 2001/2002.

OECD/UNCTAD (2002), *The World Investment Report 2002*, Geneva: UNCTAD.

Phelps, Edmund (1999), 'The global crisis of corporatism', *Wall Street Journal*, 25 March.

Pravda (2003), 'Foreign investors retreat from Latin American economy', Argentina, 10 April.

Raby, Geoff (2003), *The Costs of Terrorism*, APEC Region Conference, Australia, 24 February.

Richter, Stephan (2001), 'Bin Laden: promoter of globalisation', *Globalist*, Washington, DC, 28 November.

Ruggiero, Renato (2003), 'Regionalism vs. globalism', *Globalist*, Washington, DC, June 20.

Samuelson, Robert J. (2003), 'Globalisation goes to war', *Newsweek*, 24 February.

Saywell, T. (2002), 'Shipping News', *Far Eastern Economic Review*, 17 October.

Shapiro, Robert (2003), *How Much Would Terrorism Damage the US Economy? Less Than You'd Expect*, Sonecon, LLC, 28 February.

Skanderup, Jane (2002), *Japan–US Security Relations Post 09/11: Maintaining the Momentum*, Washington, DC: Center for Strategic and International Studies.

Stiglitz, Joseph E. (2002), *Globalisation and Its Discontents*, New York: W.W. Norton and Co.
Todd, Emmanuel (2002), *Apres l'empire: Essai sur la decomposition du systeme americain*, Paris: Gallimard.
UBS Warburg (2001), 'Talking points prepared for delivery by American Express Chairman and CEO, Kenneth Chenault', presented to UBS Warburg Global Financial Services Conference, 25 April, American Express Company.
UNCTAD (2002), *The World Investment Report 2002*, Geneva: UNCTAD.
US Department of State (2002), *Patterns of Global Terrorism 2001*, Washington, DC: United States Department of State.
Yergin, Daniel (2003), 'Fighting the globalisation flu', *Globalist*, Washington, DC, 29 May.
Zedillo, Ernesto (2003), 'On the new international disorder', Institute for International Economics, Washington, DC, 19 May.
Zoellick, Robert B. (2001), 'American trade leadership: what is at stake?' (speech), Institute for International Economics, Washington, DC, 24 September.

PART III

Business operation studies

9. The tourism sector

Frédéric Dimanche

The only thing we have to fear is fear itself. (Franklin D. Roosevelt)

INTRODUCTION

The various events following September 11 dealt serious blows to tourism, helping to remind us of its great importance not only to the USA, but also to all countries in the world, particularly in Western Europe. Indeed, tourism is one economic sector that has particularly been affected by 09/11, the more recent terrorist attacks in Djerba (Tunisia) and Bali (Indonesia), and the wars in Afghanistan and Iraq. The 'war on terrorism' resulting from the attacks on the World Trade Center and the Pentagon, and more specifically the conflict between the USA and Iraq, greatly contribute to a state of uncertainty in several world regions and economic sectors, and particularly with respect to the economic well-being of tourism. As a whole, travel and tourism has become 'the biggest business in the world', worth more that US$4.4 trillion a year, and it is a key economic tool for developing as well as for OECD countries. The short-term impact of the 09/11 attacks, combined with a US economic downturn, had immediate and disastrous consequences for many companies, as travellers suddenly changed their travel patterns and cancelled business and pleasure trips. Somehow, the World Tourism Organization recently reassured business observers by confirming that 2002 had been a better year than expected (after a 9 per cent decline in international tourist arrivals in September–December 2001) with a 3 per cent positive growth in international arrivals. Certainly, regional differences appeared: for example, the Americas suffered whereas other regions such as Asia and the Pacific comparatively thrived. However, 09/11 sowed the seeds of profound transformations and confirmed trends that must be taken into consideration by government and tourism officials. After presenting the characteristics and specificities of tourism as an economic sector and reviewing the transformations and evolutions that are taking place, this chapter will suggest four main conclusions:

1. Because of its nature, tourism is likely to be a major target for future terrorist attacks; the terrorism risk is now an integral part of contemporary travel.
2. Accepting the terrorism risk and related geopolitical problems is required for the tourism industry to effectively manage them.
3. A destination that is not safe (or perceived to be safe) cannot successfully take advantage of tourism's economic benefits.
4. Tourism has become a necessity and is a resilient economic sector.

9.1   THE TOURISM SECTOR

Tourism is an unusual and complex economic sector in that it is rarely well defined and analysed by economists. It can be called 'the elusive industry' because one can rarely read the contribution of tourism to a country's economy. Indeed, because of tourism's diversity, it is difficult to measure its benefits to an economy. In addition, the sector is complex because of the diversity of its elements.

> Tourism can be viewed from different perspectives. It is an activity in which people are engaged in travel away from home primarily for business or pleasure. It is a business providing goods and services to travellers, and involves any expenditure incurred by or for a visitor for his or her trip. Tourism is an overarching business comprising hundreds of component businesses, some huge but mostly small businesses, including airlines, cruise lines, railroads, rental car agencies, travel marketers and expediters, lodging, restaurants, and convention centers. (Lundberg et al., 1995, p. 5)

There are also travel reception services, global distribution systems, e-tourism service providers, and others.

The diversity and complexity of the sector make it difficult to assess its economic impact, especially when one adds related industries. It is difficult, for example, to assess tourism's contribution to the automotive industry (car makers) or to the film and video industry (film and camera makers). Also, unlike other business sectors, tourism has had difficulties in determining the numbers of customers (visitors) and trips taken. It may be easy in the case of a politically closed destination requiring entry visas, but in the case of a European country with open borders, the methods become very complicated and the estimates questionable. The case of domestic tourism (or travel within a country) makes it even more difficult to assess. For these reasons, tourism has remained a difficult sector to assess.

Despite measurement difficulties, the World Tourism Organization (WTO) (www.world-tourism.org), an affiliate of the United Nations whose role is to assess the world tourist flows and related economic activities, has long declared that tourism is the world's largest industry. This evaluation is seconded by the World Travel and Tourism Council (WTTC) (www.wttc.org), an industry association comprising the major tourism-related companies, which states that in 2003, travel and tourism are expected to generate worldwide US$4544.2 billion of economic activity (total demand). The industry's direct impacts include over 67 million jobs (2.6 per cent of total employment) and US$1280.4 billion of gross domestic product (GDP) equivalent to 3.7 per cent of total GDP. Considering the other sectors of the economy affected by tourism, its real impact is greater with 7.6 per cent of total employment and 10.2 per cent of total GDP. To small island nations, tourism can generate up to 40 per cent of GDP, and in many developing countries, tourism has become the number one export industry. The long-term outlook, barring significant international conflicts, appears positive: the WTTC expects total demand to grow by 4.6 per cent per year plans for 2013.

To understand why tourism may be a target for terrorists, it is necessary to realize the significance of tourism to the world economy and its increasing importance to developing countries. An attack, whether in Luxor, New York or Bali, will have tremendous and immediate negative economic implications. We will explain later some of the reasons why tourism is such a choice target, but economically, the weight of tourism is such that 'a hypothetical 10% decrease in travel and tourism demand worldwide would result in the loss of 8.8 million jobs and a 1.7% reduction in GDP' (WTTC, 2002). More specifically, this would mean the following for:

- the United Kingdom: decrease of 1.9 per cent of total GDP for the UK economy and the loss of 190 000 jobs;
- the European Union: decrease of 1.9 per cent of total GDP for the EU economy and the loss of 1.2 million jobs;
- the United States: decrease of 1.8 per cent of total GDP for the US economy and the loss of 1.1 million jobs.

The stakes are indeed high, and the current situation at the end of the war in Iraq shows that those dire predictions are quite plausible.

According to the WTO, 'international tourist arrivals amounted to 693 million in 2001 (−0.6% compared to 2000), 4 million down from the 697 million of 2000 due to the weakening economies of major tourism generating markets and the impact of the terrorist attacks of September 11'. Similarly, US$463 billion in international tourism receipts were recorded in 2001, that is −2.6 per cent over 2000 (2002 WTO estimates were not yet available at press time). In 2002, tourism recovery was under way: fear was apparently fading away and business was returning to normal, with intra-regional travel stronger than intercontinental travel. The Americas seemed behind the Pacific, Europe and Africa in terms of recovery. But in 2003, the war in Iraq and the fear of resulting acts of terrors are again hurting consumer confidence. People make fewer trips and adjust their behaviour to avoid some international destinations in favour of more regional travel.

9.2 TOURISM POST-SEPTEMBER 11

9.2.1 Consumers

The impact on consumers was tremendous. In the hours following the attacks on the World Trade Center and the Pentagon, the US air space was frozen, forbidding any travel to, from, and within the country, in fear of another attack. This resulted in a climate of fear that was not reduced by the new security measures enforced soon after 09/11 by the government and airlines. Surveys made in October in the USA revealed that increased security measures would not get some consumers to take off again as people expected another attack. Business and leisure travellers cancelled trips by the thousands, and changed their remaining travel habits by going on shorter, closer to home, and less-expensive trips, often booking late and on-line. Despite the down effect most businesses experienced, the major winners appear to be on-line service providers. Indeed, on-line travel sales increased 55 per cent from 2001 to 2002 as reported by the Centre for Regional and Tourism Research in Denmark. Early reports in 2003 seem to confirm the trend. Consumers are not only changing their purchase behaviour, they are also redefining the tourism destination maps, substituting long-haul destinations with short-haul destinations considered to be safe. Trends show a desire to take those shorter trips to allow for holidays that are 'experiences' rather than the more typical rest and relaxation on the beach. One of the challenges that tourism professionals face is to offer a total experience rather than mere locations with hotels and attractions.

But the main lesson to learn from the past few months is that fear has become a significant variable in consumer travel behaviour. This fact has recently taken an even greater effect with the outbreak of the Severe Acute Respiratory Syndrome (SARS) which is slowly hurting businesses everywhere, but particularly in Asia where tourism counts for 3–4 per cent of GDP. Strong regional airlines such as Cathay Pacific are crippled, and travel to China and Hong Kong is brought to a halt. One has to wonder, though, whether cancelling trips to Australia or Thailand because of SARS is an adequate response to a crisis. The common denominator between terrorism and SARS is the resulting fear, fuelled by the media. In the first case, fear is the objective of terror, whereas in the second case, fear is an undesired consequence of an event: the disease. In both cases, one may suggest that the resulting fear is excessive and uncalled for, as it was when Great Britain experienced a sharp decrease in visitation as a result of Foot and Mouth disease in 2001. The downturn of some destinations today may have more to do with ignorant stereotypes and fear rather than rational thoughts. The fact remains that fear is increasingly a factor in travellers' minds, be it the fear of terrorism, disease or crime. The question of security for tourists is not new. In the 1980s, specialists warned (American) travellers of terrorist threats, but both tourists and industry leaders did little to acknowledge or express concerns. This has changed with the 9/11 attacks. Tourism security specialist Peter Tarlow (2001) talks of a paradigm shift. Tarlow argues that the travel industry was blind to the public's increasing security concerns and demands, and that 'the new paradigm for the travel and tourism industry is based on the fact that tourism security is now a major part of a location's marketing strategy'. A corollary to this new paradigm is acknowledging that perceptions of insecurity and fear are strong barriers to tourism development and travel business.

9.2.2 Businesses and Destinations

The aftermath of 09/11 has shown the world the economic significance of travel and tourism by suddenly destroying businesses and jeopardizing the jobs of thousands of people in different continents. The first lesson we learnt is that tourism is vulnerable. Few had thought that travel and tourism could be so badly affected. Previous experiences with war and terrorism in the 1970s (Palestinian commandos blowing up planes in Jordan, and the attack at the Munich Olympic Games), the 1980s (various bombings in Beirut, London and Paris following the US raid in Libya) and the 1990s (the Gulf War and additional bombings or killings such as in Luxor, Egypt) had impacts on tourism that were typically limited to the region where the event took place. Through all those years, even in 1991 for the Gulf War, tourism never experienced a worldwide decline or recession. When a region was affected, travellers simply avoided it and went elsewhere. As the Secretary-General of the WTO, Mr Frangialli, declared in a letter sent to member states in March 2003:

> the need to travel, whether for business or leisure, is too deeply ingrained in our societies to be easily effaced. In spite of all the obstacles and risks consumers may perceive, they will do what they can in order to travel, even if it means reducing their expenditure, changing their destination, postponing their trip, shortening their stay or favouring domestic tourism to the detriment of international tourism.

Travel has become a necessity and the desire and need to travel are stronger than any threat. The words of Mr Frangialli are true, but the behavioural changes he identified will nonetheless lead to less money being spent and tourism businesses being in dire economic difficulties. A delayed shorter trip to a domestic rather than international destination means less receipts for travel businesses. Alternative destinations will benefit, of course, such as the Alpine skiing resorts which experienced a 20 per cent growth in winter 2002–2003 as European travellers shied away from long trips abroad and favoured winter sports at home.

Tourism has always been thought to be a very resilient industry and one could not have imagined the extent of the impacts experienced since 09/11. Even in 2002, tourism industry officials remained optimistic as recovery was under way. The problems, though, are now persisting with the war in Iraq, the SARS outbreak, a weak economy, and the fear of an uncertain future. The crisis has not affected everyone to the same extent. As tourist behaviour evolved, certain segments of the industry suffered more than others. Large national airlines, travel agents, business tourism receptive agencies and luxury hotels were particularly affected. On the other hand, low-cost airlines, domestic travel services or short-break operators are in a better position.

The biggest casualties have been the airlines. First, Swissair and Sabena disappeared, but many thought the outcome was predictable in any difficult economic time for these weak companies. But the bad news kept coming: UAL, United Airlines' parent company, filed for Chapter 11 bankruptcy protection, and the airline recorded losses of US$3.2 billion and cut back 8 per cent of their flights. American Airlines, the world's largest, must reduce payroll costs by US$4 billion. Delta Airlines, the world's number two, announced a 12 per cent reduction in capacity. Other North American companies announced similar problems and cutbacks. European airlines are also facing difficult times: Lufthansa retired nearly 50 aircraft; Air France cut 7 per cent of its flights; and British Airways will have reduced staff by 13 000 in the two years after 9/11. Similar news is echoed throughout the airline sector. The consequences are economic and social, but the lessons are managerial. We realized that an airline that is prevented from flying for just a few days can remain down, unless governments come to the rescue as they have in the USA and in Europe. The mayhem is bringing up a discussion of the adequacy of traditional airline business models, especially at a time when low-cost airlines in the USA (Southwest) and in Europe (EasyJet or Ryanair) keep recording encouraging growth figures by focusing on cost-conscious leisure and business travellers on relatively short intra-continental routes. Some traditional airlines have attempted to profile themselves as low-cost carriers, but they lack the ticketing flexibility and the

true low-cost structure of their competitors. Airline alliances and participation in networks are increasingly seen as a critical success factor and as
the counter-strategy to the low-cost challenge. New mergers and acquisitions, if allowed by antitrust authorities, are likely to be seen. The very
structure of the sector will be called in to question as industry leaders and
governments come to face the consequences of the downturn. Future discussions will include the revision of penalizing labour relations and the role
antitrust authorities play when preventing the consolidation of the sector.
Another central issue to be discussed will be that of the increased costs that
airlines and airports must face, from insurance premiums to security measures, to respond to security concerns. For example, airports such as
Aéroports de Paris are encouraged to reach a 100 per cent checked luggage
inspection rate, up from 40 per cent in 2001. Also, the US government and
the Federal Aviation Agency are lobbying for aircraft to be equipped with
secure cockpit doors. The cost, however, at about $US50 000 per aircraft, is
likely to be prohibitive unless governments contribute. If those costs are to
be passed on to the consumers, the challenge to woo travellers back will be
even greater. The current airline crisis is shaking the sector. Heavy costs
continue to handicap large national airlines. They must act quickly to organize themselves to lower operating costs and to attract travellers back. The
growth of on-line booking and the increasingly self-effacing role brands
will play in global alliances may be the first conditions towards a successful future.

Although not typically considered as 'businesses', destinations and the
large number of outbound and inbound service providers that constitute
the tourism supply chain, from travel agents and operators to attractions,
hotels and restaurants, have also suffered badly. Destinations have suffered
not only because of decreased spending, but also because tourism is a
major source for many countries of foreign exchange earnings and foreign
direct investment. In this context, some developing countries may have
been hit the most significantly. The changing consumer patterns mean a
redirection away from traditional sea and sun resort vacations in long-haul
destinations. Developing countries are facing a challenging situation as
they must reposition themselves as safe destinations that can offer alternatives to the traditional beach products. This means developing a new tourist
infrastructure at a time when foreign investments tend to disappear. The
terrorist goal of penalizing Third World countries that benefit from First
World tourists is being achieved.

In what may be the most significant response to 09/11, the tourism sector
united and cooperated, within specific countries such as the USA and at the
international level. National tourism organizations, governments and the
private sector together went into a crisis management mode. For example,

the Travel Industry Association of America's response was exemplary in its quick decision to put into action several strategies to help the recovery of the sector soon after 09/11. In an unprecedented move, several advertising spots (some of which featured President Bush) were created, inciting Americans to travel and support the tourism economy and prompting international markets such as Great Britain to keep flying to the USA. Both the WTTC and the WTO led international business coalitions to work collectively and to maintain a dialogue with governments worldwide. Indeed, crises bring people together and one of the benefits of this major crisis will have been the cooperation that resulted between destinations (for example, Australia, Fiji and New Zealand cooperated to promote a greater South Pacific region), between governments and the private sector, and between private companies forging alliances.

I do hesitate here to talk about *post*-September 11 as if the attack took place once and for all. It was certainly a watershed event; 09/11 and other related international events have been catalysts that prompted some changes and accelerated others. However, it would be a mistake to assume that 09/11 was *the* turning point. We should expect other terrorist events in other countries, and we should prepare for them. We may well be evolving on a terror continuum in which tourism is taking centre stage, and we should get used to this idea. Far from being pessimistic, we must be realistic and take on the responsibility of convincing all political and business stakeholders (who may still be in denial) of the existing risk. The tourism sector must take the lead in preventing terrorist events, and in planning and implementing crisis prevention strategies, because it has become a direct target of terrorist groups. Unfortunately, few are the examples of tourism public–private partnerships that are truly developing crisis prevention and crisis management strategies, from communication with visitors and potential visitors to planning assistance to economically affected tourism businesses. Today, very few businesses have made the effort to prepare emergency plans or crisis management guidebooks in partnership with legal authorities.

9.3 WHY IS TOURISM A TARGET?

It will be harder than after the Gulf War in 1991 for consumers to regain the confidence they need to travel in 2003, 2004 and even the following years. In the past few months, the terrorist risk has been felt globally, and may not disappear anytime soon in travellers' minds; terrorism was present in the Americas, in Europe, in Africa and in Asia. In addition, the Middle East exploded from the continuing war in Israel to the US–UK invasion of

Iraq. Beyond the higher level of risk that may be perceived in regions at war or in fundamentalist countries, one may wonder why travel and tourism is increasingly felt to be dangerous. Several elements of response can be suggested.

First, tourism is essentially perceived as being a First World activity, at least with respect to its investors and its markets. Tourism can be a metaphor for the north–south conflict, and has often been criticized as being a neo-colonialist or imperialist activity, 'furthering the domination by and subservience to Developed Countries of Third World or Lesser Developed Countries' (Butler, 1992). Tourism and tourists are agents of change in the destinations, bringing with them values and behaviours that are either accepted or condemned, depending on the host culture. It is, therefore, a typically Western economic sector with its vast majority of Western companies and Western customers (nearly 80 per cent of international tourists are from Europe and the Americas) that turns into an ideal target for fundamental Islamic activists. Although many regard tourism as a means to preserve and even to enrich the cultures of the developing world and to provide significant economic benefits, others see it as a rape of local environmental and cultural resources, with economic benefits largely leaking back to the companies and economies of the First World. Tourism development policies and incentives from the World Bank and other institutions have often tended to force regional governments to increase revenue by increasing supply (building hotels and other tourist infrastructure), without considering the impact this would have on locals and their environment.

In addition, tourism is a very visible sector in a developing country. Visitors and their consumption of services are very conspicuous. Cross-cultural issues often complicate relationships between tourists and locals. Visitors bring their culture with them as they request destinations with Western standards and services, and with their high purchasing power create a 'demonstration effect' that may be difficult for locals to bear. Also, behavioural differences may contribute to resentment when Westerners do not respect locals' cultural norms. If transnational terrorism is religious, then it may target the expressions and behaviours of our permissive cultures. Tourists sunbathing naked or topless while drinking Margaritas along the Red Sea in Egypt, the Mediterranean sea in Tunisia, or on South East Asian beaches in Indonesia or Malaysia are an insult to Islamic fundamentalists. The attack on the World Trade Center was symbolic in more than one way. It was an attack on Western civilization and global trade, in reaction to the influence of the West in the developing world.

The second reason why tourism is a target is that everyone is a potential tourist in the West. The psychological effect of a terrorist attack on tourists is then greater than an attack on any other economic interest. After 09/11, the international press wrote, 'we are all Americans', to express sympathy and attachment to America, its culture and way of life. Yet, the attack was not only on America: it was an attack on us. People from more than 60 nationalities died in Manhattan. The World Trade Center was not just twin towers in New York, it was an international symbol representing the USA and the Western world's power. Anyone who has been to New York has seen the towers. They have been appropriated in our collective memories. Tourists visited New York and went up the towers. We are all tourists and therefore potential victims. This is why 9/11 was so powerful. We all know someone who has flown in and out of New York or Boston; we all know someone who has travelled to Egypt, Kenya, Tunisia or Bali. It could have been any of us visiting the temple, dancing in the disco, taking a vacation in Mombasa, Kenya, or travelling in the suicide planes. The attack on the Oklahoma federal building did not have the international media impact the recent tourism-related attacks have had. Another example: the terrorist attack that killed 11 French engineers in Pakistan in Spring 2002 brought less stupor and international indignation than the Djerba (Tunisia) attack where 11 German tourists lost their lives a few months later. We are all tourists; international travel, whether for business or pleasure is now in our collective psyche as a basic right. It affects all of us and is not the luxury and discriminating or elitist activity it once was. In addition, tourism is truly international. People from any nationality are likely to be travelling at any one time, anywhere, contributing to make tourism a very global activity. As a result of these factors, the international repercussions of an act of terrorism involving tourism will generate worldwide media attention, and enter everyone's mind. The objective of terrorism is to suggest terror, to create fear. It turns out that tourism has become an excellent vehicle for achieving terrorists' goals.

Third, tourism is a strategic economic target. The travel sector can be thought of as a meta sector. Not all travel is pleasure related. Although it may be difficult to assess the exact contribution of business tourism to the overall picture (business travellers may account for no more than one-fifth of the total travelling population, but they contribute nearly one-half of the industry's total revenue because of their high frequency of travel) one can argue that any business will rely on travel for various purposes. Business as we know it today is international and global, and as such, it needs travel services. It should be noted that the drop in travel following 09/11 can be correlated to a general drop in business. Companies have limited their travel budgets and cancelled meetings of all sorts with partners, clients, distributors and so on. The primary (first) losers have of course been the airlines and other travel-related companies, but many non-travel businesses have also been significantly penalized. The US government has decided to intervene and help private airline companies, and the European Union supports similar actions in Europe. Other governments may need to inject cash or offer alternative financial solutions to save their airlines. A country will contribute and attempt to save some aspects of its own travel sector, as it has become so essential to the well-being of that country's economy. However, the question remains whether governments will have the financial ability and the willingness to continue supporting their battered airlines. But choosing travel as a target is not only hurting economies, it is also disturbing globalization. By hitting travel companies, terrorists are hurting the growth and development of tourism worldwide as the number of foreign visitors, the size of foreign direct investments and the stock valuation of travel-related companies decrease.

Finally, tourism may have become a chosen objective because it is an easy target. Thousands of people travel on any given day, and it would be relatively easy for a terrorist to join the crowd and to activate a bomb undetected at a tourist site, on a busy train station or in an airport. Until recent security measures were put in place, it has been feasible, as journalists demonstrated, to infiltrate an airport without authorization or to board a plane with a weapon. Travel businesses around the world have been hiring employees without thorough background checks, and any one employee may have access to critical areas in hotels, trains or planes. Certainly, security has improved since 9/11, but travellers know that it may be impossible to assure their safety worldwide in all destinations, and in all tourist sites, hotels, attractions, airports or stations. In the back of every traveller's mind remains a doubt, and the feeling that the terrorist risk exists, that it has increased, and that the next trip may be the object of an attack. It is difficult to think of a worse scenario than planes crashing into New York's World Trade Center. But if the USS *Cole* could be hit in a military harbour, would it not be conceivable that terrorists could hit and sink a cruise ship at sea with its 5000 passengers and crew?

So tourism may have become the ideal terrorist target; it symbolizes the Western world's domination of the developing countries, and fighting it is akin to fighting the hegemonic domination of the West and its old (and new) colonial powers. Tourism is present worldwide, in all forms, and its diversity and size make it an easy target to reach. Finally, the Western world is a tourism world. The ease and freedom to travel anywhere may be the best expression of our culture. As Georg Witschel and Gabriele Suder said in earlier chapters, globalization gave birth to global terrorism. It is logical that terrorism's main target has become tourism, which is both a cause and an effect of globalization. Choosing tourism as a target for attacks is certainly not neutral. By such acts, terrorists reach multiple goals at once: they hit and reduce our mobility and freedom; they greatly affect our economy; and they sow the seeds of terror. We are all potential victims. It could have been us flying from Boston, exploring the pyramids, dancing in the disco or visiting the temple.

9.4   ACKNOWLEDGING THE TERRORIST RISK IN TOURISM AND MANAGING TOURISTS' PERCEPTIONS OF SAFETY

Following the above argument, I would therefore maintain that, no matter how disconcerting it may be, terrorism, or rather the risk of terrorism, is now an integral part of contemporary travel. Travellers increasingly feel it and industry leaders increasingly know it. However, acknowledging the risk has been difficult for tourism professionals, who have often buried their heads in the sand, refusing to publicly address the issue. The recent events have forced professionals into action. However, beyond cooperation and increasing advertising strategies as a result of the crisis, one could have expected the tourism sector to become more proactive in implementing and communicating security-related measures. Of course, new security measures were implemented with great publicity in airports, but generally speaking, tourism businesses and destinations have been shy to talk and communicate openly about safety. For them, talking about security would have negative rather than beneficial effects on consumers. But, as discussed above, a dramatic change has taken place and businesses and governments now must communicate about security strategies. Travellers expect it, and they will increasingly make travel decisions based on their perceptions of safety in destinations, resorts or airlines. Managing and promoting security in a destination is becoming a difficult challenge. No one wants to visit a tourist area that appears to be a war zone with armed soldiers (we already see them in airports) or in a resort or compound limited with barbed wire. But a more subtle presence of security forces and procedures may be needed to help reassure visitors and prevent potential incidents. We already see hoteliers equip their establishments with video equipment and security guards, without having a 'scare effect' on their customers. A destination that is perceived to be unsafe or lacking in security measures will ultimately decline. Government and private initiatives to monitor people are bound to lead to some reaction from those who will not tolerate such intrusions into their private lives. Nonetheless, this may be the price we have to pay to satisfy our need to travel and for continued tourism development.

9.5 CAN TOURISM RECOVER?

Despite the stressful times tourism has been experiencing since 09/11, the industry is poised to recover, as it did after previous crises. Tourism, whether for business or pleasure, has become a necessity. Over the years, tourism has evolved from being a luxury consumption item to being a commodity that consumers now take for granted. It has become a mass consumption product with (still) great growth potential, particularly in Asia and the Pacific. In addition, the present difficult times have contributed to make governments worldwide recognize the economic significance of tourism. Tourism was often seen as an economic sector that 'just happened'. It brought great benefits without the need for much government intervention. We are now in a situation where it will be harder to attract tourists, particularly to long-haul destinations. The crisis will have had the benefit of revealing the structural weaknesses of some tourism sectors and the strengths of others. Only in difficult times can we understand in real terms the qualities of a sector and its abilities to react and to recover. Tourism will show again its resiliency, but this time it may take longer to get back to the levels of expenditures we were accustomed to. In times of uncertainty, people will continue to travel but they will apply various saving measures such as driving instead of flying, taking shorter sojourns and purchasing late discounted travel services (Internet bookings offering last-minutes deals have continued to grow), and will substitute travel products and destinations. Traveller behaviour has been deeply affected and it will take a long time to properly ascertain the full impacts of these changes.

Tourism has definitely entered its adult stage; it has matured. From being a pseudo-economic activity and a business lacking seriousness and recognition (the 'beach economy'), tourism is now recognized as a key economic sector. As a young industry, it grew almost anywhere, with little or no planning, sometimes with catastrophic social and environmental impacts as can be seen from the coasts of France or Spain to Goa in India or Pattaya in Thailand. In addition, tourism in developing countries was only partially beneficial, as a result of serious economic impact leakage (earnings leaving the destination to go back to foreign-owned companies and investors). Today, tourism can and must operate better, according to sustainable development principles. Also, the tourism sector, together with governments, must face head on the threat of terrorism. In fact, it is not a threat any more; it is there, and all stakeholders must work together to manage tourist fear and its consequences.

Europe, the largest travel market, has an opportunity and a responsibility to lead the sector in designing, recommending and implementing tourism development and management policies that will address security issues in destinations and assure a more equitable distribution of benefits, ultimately leading to better relationships between tourists and host populations. Doing this may help alleviate the resentment people continue to feel towards the West, the same resentment that fuels terrorists' actions. The terrorist threat will be there for years to come; it is now a significant variable in the business equation that no one should ignore. Although the academic community has been considering terrorism and tourism problems for some time (a special issue of the *Journal of Travel Research* in 1999 was dedicated to war, terrorism, tourism, their impacts on destinations and recovery strategies), 'It is high time for the academic community and tourism industry to view these problems as crises in need of management rather than periodic problems' (Sonmez et al., 1999, p. 17). Indeed, the tourism sector appears to act as if waiting for the crisis to pass. The recent problems due to the SARS crisis further showed the need for proper management in difficult times. We now see that fear has become a factor in consumer behaviour and that a publicized threat can wipe out all marketing efforts to attract tourists to a destination. Progress is needed in terms of crisis prevention and crisis management; it will only be made when tourism leaders recognize that risks and crises are truly unavoidable and should be managed adequately.

REFERENCES

Butler, R. (1992), 'Alternative tourism: the thin edge of the wedge', in V. Smith and W. Eadington (eds), *Tourism Alternatives: Potentials and Problems in the Development of Tourism*, Philadelphia: University of Philadelphia Press.
Lundberg, D., M. Stavenga and M. Krishnamoorthy (1995), *Tourism Economics*, New York: John Wiley & Sons.
Sonmez, S., Y. Apostolopoulos and P. Tarlow (1999), 'Tourism in crisis: managing the effects of terrorism', *Journal of Travel Research*, **38** (1), 13–18.
Tarlow, P. (2001), *Tourism Tidbits*, October.
WTTC (2002), 'Travel and tourism after September 11', www.wttc.org.

10.   The bank sector[1]

Stefano Gori

INTRODUCTION

The introduction of the euro, the slow but constant abolition of barriers leading to a single European market and the privatization of many financial institutions have had a deep impact on merger and acquisition (M&A) activity in European banking. In the past few years, a greater concentration has taken place in this fragmented sector. In 1999 the market share of the top five banks in Spain was 52 per cent while in 2003 it was 61 per cent, in The Netherlands it increased from 82 per cent to 85 per cent, in France from 42 per cent to 55 per cent and in Italy from 48 per cent to 52 per cent in the same time frame (Puledda, 2003). Even though there has been also some M&A activity in the United Kingdom and in Germany, the banking sector in these two countries is still very fragmented compared to their peers in Europe. The trend toward more concentration has also been encouraged by impressive innovations in information technology and by the diseconomies of scale and of scope in financial management caused by excessive fragmentation (De Felice and Revoltella, 2003).

The stagnant economic situation and the credit crunch that has hit the banking sector are endangering this new-found dynamism. This is especially true for Germany, where new credit lines are refused and old ones are cut (lending in 2002 reached the lowest level in more than 50 years, as percentage change compared to the previous year, *de facto* in 2003 it was flat) (*The Economist*, 1 February 2003c).

The stability of the financial architecture was even more seriously tested by the events of 09/11 and its negative spillover on the whole economy, and more specifically on the banking sector, both from an operational and regulatory point of view. After the September 11 attack on the Twin Towers and the progressing US military campaign in Central Asia and in Iraq, new tools for risk analysis and a proper international regulatory framework have become a crucial issue for financial institutions, multinationals and the so-called 'transnational' companies[2] (Vaccà, 1993).

These actors have engaged in a reassessment and repricing of risk due to a downturn in the perceived safety of overseas relations and investment. Those tragic events have had a deep impact especially on the insurance industry in the United States, Europe and Japan. This industry absorbed the biggest loss in its history, with the total liability from the attack on the World Trade Center (WTC) estimated at more than US$40 billion. More broadly, the economic scenario since 09/11 has to take into account the new military and geopolitical scenario, and a year after those tragic events the Bush administration, through the document 'The National Security strategy of the United States' explicitly expressed the willingness to use its military power as a tool of foreign policy (Rossant, 2003).

This chapter will focus more on the long-term impact of 09/11, more broadly on the war against terrorism and the emerging neo-Wilsonian nation-building policy of the US, on the banking sector, seen from a European perspective. After briefly analysing, in Section 10.1, a batch of factors that will probably have a long-term impact on this sector, and that will lead eventually to a less fragmented market in Europe and could bring about a single pan-European banking market, three interesting trends will be scrutinized more thoroughly in Sections 10.2, 10.3 and 10.4:

- a new regulatory environment (external to the firm);
- a new approach to risk assessment (internal to single financial institution);
- a by-product of the two, a weaker financial privacy for customers (especially 'marginal' customers, such as immigrants).

10.1   A SINGLE PAN-EUROPEAN BANKING MARKET IN THE FUTURE?

The endemic 'overbanking', especially in Germany[3] as was mentioned above, and more recently a lower interest rate environment, have had a relevant negative impact on the profitability of European banks. The stagnation or deterioration of efficiency levels has produced a loss in efficiency that produced higher costs for the use of capital. In the industry, the net interest margin is often used as a tool to measure such efficiency and carry out a benchmarking exercise. In the past five years this indicator in the US ranged between 5.1 per cent and 3.8 per cent, while in the UK and Italy it stayed in the 2 per cent and 2.5 per cent range. A worse performance was registered in France, between 1.5 per cent and 2 per cent, and Germany where it helplessly fluctuated around the 1 per cent threshold (*The Economist* 2003c).

The drive to improve the competitiveness of this sector in Europe will have, for sure, a positive spillover effect on the whole economy. Thus, great emphasis is being placed by politicians and opinion-makers on the significant economic gains and efficiencies that will be achieved when EU capital markets will integrate further. In fact, while financial integration is proceeding smoothly in the wholesale field, it is unfortunately lagging in the retail sector. The European Commission strongly believes that increased confidence in the euro and a sustainable and lasting economic growth will come through a more rationalized retail banking sector. Less fragmentation will have an impact not only on citizens but also on businesses, especially the small and medium-sized enterprises that have less-established relationships with the big financial conglomerates.

Many studies have been carried out by European institutions to quantify such gains. At the end of 2002 in the aftermath of the Spanish presidency of the EU a 'wrap-up' of these estimates was put in place (European Commission, 2002b). The outcome from these studies is relevant because it signals the scope of the potential gains:

1. A further integration of the retail financial markets might yield gains in terms of interest rates up to 0.7 per cent of the aggregate gross domestic product (GDP) in Europe.
2. A single market for securities and improved market access in this domain could augment the GDP in Europe in the next decade by 1.1 per cent.
3. A single infrastructure for clearing and settlement could turn out to be an efficient way to reduce costs dramatically by as much as 42–52 per cent.
4. A reduction of the costs of cross-border credit transfers to the most 'cost-efficient' countries would yield at least 41 per cent in savings of these fees.
5. Concerning the M&A activity, mentioned in the introduction to this chapter, so far in Europe this has been mainly at the national level, while a more integrated financial market would lead to cross-border M&A activity that could reduce operating costs for the sector by as much as 1.2–1.3 per cent.
6. Overall in the banking sector there would be a drive to eliminate the present inefficiencies with a potential gain of about 1.4–1.6 per cent of GDP.

We can expect that the new stable macroeconomic situation, due to monetary union and the impending competitive pressure leading to a more united financial market, will unleash a new wave of M&A activity. However, such activity will be enhanced by a series of other factors, some external to the single banking institutions and others involving the internal structure of such companies.

The first set of factors embrace mainly the agreement that is taking shape at the Bank for International Settlements, the so-called Basle II deal, changes concerning the rules governing corporate governance and the drive to step up a regulatory framework to prevent the financing of terrorism. These two last items appear to have created a drift between the US and Europe. The internal issues will concern the responses to the more competitive environment, a more complicated regulatory framework, the emergence of new types of risk and the growth of new market niches (Islamic banking and more broadly 'ethical' banking). Such responses will lead to new risk management and marketing tools that will be reached efficiently only through economies of scale.

10.1.1   External Factors

Taking into account the relevant geopolitical instability in the aftermath of September 11 and the lasting arm twisting in Iraq, that will probably spoil relations between the US and some European countries, the European Monetary Union seems to have had a positive effect because it somehow mitigated the rise of systemic risk.

In this scenario, however, there are other factors that will influence the banking sector in Europe in the medium and long term:

1.   a rethinking of competition law that still needs to take shape (Stroobants, 2002);
2.   an overhaul of the rules on corporate governance;
3.   a new deal at the international level concerning the practices for the management and supervision of risk and capital adequacy standards under the auspices of the Bank for International Settlements;
4.   the new European directive on financial conglomerates;
5.   the new regulatory framework for curtailing the financing of terrorism. This last item will be scrutinized later on, especially in Sections 10.3 and 10.4.

Concerning the issue of corporate governance, in this already rapidly changing regulatory environment the scandals, for example the recent unveiling of accounting irregularities carried out by the Dutch company Ahold, could spur efforts to overhaul accounting standards and could be used by those pushing for more pan-European rules. European regulators have generally resisted efforts to impose changes as sweeping as the Sarbanes-Oxley Act. Though several countries have moved to tighten standards and the European Commission in Brussels is poised to propose new guidelines on corporate financial reporting, European regulation still remains an incoherent patchwork of national rules. In the Netherlands, for example, there is no institution like the US Securities and Exchange Commission (SEC) with broad regulatory and enforcement power over financial markets.

In order for European companies to have a proper access to US financial markets, without paying a risk premium, strong persuasion by the European Commission on the SEC and American financial institutions will be necessary. It will have to convince US regulators that European accounting standards are adequate and comparable to those in the US (Pfanner, 2003). A step in the right direction is the work that is taking place in matching the International Accounting Standards (IAS), used in Europe, and the US Generally Accepted Accounting Principles (GAAP).

Concerning the issue of capital adequacy, since the late 1990s central banks have been working on the Basle accord for a new way of supervising banks' credit exposures. The main objectives of this process organised by the Bank for International Settlements are:

1. the convergence of the internal capital adequacy management system and the capital adequacy regulatory system, and
2. an increased attention to other types of risks in addition to the traditional credit and market risks.

With the implementation of such measures, banks operating in emerging markets will probably experience a rise in capital requirements, or they could face an increase in the volume of risk-weighted assets and a decline in capital adequacy, having a negative impact on their rating. For the banks located in OECD countries most probably the opposite will be true. In the short and medium term, however, the direct operational costs associated with introducing the new framework for banks or possibly for the overall economy may turn out to be significant in both OECD and emerging economies (Czech National Bank, 2002).

Going back to the regulatory issues, at a regional level the adoption of the new European directive on financial conglomerates will encourage internalization and consolidation in the financial sector. This will lead to the blurring of boundaries between financial sub-sectors and the emergence of cross-sector financial groups involved in banking, insurance and securities activities (European Commission, 2002a). Such a directive will enhance an effective supervision of financial conglomerates across different financial sectors and across borders, and promote convergence in supervisory approaches. Thus a comprehensive implementation in this domain will also help to meet the objectives while developing a stable international financial architecture under the auspices of the Bank for International Settlements.

More specifically, the new directive sets out requirements on solvency, such as preventing the same capital being used at the same time by different entities in the same conglomerate, as a buffer against risk (the so-called 'multiple gearing of capital'). Furthermore it sanctions so-called 'downstreaming' by parent companies, where the proceeds from the issue of debt are used as equity for their regular subsidiaries ('excessive leveraging'). This is to ensure that the concentration of risk at the group level and the transactions between entities in the same conglomerate are taken into consideration for appropriate risk management and internal control systems. However, the task of establishing a single supervisory authority to coordinate the overall supervision of a conglomerate could be harder to put in place, since it would consist in coordinating many different authorities dealing with the different parts of the conglomerate's activity. Probably the most lasting effect and relevant impact of this directive is the amendment of some existing rules for homogeneous financial groups (such as banking groups, insurance groups, investment firm groups) in order to go beyond the different supervisory regimes (European Commission, 2002c).

10.1.2 Internal Factors

The reinforcement of geopolitical and systemic risk and a low interest and low growth economic environment are hampering risky behaviour and, as we will see in Section 10.2, this will force banking institutions to readdress traditional risk assessing methodologies. A daunting regulatory framework to curtail the financing of terrorism will raise bureaucratic costs probably without seriously impeding such practices; such topics will be more carefully analysed in Sections 10.3 and 10.4.

From a commercial point of view, 09/11 has emphasized the growing opportunities of two new types of markets: ethical finance and, more specifically, Islamic banking and international money transfers that need tailor-made marketing and risk management tools. Both services, especially Islamic banking, are raising security issues; this topic, which will be scrutinized in Section 10.3, could end up producing a drift between the US and Europe.

International money transfer is attracting the attention of many banking institutions on both sides of the Atlantic. The US Treasury puts the number of Americans lacking bank services at more than 35 million. With the increase in the number of immigrants, primarily Hispanics, marketing experts are focusing their attention on the financial services required by the non-banking population. Last year about US$24 billion of remittances were sent to Latin America (the total international wire transfer market is around US$120 billion). The mere size of these services accompanied by the acknowledgement of the existence of millions of illegal immigrants from Mexico, has led to the tacit acceptance by numerous banks of the *matricula consular*, a card issued by Mexican consulates, as identification adequate to open a bank account. The search for new types of customers has become a struggle between the marketing division and the risk control unit that monitor the profiles of clients, especially after the new tougher regulations post-09/11 (*The Economist*, 2003a).

10.2   IS IT PERCEIVED OR IS IT REAL RISK?

Global competition drives companies and financial institutions into distant, unfamiliar markets. Businessmen, banks and other financial institutions are searching for ways to minimize their uncertainty. The new economics of uncertainty makes growth and earnings hard to forecast for all sectors. Nevertheless, it is clear that the nature and size of risk have changed, and markets are recalibrating their international exposure. More and more, the spotlight is on the political risk factor and how it must be incorporated into expected performance. The most striking economic result of September 11 is that consumer confidence in OECD countries depends heavily on geopolitical factors and more specifically on the execution of international military and diplomatic operations to fight terrorism and raise domestic security (Nussbaum, 2001).

Risk management involves multifaceted factors, more specifically it encompasses factors such as political framework, economic and financial infrastructure, social and cultural background, legal and regulatory framework, regional factors (contagion) and systemic risk (global economic and financial situation).

The management of any kind of risk needs a series of tools for gathering information, measuring risk and assessing the impact of this on a particular financial institution, multinational or transnational company, country and region. A series of sophisticated tools have acquired relevance, to address specific types of risks or country risk in a broader sense.

Risk analysis has faced a persistent tension between those who assert that the best decisions are based on quantification and numbers, determined by the patterns of the past, and those who base their decision on a more subjective belief about the uncertainty of the future (Bernstein, 1996). This is a controversy that has not been resolved, and with time it has

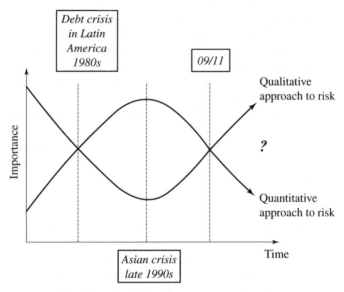

Figure 10.1   A paradigm shift in country risk analysis?

turned into a sort of theoretical pendulum ranging between quantitative and qualitative 'purists'. Such shifts in paradigms have been deeply affected by events such as the Latin American debt crisis in the 1980s, the Asian financial crisis in the late 1990s and the attack on the Twin Towers (see Figure 10.1).

In a post-September 11, 2001, arena it is becoming more and more important to use qualitative tools to address, from a dynamic point of view, the issue of international risk. In the past decades public institutions (for example, the Overseas Private Investment Corporation – OPIC) and private institutions (Business Environment Risk Intelligence – BERI, Price Waterhouse Coopers, Euromoney, Institutional Investor, Economist Intelligence Unit, Caisse des Dépôts et Consignations – CDC), international organizations (United Nations Development Program – UNDP, International Labour Office – ILO), non-governmental organisations (NGOs such as Transparency International) and rating agencies (Moody's, Standard and Poor's – S&P, Fitch) have developed qualitative tools to assess risk (Haque et al., 1998 and websites of different organizations).

These institutions use sometimes the Delphi Method (interviews to opinion-makers) and sometimes quantitative indicators (for example, for non-economic risk the UNDP Human Development Index (HDI) is based on three factors:

1. life expectancy;
2. educational attainments (literacy rate);
3. standard of living, measured by purchasing power parity (PPP).

In a post-September 11 scenario, taking also into consideration the longer than expected military campaign in Iraq, the old tools of risk assessment need to be reconsidered since the nature of risk itself has changed. Four trends seem to have emerged in the domain of risk:

1. More emphasis on domestic political and regional geopolitical factors in a post-Cold War unstable scenario (for example a new enhanced role for Russia, China and Pakistan in Central Asia).
2. The future of the United Nations and other political and economic multinational institutions is uncertain, especially after the pre-emptive military strike on Iraq.
3. The velocity in the transmission of risk is relevant due to globalization.
4. Qualitative analysis is becoming more important.

Markets are rapidly recalibrating their international exposure by incorporating these factors. However, it is crucial to avoid using an inflexible eurocentric cultural approach based on rational expectations, which does not fit a diversified cultural, political and social substratum (Gori, 2002a).

Risk goes hand in hand with opportunities (to manage, assess and speculate on risk), but we have to keep in mind a few things: as the former chairman of Citygroup Walter Wriston once said, countries never go bankrupt, but to that we can add, unfortunately, that banks, airlines, insurance and re-insurance companies can (Bouchet, 2001). Thus, risk in both emerging and developed countries (for example Long Term Capital Management – LTCM, Barings, Orange County, Enron) needs to be measured, assessed and monitored, especially in an uncertain scenario. Responsiveness becomes the keyword and being forward-looking is the key to interpreting highly dynamic scenarios.

Hence, in a globalized arena, the banking sector more and more needs to assess its risk by scrutinizing the direct and indirect risks of its clients and of its investments. The ongoing technological innovation can help to address these issues; nevertheless, the abundance of information without appropriate filters could create distortions in risk assessment and exacerbate problems. The events of September 11, 2001 were an alarm bell that made visible the faults of the traditional risk assessment methodologies.

Banks, not only in Europe, need first of all to assess internally the impact of external risk (something they cannot control) and the volatility that comes with it on their balance sheet. This is even more crucial nowadays in

Europe due to the widespread privatization of banks that has reduced the role of the state in this domain (even though it is *de facto* the lender of last resort), while the importance of shareholder value has been augmented (the slogan could be: 'privatizing the gains and nationalizing the losses').

10.3   IS FINANCIAL REGULATION AN EFFECTIVE TOOL TO ADDRESS AND FIGHT TERRORISM?

In the past year much emphasis has been placed by opinion-makers on the opacity that has emerged in international financial flows that allowed the funding of terrorism before September 11. The European Commission in the aftermath of the terrorist attacks took a tough stance on combating international terrorism:

> to prevent the financing of terrorism under conditions limiting any distortions of competition or negative effects on the functioning of the common market to what is necessary, while at the same time responding in an adequate manner to the threats of terrorism to international peace and security and the exceptional situation resulting from it. (European Commission, 2001)

This position was reinforced by the global body set up to fight mainly money laundering, the Financial Action Task Force (FATF), that published recommendations to fight terrorist financing and committed itself to check what countries were doing to monitor the submerged links between charities and terrorists. Nevertheless, it seems that the members have not yet agreed on the definition of 'charity' (*The Economist*, 2003d).

The new risk and regulatory scenario also needs to take into consideration the rise of Islamic banking in Europe and North America. The boom in Islamic banking started with 'petrodollars' in the 1970s. There are currently around 250 Islamic institutions in some 50 countries that are managing funds worth over US$200 billion. Many devout Muslims do not save in conventional banks because they regard fixed interest payments as usurious and the Islamic religious law, *Sharia*, forbids usury (Kassem and Greil, 2001).

US and European authorities have said repeatedly since September 11 they believe Muslim banks based in the Middle East and North Africa moved money to fund the terrorist actions around the world, allegations the industry strenuously denies. Former US Treasury Secretary Paul O'Neill visited Gulf states in early 2002 in a bid to convince local authorities to prevent charitable fund from reaching the al-Qaida network. However, no major Islamic bank has been conclusively linked to terrorists or terrorist activities. Islamic banking must not to be confused with *hawala*, a system of money transfer that is prevalent in the Gulf and South Asia. Most of the *hawala* transfers go through unlicensed moneychangers and in many countries there is no monitoring on non-banking financial services. This task is hard even in emerging countries such as Pakistan where tougher formal regulations have been put in place to attempt to redirect money remitted through the banking channels. The large retail networks and the scarce investments in technology and in human resources *de facto* make it difficult to monitor financial transactions and suspected individuals.

The events of 09/11 have certainly harmed the image of Islamic banks, often mistaken with *hawala*, but have not affected their activities. The appeal of Islamic banking can be linked to the growth of ethical investment, since investments in alcohol, pork, gambling and pornography are banned. In recent years, the telecommunication and technology sectors have become popular with Islamic funds; this, more than September 11, is the reason that many of these funds have sustained heavy losses in the past few years (Arab American Business, 2002). Thus, it could turn out that the extensive media coverage on Islamic banking after 09/11 could ironically help the expansion of this banking product in non-Muslim countries with a large number of immigrants. Many of these 'marginal' clients already consider it an ethical way to invest money, especially due to their scarce knowledge of financial products; but this is also so for more informed clients since equity markets have not performed well in the past few years. This will be reinforced also by the re-emergence of religious affiliation, which normally takes place in times of economic, social and political crisis (Beard, 2003).[4]

10.4   A DRIFT BETWEEN EUROPE AND THE US ON FINANCIAL PRIVACY?

The financial press on both sides of the Atlantic are overemphasizing the diverging approach to corporate governance. The media in the US believe that despite the emergence of a growing number of major accounting irregularities in Europe, regulators have avoided imposing such sweeping changes as the US Sarbanes-Oxley Act of 2002, that are aimed at improving the accuracy and reliability of corporate disclosure. As we have already mentioned, this drift is more evident after the financial scandals that have hit the Dutch grocery company, Royal Ahold NV and its handling of its American subsidiary (Pfanner, 2003).

Instead, less attention has been given by the media to the growing drift in the realm of financial privacy. Most opinion-makers believe that a more globalized financial market *de facto* makes boundaries less tangible, however after 09/11 there is a risk of a drift between European and US banking regulators on security issues. Before September 11, the US lagged behind Europe in fighting money laundering. With the USA Patriot Act of 2001, American legislators and regulators went beyond their European counterparts. However, as an article in *The Economist* of December 2002 said, terrorist money is a 'needle in the haystack' (*The Economist*, 14 December 2002) compared to the large amounts from drug trafficking, and furthermore terrorists use 'clean money' that they often receive from non-suspect sources, such as charities.

The Patriot Act did not specify how to tackle this issue and emphasized only the need to have deeper knowledge of their client base and be able to detect 'not normal' patterns in transaction. Such broad guidelines, with little operational relevance,[5] have also been accompanied by the establishment and reinforcement of special departments, agencies and projects that seem to derive more from spy stories than real life. The fact that 09/11 terrorists were able to open bank accounts with fake social security numbers has struck the media and put pressure on political figures to take a tough stance on this issue.

The name of the law itself is a daunting acronym USA Patriot: Uniting and Strengthening America by Providing Appropriate Tools Required to Intercept and Obstruct Terrorism. It gives unprecedented powers to federal agencies such as the FBI, CIA, DEA, INS, IRS, Customs, Secret Service and Postal Inspection Service to gather and share information on suspects. The Total Information Awareness (TIA) project, conceived by the Pentagon and the Department of Defense, is basically an enormous database that would tap available databases ranging from applications of any kind to local authorities to international financial transactions. A former Reagan advisor on security issues, Admiral John Pointdexter, heads the coordination of such information-gathering to combat terrorism. The huge financial and technological investments needed, the mere number of federal agencies involved and the presence of Admiral Poindexter (who disappeared *de facto* from the political arena of Washington after he was convicted of lying to Congress in the Iran Contra affair in the 1980s) signals a clear political will to tackle the issue of stepping up the Intelligence network. It seems, however, that the US Congress wants to curb this ambitious plan and the so-called Wyden Amendment will restrict funding on TIA until an official and transparent report is presented to Congress (Chaffin, 2003).

September 11, 2001 had a dramatic impact on the American population primarily because it happened on American soil and was comprehensively covered by the media; this has pushed American political power to demand tougher regulations. Ironically this has led the current Republican admin-istration to move away from the supply-side 'Reaganomics' of the 1980s based on deregulation. In the US financial privacy could turn out to be a luxury since the new legislation allows the above-mentioned agencies to take a closer look at bank accounts without permission and without prior notification.

This is less evident in other industrialized countries, raising the question whether this drift really exists, and if it will last in the future. At first sight, the different attitude by regulators on the two sides of the Atlantic appears to be more rhetorical than real. In a recent speech by the European Commissioner Frits Bolkestein (Bolkestein, 2003) it was clear that there is a need for dialogue between the two economic superpowers and that this process has just begun. Last year, the European Commission and a range of US authorities started to meet on a regular and informal basis to exchange information on legislative and regulatory developments in what it is now called the 'financial markets dialogue'. In this context, criticism from the EU on the Sarbanes-Oxley, and from the other side concerns over the Financial Conglomerate Directive, were expressed; nevertheless, up to now a compromise has not yet been reached.

The psychological impact of 09/11 on American public opinion enhanced a patriotic approach to financial regulation; however, the high cost of implementing new measures will raise the breakeven level of depos-its, cutting off even more the so-called socially excluded (clients with no or little revenues and small amount of savings, often without access to the banking system). These constraints, put in place in a highly competitive environment, will probably not last long and, as the above-mentioned article of *The Economist* (14 December) emphasized, it will turn out that the rigorous monitoring will apply only to foreigners or Americans with an Arab background. Hopefully, such discrimination will be avoided and, as many financial operators are pushing for, there is a need to encourage a risk-based approach at the international level to really tackle the issue of the financing of terrorism.

The idea is that especially in the domain of correspondent banking (where US regulators are demanding scrutiny by a bank of not only the cor-respondent bank but also of its customers) it would be more appropriate to analyse only the accounts, the track record of the correspondent bank, while relying on a due diligence by the correspondent bank on its customer base. This would create a chain of checks to attempt to combat terrorist financing, meanwhile avoiding excessive, costly bureaucracy and too much red tape that slows down procedures[6] (McDonald, 2002) without having a real impact.[7] This, at least, seems to be the second-best solution while we wait for future technological discoveries that could link banking to advanced studies in biometrics[8] (Bruce, 2002) with a significant impact on financial security.

After the commencement of the unilateral neo-Wilsonian nation-building policy in Afghanistan and Iraq, the issue of the drift on financial privacy needs to be seen as an example of the new American foreign policy inspired by the neo-conservatives. It is becoming evident that the US, on top of the apparently stricter domestic legislation, is willing to use military power to address national security issues and sees it as a complementary tool of economic power to project its political and economic interests abroad. In a recently published book *Of Paradise and Power*, by Robert Kagan (Kagan, 2003), it clearly emerges that the American neo-conservative elite is conscious of the economic and military hegemony of their country. Kagan thinks that Americans come from Mars and Europeans from Venus, and he believes that this interplanetary conflict will be won militarily and economically by Mars. The jury is out.

10.5   CONCLUSION

This chapter focused mainly, using a European perspective, on three long-term tendencies affecting the banking sector that have been by-products of the dramatic events of 09/11 and the subsequent campaign in Central Asia and Iraq. Three peculiar trends have emerged:

1. more regulations,
2. more risk, and
3. more attention being placed on 'marginal' clients (immigrants and customers sensible to ethical causes) and its implication on a diverging attitude between the EU and the US toward security.

All this is happening while a heated debate on the overhaul of financial regulation has already taken place in Europe itself. The patchwork of regulations and the fragmented market will need to be tackled, especially as globalization will probably speed up again when the economy moves out of the doldrums.

Currently European countries cannot agree on the future of cross-border supervision of securities. The issue at stake is if the current system of mutual recognition among the 15 (in the future 25) national securities regulators should be kept in place or if it is more appropriate to have a single European regulator. This is in fact a 'Trojan horse' for the whole European financial environment; the insurance sector could be the next in line and after that the banking sector (*The Economist*, 2003b).

A great push for a more centralized financial regulatory framework has come from the implementation of the European Monetary Union, the reduction of the fragmentation of the markets, developments in information technologies, the liberalization of financial markets and the growing impact of globalization. On top of these factors, the attacks on the Twin Towers and the Pentagon have built up support at the international level for more collaboration and at the regional level for more integrated and centralized regulatory bodies. September 11 has raised the issue for a more common approach to internal control and capitalization issues. The long-term impact on European banking will be to speed up a more holistic approach to financial stability and risk management at the 'sovranational' level, but also going beyond specific financial sectors (such as the European directive on financial conglomerates).

Since 1998 national bank regulators have been working on the Basle Accord II for a new way of supervising banks' credit exposures, and important decisions are about to be taken about the way banks are allowed to run the risk, and how much they need to disclose. After September 11 the debate was extended also on how the blueprint should take into account the operational risks that banks run: of wars, system failure, terrorist attacks, human error and fraud (Shireff, 2002).

From the analysis above it appears that even though steps have been taken to create a convergent regulatory framework on both sides of the Atlantic, there are relevant issues that still need to be addressed concerning security, corporate governance and common tools to address new types of risk. The regulatory drift between the US and Europe is linked to the debate concerning different socio-political and economic models: national and regional peculiarities could take time to converge. Williamson (2002), in a paper published in the *Journal of Economic Literature*, tried to explain the existence of differences between different institutions, countries and regions by identifying four levels of socio-economic factors influencing the functioning of complex institutions:

1. 'embeddedness' (traditions, norms, religions) that involves trends that take hundreds of years to change;
2. institutional environment ('rules of the game', bureaucracy, property rights) that has a time frame of different decades;
3. governance ('the play of the game') taking place in couple of years;
4. the continuous search for optimal resource allocation.

Globalization has reduced the time frame where these mega, mesa and micro factors operate; however they signal the difficulties for regions with a different social, economic and political background to agree on a common financial architecture.

In a conflicting regulatory environment, the banking sector has been engaged in an operational reassessment and repricing of risk due to a downturn in the perceived safety of overseas relations and investment. Nevertheless, compared to other events of the past, the impact of 09/11 in an increasingly interconnected world has also been felt a lot by the common citizens, encompassing their private sphere and the feeling of insecurity, going beyond the institutional interplanetary drift mentioned above. From an economic point of view, the most striking result of September 11, 2001 and the military campaign in Iraq, is that consumer confidence and economic growth, not only in OECD countries, depend more and more on the war against terrorism and the issue of domestic security (not only international terrorism, but also on snipers, anthrax scares, biological warfare and even the Severe Acute Respiratory Syndrome, SARS).[9] More broadly, economic prospects depend on psychological factors and less on rational expectations, hence going beyond the neo-classical *Homo economicus* (Gori, 2002b).

I believe that, not only from an academic point of view, the outbreak of social and economic anxiety, curtailing rationality, has signalled the swing of the pendulum to a more cognitive approach to business, economics and more broadly social sciences. Such a shift in paradigm will have a deep impact on the daily behaviour of all economic actors, including the nervous system of the economy, the banks.

NOTES

1. I would like to thank Prof. Bertrand Groslambert from CERAM for the material he provided me on European M&A in the banking sector and two Italian attorneys Francesca Falcioni and Claudio Lettieri for patiently reading my drafts. I would like to express my deepest gratitude to Prof. Michel Bouchet from CERAM for the intellectual guidance in the realm of international finance.
2. The concept of transnational companies goes beyond the concept both of multinational and international company. In a globalized knowledge-based market place, more and more it is important to be part of a network of relations, where the size of a firm is irrelevant while it is important the role it plays inside the network. A 'transnational' company is part of an international and highly technological network.
3. Germany's large private banks manage barely 4 per cent of the money in savings accounts and make only 14 per cent of all loans to companies and households. The country's more than 500 municipally owned savings banks, *Sparkassen*, manage more than half of all savings deposits and make 20 per cent of all loans; the 12 regional banks, *Landesbank*, owned by federal states and the regional associations of *Sparkassen*, have about 16 per cent of the lending market. On top of these local institutions, there are about 1500 co-operative banks.
4. In the US, similarly to the aftermath of 09/11, at the beginning of 2003 the sales of Bibles, testaments and prayer books increased by 37 per cent.
5. The responsibilities of banks, brokers, dealers and insurance companies and money transfer services include: (1) the identification and verification of customers seeking to open new accounts, (2) checking new account applicants against various government lists of

suspected terrorists, (3) reporting suspicious account activity to the Financial Crimes Enforcement Network (FinCen) and to the Treasury Department's central anti-money laundering database, (4) conducting enhanced due diligence for correspondent accounts for foreign banks and private accounts of non-US persons, and (5) complying promptly with requests from federal investigative agencies for financial records.

6. The American Bankers Association identified several problems concerning account-opening procedures such as: photocopying the government-issued picture identification document could expose the institution to loan discrimination charges under the Equal Credit Opportunity Act; and the use as an identification document of the driving licence could create a problem since many states do not print Social Security numbers on licences.

7. Checking the financial guarantees and personal history of the client base of a correspondent bank in a foreign country could turn out to be very difficult and can be easily overcomed by shortcuts. Furthermore, it would reduce the responsibility of the correspondent bank itself, hence stimulating moral hazard.

8. It is the world of iris scans and hand and voice recognition devices. These futuristic instruments nevertheless may be not appreciated by customers because it could be considered as an intrusion in their financial privacy.

9. In China a part of public opinion believes that SARS was created artificially in American laboratories and spread to mainland China to punish the population for the 'ambiguous' attitude of their government concerning the US–UK military campaign in Iraq.

REFERENCES

Arab American Business (2002), 'Islamic bank's investments increase in the aftermath of 09/11', www.arabamericanbusiness.com .

Beard, A. (2003), 'Geopolitical tensions boost US Bible sales', *Financial Times*, 22 March.

Bernstein, P.L. (1996), *Against the Gods: the remarkable story of risk*, New York: John Wiley & Sons.

Bolkestein, F. (2003), 'EU-US regulatory co-operation on financial markets: A matter of necessity', speech at the Breakfast Meeting at the European Business Council, 24 February.

Bouchet, M. (2001), *Country Risk Analysis*, CERAM course material, Spring.

Bruce, L. (2002), 'Banks not yet banking biometrics', www.bankrate.com, 23 July.

Chaffin J. (2003), 'Congress curbs plan to monitor electronic mail', *Financial Times*, February 13.

Czech National Bank (2002), *Comments on the New Capital Adequacy Framework*, Prague.

De Felice, G. and D. Revoltella (2003), *Towards a multinational bank? European banks' growth strategies*, Paris: Banques & Marchés no. 62, January–February.

Economist, The (2002), 'The needle in the haystack', 14 December .

Economist, The (2003a), 'Banking for immigrants: reaching out', 22 February, p. 77.

Economist, The (2003b), 'European securities regulation: Trojan horses', 15 February.

Economist, The (2003c), 'German banks: that sinking feeling', 22 February, pp. 73–74.

Economist, The (2003d), 'The iceberg beneath the charity', 15 March.

European Commission (2001), *Specific restrictive measures directed against certain persons and entities with a view to combating international terrorism*, Brussels and Luxembourg, 30 November.

European Commission (2002a), *Common Position of the Council on the adoption of a Directive of the European Parliament and of the Council on the supplementary supervision of credit institutions, insurance undertakings and investment firms in a financial conglomerate*, Communication from the Commission to the European Parliament, 20 September, Brussels and Luxembourg.

European Commission (2002b), *Financial Services. Meeting the Barcelona Priorities and Looking Ahead: Implementation*, 7th Report, 3 December, Brussels and Luxembourg.

European Commission (2002c), *Financial Conglomerates: Commission Welcomes the European Parliament's Adoption of Directive*, Press release, 20 November, Brussels.

Gori, S. (2002a), *A Critical Assessment of Country Risk Analysis in a post 11th of September Scenario*, Global Finance Chair paper, CERAM, 13 January.

Gori, S. (2002b), *A Cognitive Approach to Political Risk*, Global Finance Chair paper, CERAM, 26 April.

Haque N.U., N. Mark and D.J. Mathieson (1998), *The Relative Importance of Political and Economic Variables in Creditworthiness Ratings*, IMF April.

Kagan, R. (2003), *Of Paradise and Power*, New York: Alfred A. Knopf and London: Atlantic Books.

Kassem, M. and A. Greil (2001), 'Islamic banking reputation suffers in wake of September 11', Dow Jones Newswire, 6 November.

McDonald, J. (2002), 'New law declares open season on bank records', www.bankrate.com, 23 August.

Nussbaum, B. (2001), 'A shock to the equity culture', *Business Week*, 8 October.

Pfanner, E. (2003), 'Ahold reveals Europe's regulatory gaps', *International Herald Tribune*, 26 February.

Puledda, V. (2003), 'Concentrazioni, Italia fanalino in Europa', *Affari e Finanza*, 17 February.

Rossant, J. (2003), 'Continental drift', *Business Week*, 21 April.

Shirreff, D. (2002), 'Banks reinvent themselves', in *The World in 2003*, December, London: The Economist.

Stroobants, J.P. (2002), 'Concurrence: Les camouflets obligent la Commission européenne à redéfinir son rôle', *Le Monde* (2002) *Bilan du Monde Edition 2003*, December.

Vaccà, S. (1993), 'Grande Impresa e concorrenza: tra passato e futuro', *Economia Politica Industriale*, no. 80.

Williamson, O.E. (2000), 'The new institutional economics: taking stock, looking ahead', *Journal of Economic Literature*, September, pp. 595–613.

Websites of organizations: http://www.beri.com, www.euromoney.com, www.tacfinancial.com, www.transparency.org and www.undp.org.

11. The evolution of contingency planning: from disaster recovery to operational resilience

Till Guldimann

Since September 11, 2001, the word 'disaster' has become inextricably linked to terrorism. Renewed attention is given to recovery after a catastrophic event to ensure financial services firms can get back up and running quickly, and to minimize systemic risks. This attention is crystallizing the need for a new perspective on the challenge of disaster recovery. The fact is that financial services today are managed and delivered through an amalgamation of networks – tightly intertwined and electronically linked – and the network's vulnerability is a source of increased concern. We have become dependent on the network, and therein lies the real threat to firms and the financial system as a whole.

The old paradigm was redundancy: backup, backup, backup; the new one is resiliency: keep your operations humming and ensure your node on the financial network remains 'on-line'. The contingency challenge has shifted from disaster recovery – cleaning up and getting back to work after a cataclysmic event, to operational resilience – designing your enterprise to operate effectively right through a disruption.

This new vulnerability is not a consequence of terrorism; rather, it is driven by the relentless application of technology to the business of finance. Technology has transformed finance, and generated substantial new risks for every market participant because technology is vulnerable to natural disasters, to terrorist attacks like 9/11, and to cyber-terrorism, the rapidly emerging epidemic of computer bugs, worms and viruses.

Based on data from Swiss Re, Figure 11.1 shows while natural disasters continue to take their toll – particularly in terms of human life and particularly in the developing countries – man-made disasters like terrorist attacks are getting more expensive.

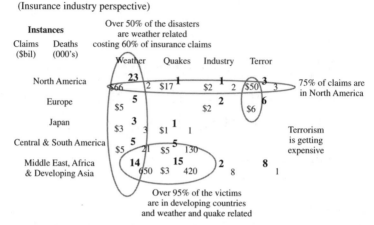

(Insurance industry perspective)

Adapted from: SwissRe – Natural catastrophes and man-made disasters, sigma 1/2002

Figure 11.1   Big disasters 1970–2001

11.1   TWO EXAMPLES: 1985 AND 2001

To highlight the new reality, compare a severe market disruption of 1985 to the one caused by the attack on the World Trade Center in 2001. The earlier event demonstrates the risks posed by a software problem at a single firm; the latter demonstrates the risks of highly interdependent networks.

On 20 November 1985, the clearing operation of a major New York bank handled more than 32 000 Treasury security trades for the first time. This record volume triggered a software problem, preventing the firm from delivering Treasuries to the buyers. The next morning was settlement day, and the bank began accumulating undelivered securities, which had to be financed by borrowings at the discount window of the New York Federal Reserve (the bank had to borrow a staggering US$23 billion by the end of the day). The following morning, with the software still malfunctioning, the Fed told dealers not to deliver more Treasuries through the affected clearer, which led to a broadening of the disruption. Fortunately, the software was corrected later that day and clearing normalized.

The lesson: because of a high concentration in the market for clearing services, a single malfunction in a single firm's system led to an expensive crisis and highlighted systemic risks in the US Treasury market. No systems back-up could have prevented the problem – the back-up system would have had the same software bug.

Now compare this to what happened in the same market on September 11, 2001. Again, a major New York bank is an active player, clearing more than half of all US government securities transactions. Volumes are far greater, and the bank's systems far more robust, with multiple data centres and recovery sites primarily located in New Jersey and therefore physically unaffected by the terrorist attacks. What is different this time is the critical role of the telecommunications infrastructure handling all the data traffic created by the trading activity. When the network hubs in the World Trade Center were destroyed, traffic was automatically routed to another hub nearby, which happened to be the principal access point serving the clearer. The ensuing enormous surge in telecom traffic swamped that facility, temporarily disrupting communications for the clearing bank. Trades stopped being executed and settled; the business shut down.

Even though the bank was physically removed from the World Trade Center destruction, the bank's dependence on the network infrastructure had a profound ripple effect throughout the government bond market.

11.2 TECHNOLOGICAL PROGRESS AND ASSET GROWTH: DRIVERS OF THE NEW REALITY

To understand today's environment, we must take a look at the most profound drivers of the financial industry since 1975: the precipitous fall in technology (hardware) costs and the dramatic rise in investment assets (see Graph 11.1).

In effect, the marginal cost of hardware is close to zero; this has had a huge impact on financial markets. Access to information is cheaper and

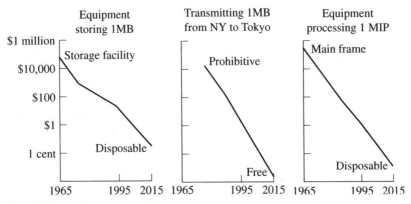

Graph 11.1   Precipitous shifts

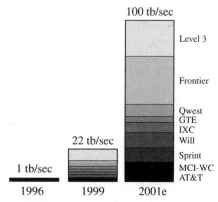

Source: Fortune Magazine 3/1999

Figure 11.2   Capacity of the US telephone network

broader, markets are more efficient, volumes have skyrocketed, and cycles have accelerated. Combined with financial deregulation on a global scale, the result is greater competition, more specialization, and a deeper reliance on network infrastructures.

By any metric you care to look at, the hardware costs of processing, storing and transmitting information have plummeted, and the trend line is clear: the hardware-specific costs of IT are dropping to essentially zero (see Graph 11.1). To cite just one example: in a report published by *Fortune* magazine in 1999, the entire US long-distance telephone capacity in 1996 was shown to be one terabit/second – enough for about 15 million simultaneous phone calls. By 2001, that capacity had increased by a factor of 100 – two orders of magnitude – with the obvious consequence: lower costs and higher traffic (see Figure 11.2).

If technology has changed the nature of finance, so too has the opportunity created by the massive shift from bank deposits to investment assets. In 1980, bank deposits accounted for more than half of the roughly US$2.8 trillion in personal financial assets in the United States; by 2000, the assets had grown to US$17 trillion with less than 20 per cent of that money in bank deposits.

It is axiomatic, but all these new dollars in securities had to be managed. The growth and competitive frenzy of the asset management industry, coupled with an ever-increasing, technology-driven capability to assimilate and analyse raw data, generated more and more market activity, which in turn generated more and more data, and so on in a cycle that brings us to today, with volumes of trades and information that were unthinkable only a decade ago.

Driven by the need to create and exploit economies of scale, most growing manufacturing industries eventually consolidate. Growing financial markets are no different (the quest for scale and efficiency has certainly generated lots of mergers). But while scale benefits financial operations, it is inimical to investors. The ability to exploit information and market insights is limited when managing very large pools of assets, simply because the markets are not liquid enough. The liquidity issue forces asset managers to restrict the sizes of investment portfolios, making distribution relatively more expensive as trading costs go down.

11.3   TWO KINDS OF PLAYERS EMERGE

The result has been a profound evolution in the structure of the financial services industry, with two kinds of enterprises on the ascendant: specialized component producers that do one thing extremely well on a global scale (exploiting technology to achieve economies: clearing or custody, for example, or processing credit card transactions) and 'megabranders' that package a wide range of products and services for a huge global market (exploiting the power of their brands to reach consumers and the power of technology to manage relationships – for example Citigroup, Morgan Stanley).

This evolution suggests what the future of the industry will look like in technological terms. Today, the biggest cost component (and therefore the largest cost savings opportunity) is not in processing itself but in the communications between specialized providers, in managing the interactions of all those systems and messages. For specialized component producers, therefore, the best way to cut the costs of production is by moving to Straight-Through Processing, or STP. Basically, instead of people reformatting, translating and relaying the myriad messages associated with transactions, STP means systems talking directly to systems and processing transactions in real-time.

Figure 11.3 illustrates how many parties and systems are involved in executing a hypothetical share trade between an institutional and an individual investor. Each arrow represents a connection between systems, a communications channel that often involves an expensive 'linkage': a person translating and relaying information. Even straightforward transactions can involve as many as 100 different systems and 200 separate messages.

The adoption of STP combined with the increased specialization of producers will result in a monumental shift in financial services processing: from batch to continuous. Batch processing works well when transaction

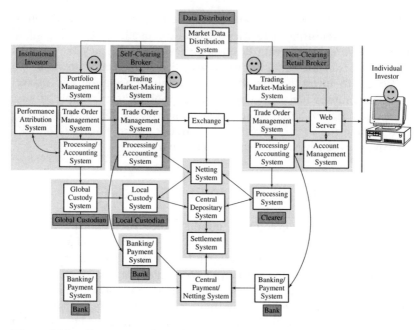

Figure 11.3   Executing a hypothetical share trade between an institutional and an individual investor

cycles are long and single firms handle an entire value chain. But as trading volumes increase, transaction cycles shorten, and firms focus and specialize, serialized batch processes become a severe operational bottleneck. The network can no longer be accelerated, while the cost of error-handling goes through the roof.

Implementing STP and continuous processing will require huge investments. One consulting firm, The Tower Group, estimated in 2002 that the financial services industry will spend more than US$15 billion to implement STP through 2005. A fundamental rethinking of workflows will result in new ways of doing business, and that change is expensive. The silver lining of this challenge is that rethinking workflows enables firms to really exploit the benefits of technology. It is a golden opportunity to make operations dramatically less expensive.

11.4   LESS REDUNDANCY; MORE RISK

The specialization of finance goes hand in hand with consolidation and concentration. In the 1980s, there were 20 substantial credit card processors; today there are five huge ones. These five have certainly achieved economies of scale, but they have also squeezed redundancy out of the system, generating new kinds of systemic risk. This is a natural, predictable but unfortunate by-product of the invisible hand of the marketplace and its ruthless quest for efficiency – and it poses new challenges for participants and regulators alike.

Indeed, the new systemic risk in the financial industry is no longer characterized by institutions that are too big to fail but by institutions that are too critical to the network because they are a dominant provider of a highly specialized service. More and more firms are dependent on third-party specialists (consider, for example, the current oligopoly in market data services: Reuters, Bloomberg, and so on). Furthermore, the increased degree of automation and faster transaction cycles mean that problems anywhere on the network make the whole system more vulnerable. Automation reduces flexibility in responding to emergencies and allows errors to propagate much faster.

These technology-driven issues will continue to evolve the structure of the financial industry in the future, and they create new risk management challenges for managers and regulators. In an environment characterized by highly interconnected, interdependent service providers, network risk becomes paramount when planning for contingencies and disasters. How secure is the network? How redundant is the network? How automated is the network? And, ultimately, who regulates the network which transcends national boundaries?

While earthquakes and jetliners can have catastrophic effects on financial networks, the bigger and more worrisome threats stem from cyber-terrorism: computer viruses, worms and other forms of artificial 'life' aimed directly at the network infrastructure critical to contemporary finance. According to the CERT Coordination Center at Carnegie Mellon University, which tracks computer emergencies and responses, more than 80 000 computer security incidents were reported in 2002; that number is expected to increase another 50 per cent this year. Losses attributable to viruses in 2001 were estimated at US$15 billion (see Graph 11.2). And the threat can only increase as network access points proliferate (think of the potential for viruses to enter the network when every mobile phone can access the Web and 802.11b wireless computer networks become truly pervasive).

11.5 WHAT TO DO NEXT

What should you do in this new environment of contingency planning? From a macro perspective, you need to adopt a new distributed architecture

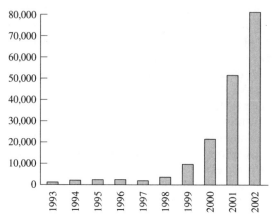

Source: CERT Coordination Center, Carnegie Mellon University

Graph 11.2   Computer security incidents

for the processes truly critical to your ability to function. A networked operation is far more resilient than a concentrated, standalone operation. A few
guiding principles to keep in mind are described below.

First, identify key businesses and dependencies. Operating your entire
company on a fully redundant basis is not necessary and would be far too
expensive. So begin addressing the challenge of operational resilience by
identifying which parts of your business need what kind of resilience.
Landscaping around your corporate headquarters, for example, will rank
low; customer relationship management will rank high. You also need to
understand your dependencies on third-party service providers and, most
important, whether the third parties you depend on most regard you as critical to their business.

Second, backup processes, not just data. Under the old paradigm, the
focus was on backing up data, but that does nothing to ensure your ability
to operate continuously. In the new world, you have to back up data as well
as the network and processing capacity, people and third parties upon
whom your enterprise depends. Lots of firms have back-up data centres
and even back-up trading rooms, but how many today have their call centre
operations spread out across the country?

Third, plan and test for network-related contingencies. Once you have
begun backing up processes and data, you can begin planning for network-
related contingencies and actually testing your resilience. The goal should
to be remain operating (and to be prepared for substantial – perhaps record
– volumes as other financial market participants and their systems come
back on-line). You need to establish clearly defined responsibilities in the

event of an emergency and to share your contingency plans within and outside your enterprise (to critical partners, for example). And test your resilience: prove to yourself that your contingency plans will work. (Don't forget to include your firm's senior managers in the tests so they can see first hand how they will react and what really needs to be done in the event of a disaster.)

Recovering after the impact of a disaster, whether it is an earthquake in Tokyo, a terrorist attack in Manhattan, or a computer virus unleashed in London, will no longer be sufficient to ensure enterprise safety or systemic integrity. In today's networked financial services economy, financial enterprises must keep going continuously in the event of a catastrophe. Markets can melt down or freeze (choose your favourite metaphor) with great speed, and that speed will only increase as market participants and their systems become more closely intertwined.

We will never be able to make ourselves immune to the human costs of attacks like September 11, 2001, but we owe it to our companies and our industry to make our enterprises as immune as possible to the operational risks posed by them and other threats. Ultimately, it is a matter more of commonsense applications of technology and other resources ('What do I need to do to keep running in the worst-case scenario?') than fancy analytics or sophisticated risk quantifications. Addressing these new risks is vital to the ability of our firms to function and the ability of our system to thrive.

11.6 AN EVOLUTION: FROM DATA BACK-UP TO PROCESSING REDUNDANCY

As technology became more pervasive in the financial business and dependency on technology increased, IT and operations professionals have become more sophisticated about backing up data, from 'batch' back-ups to continuous back-ups to on-line data mirroring (see Figure 11.4). Processing capabilities have followed a similar trend line, from scheduled downtime to high availability to uninterrupted processing. Because data processing is now so deeply embedded in every business activity of practically every employee, protecting the data and the main processing centres no longer assures survival. It is the combination of data, processing and workgroup availability that ensure operational resilience.

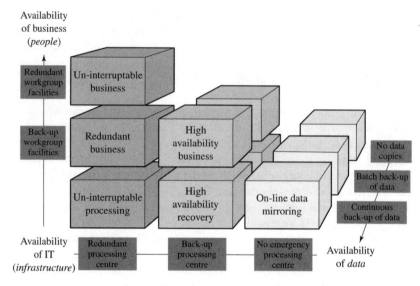

Figure 11.4   From data back-up to processing redundancy

PART IV

Implications of crisis in a synergetic world

12. Disaster management after September 11: a 'normal accident' or a 'man-made disaster'? What did we know, what have we learned?

David H. Weir

INTRODUCTION

It has almost become a commonplace that after the events of September 11, the world will never be the same again. The date has become iconic, evoking instant recognition in many contexts, though not in Chile where the date symbolizes for most people the *coup d'état* in 1973 of General Pinochet with US backing against the elected government of President Allende, leading to his assassination. Nonetheless, these are strong claims: are they justified? Have the responses of the world community been commensurate with this discourse? What has changed and are such events now more or less likely in the future?

In some senses, for students of disasters, such catastrophic events are not so unusual and by some criteria it is arguable that September 11 was quite a 'normal' disaster. It was predictable and it was predicted: it affected a relatively circumscribed and limited group of people, and its etiology is not in doubt. We shall argue that there is extant research and conventionally accepted patterns of explanation within the scientific community which can assist in the work of interpretation

12.1 NORMAL ACCIDENTS

The term 'normal accident' was first coined by Charles Perrow in 1984 to define a type of occurrence which may be system-induced in the sense that it is an inevitable outcome, at some time or other, of the way that a complex system with multiple interactions operates. Thus an accident of this kind, however major or catastrophic, cannot be considered as 'abnormal'. It *will* occur; only the timing and perhaps the periodicity is obscure.

These disasters tend to occur in complex, interconnected and interpenetrated systems which are highly reliable under conditions of normal operation, but in practice are vulnerable and may succumb to certain types of attack because of the very tightness of their internal bonding. We have previously referred to these systems as 'over-controlled' (Weir, 1976; Weir, 1996; Mars and Weir, 2000).

Perrow's initial empirical data is based on the operation of the nuclear power industry in the US and in particular from a review of the sequence of events that led to the accident at the Three Mile Island Unit 2 nuclear plant at Harrisburg, Pennsylvania on 28 March 1979 (Perrow, 1984). The conditions which especially favour these events include what Perrow defines as 'interactive complexity' and 'tight coupling'. In these kinds of systems, on the whole, things will go wrong not as a result of random, unpredictable and exogenous shocks, attacks and incursions, but as the consequence of a complex string of events, antecedent conditions and small but cumulative defects and deficiencies in operating systems. Perrow warns that 'neither better organization nor technological innovations appear to make them any less prone to system accidents. In fact these systems require organisational structures that have large internal contradictions, and technological fixes that only increase interactive complexity and tighten the coupling; they become still more prone to certain types of accidents' (Perrow, 1984, p. 5).

What, in the case of the September 11, 2001 disaster, can we identify as 'the system'? Does it meet the constraints implied by the theory? There is no doubt that the international geopolitical system demonstrates interactive complexity but can hardly be described as tight-coupled, so the basic requirements of Perrow's formulation do not seem to be present. The theories we are considering were not derived from studies of major terrorist incidents. Perrow's empirical work refers to the failures in the nuclear power industry, Vaughan's to the Challenger Space Shuttle disaster, my own and others to crashes of big commercial passenger jets. Nonetheless the theory has indeed been found to have wide applicability (Vaughan, 1996; Weir, 1996).

Perrow notes that 'interactive complexity' is a feature of many complex high-technology systems in industries like that of nuclear power, and introduces the notion of 'tight coupling' in which sequences of events, once started, lead apparently irreversibly to catastrophic outcomes even when only small or unimportant problems can be identified as the original 'cause' of the chain reaction. This tight coupling is a consequence of the very nature of the technology in a high-risk situation which prescribes invariant behaviours and tightly prescribed sequences of actions precisely because the risks of failure are objectively great. He concludes 'this interacting tendency is a characteristic of a system, not of a part or an operator' (Perrow, 1984, p. 4).

Nonetheless the interactions prescribed in a tight-coupled system themselves become causes of system failure because once the first mistake occurs and the failure sequence is initiated, it is other behavioural characteristics, of innovation, creativity, 'thinking outside the box' and even simple ingenuousness which may be required in the critical situation. Further, Perrow notes:

> for most of the systems we shall consider . . . neither better organisation nor technological innovations appear to make them any less prone to system accidents . . . the odd term normal accident is meant to signal that, given the system characteristics, multiple and unexpected interactions of failures are inevitable. (Perrow, 1984, p. 5)

The second relevant theoretical formulations come from the work of Turner and others on 'man-made disasters' (Turner, 1976; Turner, 1978; Turner and Pidgeon, 1997). This term identifies a category of events which at first appear to be tragic accidents but in the etiology of which acts of human commission and omission are of prime significance.

Some of these events occur within systems that appear to be safe in terms of their design, but in which the experience of operations has deviated from the designed plans and operating routines have been introduced which subvert the safety features of the system. Many of these deviations from plan are introduced to save operating time, often to reduce production costs, or are associated with short-cut procedures which serve the purposes of groups with special interests: thus it is appropriate to describe the actual processes and procedures of operation as constituting a 'degraded mode'.

The multitudinous corrections, updates, program improvements, short-cuts and paste-ins which develop in complex systems imply that no such system ever operates in fact in the way described in its operating manuals and design specifications. In practice, therefore, all such complex systems operate in degraded mode.

An associated consequence is that the monitoring procedures and records and statistics which purport to reflect the operation of significant events do not in fact do so. Accordingly it becomes difficult if not impossible for higher levels of management to monitor the real states of the system. In addition, differences of grade, authority and expertise combine to decrease the transmission of accurate information, and the communication system also evidences degradation. This especially affects the upward transmission of information which contradicts the expectations of the hierarchy about system performance. Since in principle, therefore, all systems operate in degraded mode, it is impossible to infer from an *a priori* specification of the design of complex socio-technical systems to specific conclusions about actual events (Weir, 1991).

When reviewing the causes and sequences of failure in these complex systems it is important to avoid moralistic condemnations and the search for scapegoats. These approaches diminish the chances of improving the systems in future. Thus the routine findings of 'pilot error' do little to create the organizational climates in which pilots will routinely report near-misses and mistakes, knowledge of which can in a 'no-fault' reporting system such as those now operated by major carriers like British Airways, improve operational safety. The discourse of morality and personal blame leads to mind-sets that are unhelpful to objective judgements of causes and understanding of motives in complex socio-historical contexts (Beaty, 1991).

It is important to distinguish between the experience and knowledge of the first-line operators in a complex system, and the managers higher up who may have overall responsibility for system operations at a strategic as well as operational level, because as Turner and Pidgeon comment, 'the front-line operators of socio-technical systems such as pilots or process plant personnel frequently inherit, and are blamed for, the consequences of what are in reality latent failures, in particular those stemming from organisational and management inadequacies' (Turner and Pidgeon, 1997, p. 180).

Therefore a prime focus of enquiry into why disasters happen must be the structures of power, control and cultural mediation in systems which are especially disaster-prone to understand why disasters of this kind typically occur in imperatively-coordinated associations characterized by certain patterns of communication. We can identify these systems as especially vulnerable (Weir, 1993).

Samuel Huntington characterizes the emerging world order as increasingly vulnerable due to the increasing risk of a clash of civilizations, in particular between the Muslim and the Western worlds (Huntington, 1996). This analysis is representative of a new breed of geopolitical 'realists' who are not afraid to think what for much of the last generation has been an almost unthinkable dogma: that is, that the correct and appropriate ways to settle international disputes may be by overt confrontation, if necessary involving military force. But Huntington is distinctive in that he sees such conflicts as rooted not in geopolitical or economic terms but ultimately in inevitable and deep-rooted cultural differences. In specific terms he sees the differences between the Western and Islamic paradigms of social organization as constituting nothing less than a coming 'conflict of civilizations'.

Huntington argues that the differences between what he describes as

'Western' and 'Islamic' civilizations are so disparate that the only conceivable relations between them are those of confrontation, rooted in cultural misunderstanding, and that the most likely outcome of this essentially hostile pattern of relations is explicit and damaging conflict. If this analysis is correct, the world geopolitical system is indeed increasingly vulnerable.

It is not our purpose in this chapter to debate in depth the relevance of Huntington's analysis but it is important to note that his characterization of the Islamic world is partial and to some extent incorrect. Much other research into management styles and culturally rooted patterns of behaviour in relation to the characteristic modes of decision-making in the Arab world and the frame of reference of decision-makers in the Arab Middle East leads to the conclusion that this world is by no means well described in the apocalyptic terms used by Huntington. Nonetheless it is different, and warrants intensive study. In terms of management, the Arab ways of doing business and managing organizations constitutes a 'Fourth Paradigm' of management, which needs to be carefully distinguished from the prevailing and dominant Anglo Saxon orthodoxy and also from European and Japanese traditions (Weir, 2000a).

But these behaviours constitute a system of management cultures and business structures which fit very well the emerging patterns of globalization with its associated patterns of decentralized consultative decision-making, network capabilities and high professional and technical competence (Weir, 2003). Nonetheless it is clear that at the crucial levels of decision-making within Western society, and in particular within the hierarchy of the US intelligence and counter-terrorist agencies, there existed certainly before September 11 a gross deficiency in street-level knowledge of what was going on. This deficiency relates to many background features of the American educational system, to the increasingly centralized structures of the intelligence community, to lack of linguistic competencies and to reliance on technology-based rather than people-rich sources of information, and has been widely documented (see for example, Weir, 2000a).

It is apparent also that the official public responses to the attacks were heavy in emotional and judgemental discourse, and relatively lighter in objective dispassionate analysis.

12.2   THE MAN-MADE DISASTER

There is now a considerable literature on 'man-made disasters': but the term was coined as a sociological term of art by the late Barry Turner in his book of the same name, published quietly by a little-known publisher in the mid-1970s (Turner, 1978). The idea, though, is as old as mankind and recorded literature: certainly Shakespeare was in no doubt when relating the misadventures of struggling humanity that 'the fault is in ourselves' and not in 'our stars'. The notion has been extended from its initial meaning in ways that are important for our understanding of disasters and the possibility of preventing them.

While all commentators of the human condition have understood that deficiencies of character in individuals could lead to unfortunate outcomes for them and others, it is a more sophisticated understanding of systems that has crystallized the understanding that certain conditions may be regarded as iatrogenic, that is to say, as produced by the very mechanisms that had been designed to control or remedy them.

So high-tech hospitals designed to cure diseases in conditions of absolute sterility and the scientific destruction of potentially threatening microbial and bacterial life-forms provide the milieu for the spread of disease of even more virulent capabilities. Political and juridical measures designed to solve 'evils' by seeking out and eradicating evildoers, only create the conditions for the intensification of 'evils' to generations unborn, innocent of the transgressions that stigmatized their parents' generations but doomed to suffer the consequences of their correction.

In the case of the complex socio-technical systems that form the basis of contemporary post-industrial society, it is the measures to maintain control that create the triggers that send these same systems spinning out of control. In some cases we can talk of such systems as being 'over-controlled', as when the application of ever tighter discipline in institutions of penal correction creates forces of reaction that break the bonds of sensible and calculative response in an outburst of self-defeating rebellion.

We also understand from a wide range of scientific evidence that no event, however apparently unique or idiosyncratic in its occasion, is without its precursors. If it has happened, it has happened before, and will certainly happen again. Earthquakes are betrayed by initial tremors, and wars by riots, disturbance, confrontation and the raging undertones of wrongs unnoticed except by those suffering them (Bignall and Fortune, 1984).

Systems scientists since Turner have drawn our attention to the significance of what we now call 'soft signals'. These are only likely to be noticed by those familiar with the normal operation of these systems. They may be intermittent, of low power or limited variety and often unquantifiable. But those used to how things normally operate notice them and realize that they herald a potential change of state of the system. But they may appear too insignificant or irrelevant to the senior management in the system which has its eyes and ears attuned to bigger waves, stronger impulses.

Those who do notice them may be of low status in the system and their intuition that 'something is not quite right' may be easily disregarded by the powerful. So it is the almost universal fate of whistleblowers to be unheeded, and of small Jeremiahs to be perennially calling in their wilderness while these soft signals pass unnoticed as the senior managers in complex systems move about their diurnal procedures. This knowledge thus remains in a sense subterranean: it is there but it has to be excavated carefully by those who know where to dig.

Per contra, the very regularity of the high-level defensive procedures, their programmed and predictable nature and the way in which the behaviours enjoined by these systems can become internalized as habits and roles, and their justifications institutionalized as norms and mores, in principle offers opportunity to the attackers (as the Allied prisoners of war incarcerated in Colditz and other high-security prisons in the Second World War discovered to their advantage.)

Thus, precisely in the case of September 11, the defensive capability of the USA to notice, react to and to withstand large-scale military attacks emanating from outside 'homeland airspace' was very strong: but the attacks on the Twin Towers came through commercial aircraft whose journeys commenced within the USA. Soft signals did exist and it is understood that there were increasing intelligence reports that 'something big' was planned. But the capability to operate at street level, close to the sources of these intelligence sightings, did not exist within the American defence establishment which lacked Arabic, Urdu, Farsi or Pushtu speakers, and field operatives attuned to the soft variations in communication and sentiment in the Arab world. There is nothing new in this. Throughout the Second World War major intelligence gaffes regularly occurred for precisely similar reasons of physical distance, lack of familiarity with everyday life in Occupied Europe, and cultural and linguistic inadequacies.

It is precisely within the ambit of the 'high reliability systems' so favoured by the leaders of the high-tech military–industrial complex in Western societies that the coincidence of these circumstances produces the highest probability that highly vulnerable systems will succumb to inevitable catastrophe. There is no system so secure that it cannot be threatened by the attitudes and behaviours that emanate from a strong sense of inviolability. Predictability and precision are the essential supports for behaviour in circumstances of normal operation: they are less advantageous attributes when circumstances are threatening.

Another aspect of the massive attack on core institutions that appears to characterize the September 11 events: characteristic of such events is that these assaults occurred on the 'central places' of one of the protagonists. Washington is the capital city of the USA and the White House and the

Pentagon are two of its most cherished significations as a capital of the most potent power on earth, and its military and political embodiments. New York is not the capital city of the USA but it is its most widely recognized urban symbol of economic wealth and prestige, and within it the Twin Towers were iconic symbols of American capitalism. These two cities constitute 'head office' locations and prime targets for attack.

But it does not follow that they were the best defended. Quite the contrary, indeed. The attackers would almost certainly have had less chance of success had they followed the earlier tactic of attacking American embassies and warships in overseas locations, or of assailing remote locations and branch offices, because the lessons of previous attacks had been incorporated into more effective security systems.

Studies of attacks on the integrity of computer systems show this pattern also. It is the incidents which occur in branch offices and in downstream businesses which are detected early, and the major degradations and subversions on Head Office systems which carry on undetected for a long period and result in serious financial losses. There are several reasons for this, not least the truth that head office personnel have lost, or perhaps never had the opportunity to obtain, that sense of imminent danger which is the *sine qua non* for survival on the street or upcountry, especially in what the cowboy films call 'Indian country'.

People and institutions feel safest in the places they know the best, where their friends are, and surrounded by the symbols of the institutions which care for their welfare. But it does not follow at all that these places are the safest places for them to be.

It is undoubtedly the case that the events of September 11, 2001 constituted a dreadful shock to the American government and people. But they need not have done. They were a dreadful disaster, but one that was eminently preventable. They were events of a kind that had in some form occurred before, in the case of the Trade Center in that precise location, and by the same presumed perpetrators who had communicated quite publicly their intentions of carrying out further such attacks.

The weapons utilized, commercial airliners carrying passengers, had in fact been used for similar events in the past by perpetrators espousing the same or associated causes, though not of course in precisely the same way. Suicide attacks have been a feature of several assaults in the Palestine–Israel conflict. The breaches of airport security were such as could have been deterred by the operation of the most rudimentary procedures, had they existed, and are indeed the subjects of training in most professional counterterrorism and political policing regimes worldwide. They would not have occurred at Tel Aviv or Belfast airports.

One of the most horrifying aspects of the September 11 attacks was that they took place in a people-rich, urban milieu and disrupted normal business and commercial activities; they were seen on prime-time TV. Outside of overt acts of war, these were unusual combinations of circumstance. But as urban disasters, in a historical context, compared to the cataclysms that overtook Pompeii and Herculaneum, Santorini, Peshtigo, London, Hamburg, Dresden, Grozny, Hiroshima or Nagasaki it ranks relatively low down on the list of Big City Disasters of which we have records. The life of the great city, though affected, did not stop, and for many inhabitants the interruption to the normal patterns of life was minimal. The city survived and its emergency services coped; Dresden, Grozny, Hiroshima did not.

But in another non-demographic sense, these assaults did succeed, precisely because they were perceived to be the products of a type of reasoning which is seen as alien and incomprehensible to the defenders. They have changed the frameworks of discourse. The tactic of suicide bombing is perceived by many in the Western world as somehow beyond belief. But it is by no means a new tactic. During the Second World War, Japanese Kamikaze pilots caused consternation among American defenders in the Pacific: so much so that special orders were issued by the American High Command that the crews of US ships under threat of Kamikaze attack should not be warned even when an attack was predicted because of the risk of a catastrophic collapse of their morale. In fact such attacks are very often successful. Smart defensive systems work well against smart attackers, but crude assaults are surprising, unanticipated and mystifying, succeeding by their very unlikeliness.

Thus they represent a violent assault on the basal attributes of a social order, in which control, comfort and predictability are core assumptions. The precise etiology of the September 11 attack on the continental United States, the lack of attention to 'soft signals' and the lack of preparedness for clearly predictable and crude attacks on the complex infrastructures of a highly sophisticated society are characteristic of a specific type of disaster.

12.3   VULNERABLE SYSTEMS

We can now briefly characterize the relevant characteristics of the social systems in which the events of September 11 were embedded and located, and identify the features which enable us to classify these systems as inherently 'vulnerable'. We then try to summarize the changes that have occurred since that date and whether these changes have rendered these systems more or less vulnerable to future attack.

For a system to be vulnerable it must possess certain characteristics. These may be summarized as:

- complexity
- opacity
- over-confidence
- multiple communication paths, poorly integrated or conformed
- decision-making styles prone to acting on poorly assimilated field information prone to inertia or fatalism; the belief that things on the whole tend to work out.

These theoretical predispositions are usually justified within a discourse which is moralistic or self-exculpatory in style and which relies much on the reluctance of outsiders to probe too deeply into difficult detail. Thus incidents leading to loss of life of lower participants, clients or customers are described as 'tragic accidents', or in the case of some prison riots as 'outbreaks of evil' when they are really evidence of managerial incompetence and of inattention to soft signals of impending breakdown of defensive systems.

These organizations tend to handle information according to its apparent conformity to pre-existent paradigms which formulate experience into trends and tendencies which confirm the existing power-holders in the belief in the wisdom of their own judgements and those of their predecessors in office. Thus, the British garrison at Singapore in 1940, the board of Enron and the Arthur Andersen partnership prior to the Enron collapse, and the American naval leadership at Pearl Harbor before the day that would 'live in infamy' all display symptoms of this systemic vulnerability.

'Groupthink' is an aspect of the bases for decision-making in such enterprises, and so is the overconfidence that comes from apparently overwhelming military or market superiority. Often the confidence is based on the undoubted facts of previous successes: but the failure to heed apparent soft signals of impending attack is also related to the failure to update in defensive capabilities on the assumption that enemies previously defeated will not have recovered over time even if the bases of their enmity is not dealt with in the aftermath of the previous success (Janis, 1982). Thus, to be precise about the targets of the September 11 attacks, the Twin Towers of the World Trade Center, the fact that previous attacks on their structural integrity had been survived did not imply that either the motivations for such attacks had been eliminated, that the perpetrators and their organizational back-up had been rendered ineffective or that other targets would be chosen on a subsequent occasion. *Per contra*, it was highly suggestive that only low-level perpetrators were captured, whereas the planning and execution of the attack and the magnitude of the explosion that ensued indicated that sophisticated organizational capabilities and high-profile targeting were features of the opposition team and their perception of the situation.

It is an elementary principle of criminal investigation that sites which have suffered one attack will indubitably suffer another; banks once robbed will be robbed again, and tourists attacked in one location will suffer again in the same place in the same way. Attacks by armed insurgents are seldom random and never 'accidents', so the discourse of 'accident' and 'tragedy' only serve to subvert attempts to establish etiology and actively inhibit successful preventative strategies. Vulnerable systems are typically passive in their attitudes to information, preferring mainly to rely on established statistical presentations which confirm, rather than proactively seeking sources of data which challenge, existing prejudices. They do not seek to rotate roles, experience or qualifications to produce fresh insights. They do not seek to recruit new types of people to challenge the comfort zones of existing incumbents. They rely on established communication routes and do not willingly send leading position-holders to undertake low-level and front-line tasks. They do not, in short, 'manage by walking about'. They do not simulate or self-consciously seek to invert the prevailing organizational visions by 'walking in the shoes' of the customer, still less of the potential enemy. Often they are inhibited in handling matters in these radical ways by the lack of basic skills, whether of relevant linguistic competencies in the language of the potential attacker or of 'street' awareness and comprehension of the structuring of political and social debate in other domains than their own. Rules of Engagement are seen as predictive of future encounters rather than as summaries of understandings achieved in previous ones. It would be a work of super-erogation to catalogue the manifold ways in which the internal security systems of the mainland United States conformed to these patterns before September 11, 2001. To Europeans, especially British citizens used to the airport security regimes enforced after two decades of IRA attacks, the lack of adequate check-in and in-flight security awareness among US airlines and airports was obvious. To European political analysts the insouciance about the cumulative effect on their Arab neighbours of perceived American partiality in the Palestine arena, and the support for regimes which offended the tenets of Islamic principle in the Arabian peninsula, were equally surprising.

To observers of the administrative scene, the governmental doctrines of separation of powers had appeared to degenerate into the politicization of managerial agendas and inter-agency complexity without any constraining organizational principle.

So American official attention to security concerns appeared to outsiders to exhibit symptoms of waywardness, failure to recognize significant trends, and lack of street-awareness in almost equal measure to its overweening self-confidence. This was not a feature of all American organizational life, for it was from the USA that the doctrine of 'high reliability systems' had emerged practically contemporaneously with the theories of normal accidents, and in partial response to its implications.

High reliability systems are supported by a culture in which security of information transmission is secured by the operation of multiple communication channels: in large US aircraft carriers, redundancy is designed in to their operating systems with more than 20 communications devices to ensure instant communications to any part of the ship; the flight deck itself is linked to the control tower by five such systems. These systems reinforce a culture of safety by aggressively seeking to review and understand the causes of failure, by simulating critical and disaster situations in training and stressing a culture of safe operation, and supporting networked communication about how the effective performance of small tasks contributes to the safe operation of the whole system.

These lessons are now accepted in much of industry and in the UK, for example under the direction of regulations monitored by the Health and Safety Executive, enterprises now aim to base their safety training on the creation of 'Safety Cases' in which the vulnerabilities of the systems and potential weaknesses in preventative procedures are exhaustively reviewed and documented. But experience indicates that these benefits may be short-lived. On the day they are completed and for some time thereafter, these exercises undoubtedly do much to raise awareness of the ways in which failure can occur and the sequences in which small events can develop into large-scale crises and failures, and it would be tempting to see these activities as somehow heralding that much-abused phrase 'a change in the culture'. But these management initiatives and challenging new discourses of 'safety culture' have to be incorporated into behavioural modifications and new patterns of reward and behavioural reinforcement. These take time and there is usually much back-sliding. Established patterns of behaviour which meet existing cultural expectations and offer psychic rewards are not easily controverted by management fiat.

12.4   CONCLUSION

Has there been a change in the culture of attitudes towards disasters since September 11? Is this change compatible with a trend towards 'higher reliability'? Have these systems become less or more vulnerable?

There have been serious and immediate consequences: major changes of direction in foreign policy principles; two armed conflicts; ruptures with established allies; contemptuous dismissal of established relations with the United Nations and other international agencies. All of these have been accompanied by changes of discourse as well as of action. Many of these changes are discussed in the other chapters in this book. They are of major geopolitical significance. And it may be argued, quite plausibly, that it is altogether too early to form conclusive judgements about the extent to which these changes have 'worked'. But on the more limited questions relating to the vulnerability of the systems of international travel and the liabilities of attack for American cities, it is possible to make some preliminary assessments.

High reliability systems depend ultimately for their efficacy on the possibility for central hierarchical coordination, backed by clear and massive funding streams. Such systems are normally only possible in the public sector and in domains of strategic significance for public investment. In the US governmental systems, with separations of powers both between federal and state agencies, and between private and public arenas and between multiple agencies operating to further the same objectives, there is usually a limited opportunity for such systems. The introduction of an office of 'homeland security' headed by a senior politician would appear to mark a change in this philosophy. It remains to be seen, however, whether a Republican administration can move so far away from its traditional beliefs as to make this possible.

In fact, worldwide, only in Israel have these preconditions for airline and airport security ever been approached; and the political framework and the reality of defending a siege economy, supported by massive external remittances, creates a totally different pattern of expectations. The American public will ultimately not wish to or be able to pay for a 'high reliability' solution. That is a chimera. But if the 'high reliability' route is not realistic, can we form an assessment of the increased or decreased vulnerability of the system in the light of the changes in the geopolitical framework? The US administration has announced several changes of strategic intent which will tend to simplify the situation, at the cost of taking responsibility for topics which it was previously content to see administered by others. The viability of these decisions will depend on the successful follow-through and implementation of the ensuing solutions.

But in an inherently complex geopolitical order, with different power bases, interests and cultures, the imposition of new routines, procedures and protocols from a hegemonic source is inherently implausible. In the case of such an attempt by the USA in the present situation to propose the central regulation of the industries and jurisdictions which created the present vulnerabilities, two factors combine to weaken the chances further. The first is the explicit disavowal by the US of the only existing structures through which such procedures could currently be enforced on an international basis. The USA is out of step with the majority opinions within the United Nations and most existing agencies owe their legitimacy ultimately to that organization and its dependent bodies. The second is that the industries, which are central to any such efforts, in particular the airlines and tourism industries, are in a relatively weakened position and unable to take a leading role involving major new investment streams. They have been financially penalized already by taking on such changes in physical security as reinforced doors separating flight decks from cabin areas. On a jumbo jet the typical cost of these upgrades alone is around £250000 per vehicle.

These investments are being made, despite opposition from pilots' organizations and industry professionals who believe that these modifications will not beneficially impact upon in-flight security. The economic return from improved security is far from certain. The two leading US airlines, American and United, are practically bankrupt already. The major aircraft manufacturers are feeling the heat of consistently improving European competition.

The major possibilities for decreasing the vulnerability in the system would therefore seem to lie in a successful eradication of the causes of the discontents which led to the initiation of the sequence of events which culminated in the Twin Towers attacks.

These causes may be found in the geopolitics of the Middle East and possibly in the perceived confrontation of civilizations between Western and Islamic cultures as depicted by Huntington and others. These frames of reference are not coterminous as the Bali bombing indicates. The largest Muslim nation in the world is Indonesia.

It is not clear that military intervention, however apparently decisive, can solve these underlying discontents. The peace is not yet won in Afghanistan; in Iraq the problems of post-war reconstruction have only just started to surface. A realistic peace process in Palestine that would be acceptable to the Arab world has not yet been outlined. The perception of the US as ineluctably committed to the Israeli cause has been strengthened by events in Iraq and Afghanistan, and the situation of Britain as a potential 'honest broker' has been fatally compromised for the foreseeable future, possibly for a generation. These are not political judgements, for the instigators of the September 11 attacks were not politically motivated in the conventional sense. The opportunities for creating future Osama bin Ladens competent to operate on the radical consciousness of the deprived and underprivileged as well as the intelligentsia in the Middle East region, in future will arguably increase rather than attenuate with continuing displays of Western hegemonic force. Already it is becoming clear that a political settlement of the Iraq situation will take immeasurably longer than the military confrontation; and it is less likely that such a settlement will conform to Western norms of democracy. These worlds of the Arab Middle East have become, in the judgement of many business people and political commentators, more dangerous for Westerners for the foreseeable future.

Indubitably the vulnerability to further attacks on civilians, whether tourists, journalists or aid agency workers, has been increased over the past period. Yet all past experience, whether in Northern Ireland, Kenya, Cyprus, South Africa or wherever, illustrates that the problems of terrorist violence are not amenable to purely military solutions. The political accommodation comes before the surrender by the 'terrorists' of the option of violent force.

The willing incorporation of the civilian majority in troubled areas into the processes of constraint of the men and women of violence precedes the cessation of hostilities. That is how terrorism differs from formal warfare. The overt attempt to solve the one problem by modalities attuned to the other has confused these issues and delayed a more realistic strategy for their resolution.

We conclude by arguing that the events of September 11, 2001 do not fall unambiguously and easily into the category of the 'normal accidents' described by Perrow; they are, however, well described as 'man-made disasters' and fall quite clearly into the rubric of 'vulnerable systems'. The events of September 11, 2001, while shocking and important, can be subsumed within areas of social science for which paradigms of explanation are available, whether in the fields of crisis and disaster management, system failure, political processes, or terrorism and insurgency. Nonetheless, September 11 will undoubtedly constitute a rupture of expectations leading to changed behaviours in a most significant sense because as the sociologist W.I. Thomas noted, 'What men believe to be real . . . that is real in its consequences'. And no doubt there have been and will continue to be major consequences. It is too soon to form any decisive judgement as to whether the world has become a safer or a more dangerous place. But it is not clear that there are substantial grounds for optimism in terms of lessons learned and measures taken which render the geopolitical structures less vulnerable.

REFERENCES

Beaty, D. (1991), *The Naked Pilot*, London: Methuen.
Bignall, V. and J. Fortune (1984), *Understanding Systems Failure*, Manchester: Manchester University Press.
Huntington, S. (1996), *The Clash of Civilisations and the Remaking of World Order*, New York: Simon and Schuster.
Janis, Il. (1982), *Victims of Groupthink*, Boston, MA: Houghton Mifflin.
Mars, G. and D.T.H. Weir (2000), *Risk Management*, vols 1 and 2, London and New York: Ashgate-Dartmouth.
Perrow, C. (1984), *Normal Accidents: Living with High-risk Technologies*, New York: Basic Books.

Turner, B.A. (1976), 'The organizational and inter-organizational development of disasters', *Administrative Science Quarterly*, **21**, 378–97.

Turner, B.A. (1978), *Man-Made Disasters*, London: Wykeham Press.

Turner, B.A. and N. Pidgeon (1997), *Man-Made Disasters*, 2nd edn updated, London: Butterworth-Heinemann.

Vaughan, D. (1996), *The Challenger Launch Decision*, Chicago, IL: University of Chicago Press.

Weir, D.T.H. (1976), 'Stress and the over-controlled organization', in K. Legge and D. Gowler (eds), *Managerial Stress*, London: Gower.

Weir, D.T.H. (1991), *Hazard Management and Transport: ESRC Seminar on Institutional Design and System Failure*, London: London School of Economics.

Weir, D.T.H. (1993), 'Communication factors in system failure or why big planes crash and big companies fail', *Disaster Prevention and Management*, **2** (2), 41–50.

Weir, D.T.H. (1996), 'The role of communications breakdown in plane crashes and business failure', in C. Hood and D.K.C. Jones (eds), *Accident and Design*, London: UCL Press, pp. 114–26.

Weir, D.T.H. (2000a), 'Management in the Arab world: a fourth paradigm?', in A. Al-Shamali and J. Denton (eds), *Arab Business: The Globalization Imperative*, London: Kogan Page.

Weir, D.T.H. (2000b), 'Management in the Arab world', in M. Warner (ed.), *Management in Emerging Countries*, London: Business Press Thomson International, pp. 291–300.

Weir, D.T.H. (2003), 'Human resource management in the Arab Middle East', in M. Lee (ed.), *Frontiers of Human Resource Management*, London: Taylor and Francis, pp. 69–82.

13.   A new challenge for security policy
Kai Hirschmann

INTRODUCTION

International terrorism is a phenomenon in transition. It reflects continuity, but also significant change. The terrorist's motivations, methods and targets have notably changed. New types of adversaries have emerged in addition to the old, making use of the latest technical developments and operating with higher financial resources. New forms of terrorism have enlarged the terrorist repertoire. So far, the face of terrorism has not remained the same. On the other hand, the vulnerability of modern societies has increased.

Tendencies for certain groups or individuals to radicalize cannot be denied. A growing number of controversial issues within or between societies increase the likelihood of extremist behaviour. Terrorism prevention strategies have to develop concepts against this changed background. But concerning the predictive capabilities, the range of potential new terrorist weapons, types and associated scenarios for destruction will create major problems for those responsible for identifying this new generation of terrorist threats. Nevertheless, there are some who long for the 'good old days' when a 'terror network' guided by state sponsors could be blamed for bombings, hostage-taking, skyjacking and other forms of mayhem.

Understanding September 11, 2001 as a key date in world history does not conclude that there was a sudden and irreversible change of any preexisting conditions. The terrorist attacks in the United States merely increased the visibility of previous processes that had already been unfolding out of sight for the public. In the new millennium, people have increasingly been experiencing terror in their own backyards through an internationally structured network called al-Qaida, which has been operating globally for quite some time. Under al-Qaida's ideology and training, terrorist acts have been carried out since 1993.

It is imperative to place the phenomenon of 'international terrorism' in a globally developing context: the face of the world during the Cold War was dualistic. With far-reaching influence beyond their own territories, the two opposing superpowers guided global developments. Bipolarity overshadowed regional problems, led to a disciplining of conflicting parties, and thus to a relatively stable world order. However, the super- powers largely lost the ability to discipline after the collapse of the East, which in effect led to the creation of a multi-polar world order. The number of players in the world has since increased, now not only encom- passing a larger number of independent states, but also numerous societal and ethnic groups. It has therefore become increasingly difficult to coor- dinate various groups and all their interests, while somehow reaching a reasonable consensus.

The dominant role of the nation state is dissipating as a result of devel- opments in politics, the economy and in society, all of which are question- ing national authority. The emergence of new groups within nations both triggers this development and simultaneously is a result thereof. Cross- border dependencies and flows undermine the principle of national sove- reignty. Thus, in addition to the implementation of transnational trade zones, areas of cultural identity are created. Also, identification and loyalty to groups that range across borders often dominates over national identity, for example within religious communities. However, one must broaden the scope.

Politically and structurally, two types of developments have been detected – both for which preparations have been made: first, the interna- tionalization of domestic politics through cooperation and integration; and second, the economic internationalization through globalization. A third type of internationalization has thus far been less visible: the interna- tionalization of society. A mistake, as has been discovered. Private regional groups are increasingly organizing themselves on a transregional and global basis. Amongst these groups are terrorist organizations.

Thus, international relations are viewed in a new light. The best-known model of thought assumes that security political relations are controlled by the competition over influence between powerful nations. This creates a balance of power that results in stable alliances. However, since the dawn of al-Qaida's terror, something has occurred that lies beyond the scope of this model: vested within all strong powers as a central security issue, a non- governmental phenomenon called 'global terrorism' has emerged. Based on a radical ideology, al-Qaida's networks claim no territorial possessions, nor are they dependent on any foreign protection, both of which make them impossible to localize. Everyone is equally threatened, which is an entirely new situation in world history: the United States, Russia, China, India, Japan, the European Union and Australia are all confronted with an iden- tical threat, an identical enemy. Al-Qaida unites fighters and like-minded people under an umbrella of a destructive Messianic ideology constructed by distorted belief. Basically, it is an apocalyptic sect that easily managed to acquire previously completed parts of its delusional world view from an environment that is saturated with conspiracies.

These developments provide the basis for new conflict constellations, for which a number of terms exist in the scientific literature. Van Crefeld speaks of 'low intensity wars', Daase of 'small wars', and others of 'privatized or informal conflicts' or 'new wars'. What all these terms have in common is the view that presently, nations rarely stand in conflict to each other, but rather a number of private and public groups. The state is losing its monopoly on national power. The traditional separation of government, armed forces and the populous is dissolving on all levels, private and public, interior and exterior. Regular troops or their fragments, paramilitary groups, self-defence units, bandits, terrorists, foreign mercenaries, private security firms, and regular foreign troops under international supervision, international government and non-governmental organizations: all these groups belong to the participants of the new wars.

The political and legal classification of war, however, does not go beyond the terminology, especially not in the case of the multinational-ideological terrorism of al-Qaida. The definition of war as being a 'violent mass conflict' also falls upon the terror exerted by the Islamic terrorists. However, no definition that fits to al-Qaida's strategy exists. The various types of war are defined as 'anti-regime wars', 'independence wars', 'decolonization wars' and 'other national wars'. The definitions remain within the concept of nations and its territories at war, but do not include an international societal ideology. It is therefore appropriate to add the term 'transregional ideological war' to the list. The 'War against Terrorism' which is led by the 'Anti Terror Coalition', as US President Bush calls it, is politically and legally more a hunt for criminals and murderers than an outright war, simply because al-Qaida is not classified as an entity at war. This position is not always unopposed. Some scientists criticize that politicians often identify terrorism as a special form of crime. Some political leaders share the idea that one should treat terrorists as smugglers, drug dealers or political Mafiosi, rather than what they really are: organized, well-trained and extremely destructive paramilitary units that execute and lead planned attacks against states and societies. In reality, international terrorism has always been a form of war.

Today, the classic security political constellation of state versus state is hardly relevant. In the 1990s, wars within nations posed the biggest challenge. During recent years, such conflicts have been constantly increasing on a global basis. They have mostly been the result of ethnic or religious conflicts, unfair distribution of scarce resources or of the national wealth. Unfortunately, these national conflicts tend to be more violent and ruthless than conflicts between two states. Terrorists like to justify their actions through such conflicts.

A second important security political constellation has been added since the mid-1990s: Nation (or a union of nations) versus international violent NGOs (destructive substate actors). It was difficult for countries which were operating on a national level to understand that they were seriously threatened through a globally operating ideological group. For al-Qaida, it was working out: flexible, anonymous small groups against the political and military power of states. A different enemy than was expected after the end of the Cold War has emerged, one that must be taken seriously. It is no longer a regional terror group with ethno-national demands where the threats and effects were limited, despite all the victims. This new enemy is an abstract-ideological 'Islamic International' enemy that can and will serve as a blueprint for other internationally operating violent groups.

But the next constellation as a challenge in security policy is already visible on the horizon: NGOs against NGOs on an international basis. Imaginable scenarios, for example, are violent protest groups against multinational corporations such as McDonalds or Microsoft. With a constellation of economy versus society, the loss of the importance of national entities would be most visible. The state would have to ensure safety on its territory as a strategy of 'second best'. However, the state would no longer have a direct influence on the cause of the conflict.

In conclusion, it is ascertained that often states are not structurally adjusted to the new crisis constellations. It is also undeniable that adjustment difficulties to new challenges in security policy exist, and are best depicted through the reaction to the new form of international terrorism. Adjustments are needed because one cannot face these new challenges with traditional thinking and reactionary strategies that existed in the old structures. However, this is widely spread. The national military cannot fight this form of terrorism because infrastructure targets, apart from some training camps, cannot be identified. Nevertheless, one is contemplating an 'anti-terror unit' within NATO. Soldiers against ideologies? Other international organizations seem just as helpless, as they are nearly completely structurally fixed on politics in the form of nations. Al-Qaida has completed its international build-up, for which training camps in Afghanistan were necessary. About 30000 fighters from different countries (including Europe) have been educated and trained there. After that they returned to countries where they came from, waiting for 'the day'.

Terrorists are not in a hurry. They have plenty of time to wait for the right moments and circumstances; they see their conviction as a 'duty for life'. Almost 40 per cent of the al-Qaida fighters have been recruited in European countries and bear corresponding nationalities. This is to say that they will not run out of personnel very soon. Al-Qaida's credo is to work independently and without national support.

The structural dilemma is heavily manifested in the politics of the United Nations. Here, countries construct programmes for fighting terrorism, which sounds absurd when considering that many nations do not even control the entire territory within their own boundaries. It is exactly these worldwide 'tribal areas' that terrorists need to operate out of. Most al-Qaida leaders are said to have retreated to such havens in Yemen, Pakistan and Indonesia. Al-Qaida has successfully tried to decentralize their production and training capacities to other 'tribal areas' than Afghanistan where no state authority whatsoever is present. The Ansar-al-Islami-group in Northern Iraq, heavily supported and equipped with al-Qaida resources (people and weapons) is such an example. They were operating without state assistance or any other organized connection to Saddam Hussein's repressive regime. Their central camp was destroyed by coalition forces but many members remained in the region. Proof of connections to European Islamist structures was found.

A similar dilemma exists in international law. This is the same law in the national framework, which makes it doubtful if violence in societies without national backgrounds can even be detected.

One could conclude that one is still trying to adapt new challenges to outdated structures, and not vice versa. An international structural reform is therefore inevitable. Terrorism is more than changing weapons, actors and motivations: it is a kind of struggle that is ultimately fought in the political arena and, as such, is also a long-run war of ideas and ideologies. Good intelligence and a professional security force are necessary. But most important for any democracy is a public that is informed and engaged, that understands the nature of the threat and its potential costs.

14. Conclusions

Gabriele G.S. Suder

A 22-page document entitled 'General Security Risk Assessment Guidelines 2003', which includes seven suggestions for corporate risk assessment, has been developed by ASIS with the aim of 'helping the private sector protect business and critical infrastructure from terrorist attacks'.[1] The US federal government as well as the European political organizations have been discussing ways to stimulate corporate security. The need to do 'something' to assess, evaluate and methodologize post-09/11 terrorism is recognized in the regulatory as well as in the corporate sector. Assessment process are particularly complex. What is terrorism? Why and how does it affect business?[2] Can it be classified as political risk? Do risk managers need to expand the notion of political risk and include geopolitical scenario planning? If so, what assets are prioritized and how are they categorized? What is the direct and what is the indirect impact of international terrorism to the primary, micro and macro level of the international business environment? For quantitative and qualitative risk assessment and research, it will be useful to define and narrow the criteria on which the risk ratio of emerging threat can be calculated for corporate purposes, as a basis for the extension of loss-modelling to operational resilience planning.

Corporate assets and risk identification is critical.[3] The ability to measure risk and the possible consequences is a vital part of risk assessment and risk analysis. The notion of risk is historical, quantifiable, probabilistic and modelizable, while uncertainty is characterized rather by discontinuity and is not amenable to prediction. Terrorism can translate into direct physical damage, loss of life, equipment and goods, or the operability for the provision of services. It also means loss such as that of opportunity, supplier reliability or of profit margins, as well as impacts on stock valuation, interruption in possible M&A or strategic alliance negotiations. In this case, life safety, contingency, and disaster and emergency planning and management are priorities. Only a relatively small number of companies worldwide are faced with the most direct impacts. On the other hand, dozens of companies in the World Trade Center in September 2001, have had to cope with finding new personnel, new facilities, new equipment and security databases, change their leadership and move forward, while mourning, at one and the same time. More widespread are the indirect effects of terrorism on the international business environment, that need to be added to any risk management approach today. Business continuity is something that is often overlooked. Business continuity planning is crucial to the survival of your business. A business continuity plan needs to address business continuity needs. Enterprise risk mapping determines the proper enterprise risk strategies and enterprise risk solutions that may arise through the impact of terrorism; the only sustainable competitive advantage is the ability to continuously learn faster than the competition. In the post-09/11 era this means that international business decision-making has to be adapted to global risk in a world of transitivity of globalization, vulnerability and threat. Accurate business risk assessment is vital to the longevity and resilience of business. Risk assessment and risk analysis are not optional luxuries. An essential part of business planning, a normative approach calls for a risk analysis audit on a regular basis that includes political and geopolitical risk research, using quantitative risk assessment and qualitative risk analysis that evolves into risk strategy planning, resilience and risk transfer considerations.

Chapter 2 in this volume, by Georg Witschel, analysed the nature of this threat:

- Legacies from September 11, 2001 are a symbol and metaphor that added a new size and quality of threat to the world society and its business environment.
- Terrorism is defined as premeditated, politically motivated violence perpetrated against non-combatant targets by sub-national groups or clandestine agents.[4]
- Contemporary terrorist activities share a number of common features and seem to indicate some trends which have to be analysed carefully in order to find appropriate counter-strategies. All of these common denominators are interrelated and most of them of a rather recent nature: the increasing dominance of religiously motivated terrorism, the globalization of terrorism, modern business-like leadership structures, asymmetric warfare using the victim mostly as part of a communication strategy, and the inseparability of internal and external security.
- The author highlighted the possibilities of risk management through governmental and supranational coalition building as well as counter-measures of the international community.
- This chapter concluded that prevention of terrorism and combating terrorism must go hand in hand, in a long-lasting challenge to risk management on a variety of levels.

What is the relation of this threat to the world order and economy? In Chapter 3 Yusaf Akbar introduced us to a critical approach to what he calls a possible 'new shift in the development of capitalism as the Huntingtonian-type 'clash of civilisations':

- In this case, can any reference be made to existing experience in international affairs and commerce, through the tentative study of ruptures such as wars and global economic shocks?
- The author concluded that global terrorism in the post-09/11 era can be considered as a continuous disruption to the world economy. The most likely outcome in the near to medium term is that rather than focusing on an inclusive and constructive dialogue, the foreign policies of the industrialized world will seek to isolate 'terrorism' from the mainstream world system, thereby further relegating some of the poorest societies further into the periphery.
- Threat and combat of threat are taken as long-lasting challenges to the world order and the international economy.

We are left with some optimism in regard to the underlying strength of multilateral institutions, despite the terrible attacks against the UN representation in Baghdad on 19 August 2003. Trade liberalization, while generating considerable opposition by groups who have fundamental disagreements about globalization, has increased consumption possibilities for billions of people in the world, it has brought productive and technological benefits to a number of regions of the world economy. Crucially, it has undermined the power of economic nationalists to argue for trade protectionism. There is a lot more work to be done in the world economy. The WTO has to tackle seriously its critics' claim that it protects the interests of the industrialized world. It has to cajole the EU and US to tackle honestly the problems of agricultural protectionism and to open these markets to developing country producers. It also has to broaden the trade agenda in order to consider the impact of free trade on the environment and the protection of social and cultural systems in the light of globalization. The long-term stability of the world economy is the widest possible participation in a fair and open trading system likely to outlast terrorist issues, argued Akbar. It is a return to matters of global economic importance that the post-09/11 world must consider in the medium to long term.

At the same time, and of equal importance, terrorism is considered as an important threat to the international firm. It reflects the risk of violent acts to attain political goals via fear, coercion or intimidation with a clear impact on the international business environment. Michael Czinkota, Gary

Knight and Peter Liesch linked key concepts on terrorism to the international activities of the firm. In their Chapter 4, we are provided with:

- Units of analysis, actors and facilitating factors highlighted in the relationship between terrorism and international business.
- A model that ties these elements together, and conclusions are offered with suggestions for future research. The chapter attempted to develop a conceptual model that may be used for a systematic theory on business security nexus through terrorism. The analysis started on three levels, the primary, micro and macro levels of impact of terrorism on international business, researched through producers, consumers and governments. It includes the factor of uncertainty that occurs through terrorism, and sets the difference between political risk analysis and terrorism as a challenge to risk analysis in international business.
- The authors concluded that the complexity of the study of terrorism requires a research focus leading to normative approaches that can be practically applied by managers, because the international value chain needs to be stabilized to ensure sufficient revenue in the case of attack.

In a similar and complementary approach, Gabriele Suder in Chapter 5 examined the complexity of the geopolitics dimension in risk assessment for international business. This chapter studied the pre- and post-09/11 era in regard to geopolitical theory and the perceptions generally ruling US and EU schools of geopolitical thought:

- Despite the complexity of risk assessment in this field, international business needs to examine not only the impact of foreign and domestic market threat as represented in traditional risk management, but also the implication of global terrorism, and hence global impacts.
- Despite the danger of subjectivity and dense complexity, this approach to risk assessment supports the call for truly international management of threats and uncertainties that the post-09/11 world has to tackle. The aim is to stir the debate about a formulation of models that help business to achieve operational resilience, and that include geopolitical scenario planning.
- The author concluded with the development of a model that includes probability and impact factors of three dimensions: terrorist threat, act and aftermath.

Part II analysed the impact of (post-)09/11 terrorism on the trade and investment environment. The macro level of consequences resulting from terrorism reflect that the September 11, 2001 terrorist attack coupled with the Afghan and Iraqi pre-emptive wars coincide with a major and probably long-lasting reassessment of country risk in international business. The global terrorist threat catalyses a number of emerging risks that stem from the higher and wider volatility in the global economy, including in the economic, financial and socio-political spheres. Michel Bouchet argued that more than ever, market globalization coincides with risk globalization: 09/11 and the Afghan and Iraq wars have a two-pronged impact:

- First, geopolitical turmoil reactivates and globalizes containment, given that terrorism replaces communism as a widespread security threat.
- Second, it feeds a perverse dialectic between stateless violence and enhanced security measures, both within the 30 Organization for Economic Cooperation and Development (OECD) countries and in the developing nations.
- In addition, the combination of mounting global terrorism, tighter banking regulations and a worldwide economic slowdown reduces market access prospects for emerging countries and increases the scope of liquidity difficulties. Foreign direct investment (FDI) flows have shrunk since their peak of 2000 and trade tensions are mounting between Europe, North America, Japan and the emerging market countries (EMCs). In the OECD, the protracted impact of the Internet bubble reinforces the negative wealth effect of the stock market decline and prospects of a housing market value correction. The Japanese banking system is in need of a thorough restructuring with solid capital base and sound portfolio. In the US, the banking system is about to face a rise in consumer debt equal to nearly 100 per cent of annual private income. Any rise in short-term interest rates will increase the spectre of mounting non-performing loans. The European banking sector, notably in Germany, remains fragile.
- All in all, developed and developing countries face a number of long-standing impediments to growth and their impact is compounded by geopolitical turmoil resulting from terrorism.

Rising risks that are characterized by a lack of the traditional warning signals thus require the risk analysts to be more agile, broad-minded and innovative than in the past. Volatility and complexity make quantitative assessment of country risk, including ratings and rankings, at best partial tools and at worst recipes for simplistic outlooks. The shortcomings of ratings and panel-based market consensus methods has been exemplified on the eve of the Asian crisis. They are still larger in the aftermath of 09/11.

Robert Isaak's contribution in Chapter 7 studied the impact of increased theoretical access to the Internet due to globalization on freezing inequalities, possible through IT:

- What is the impact of terrorism in the developed and less-developed countries in regard to the spread of digital opportunity?
- Using 09/11 as the starting point of analysis, terrorism threatened to hinder the process through the drying-up of venture capital and declining tolerance for risk-taking, but stimulated the spread of cost-cutting IT into 'risky places'. Does IT transform and democratize the people of the world? Does it protect or harass the integrity of cultures, marginalize people or widen their opportunities, enforce domination? To avoid a negative impact of IT, less-developed countries need governmental support for financial viability and for coordinated use, stimulated through education.
- The author argued that on the basis of Reagan–Thatcherian policies, the Anglo Saxon colouration of globalization enhanced a US hegemony, and assessed the European stake while looking at the Linux phenomenon.
- The chapter concluded that terrorism in the post-09/11 era highlights and reinforces existential issues in digital globalization, and opens a gap between the approach taken in regard to these issues by the EU and the US.

Investment and trade have been subsequently examined by John McIntyre and Eric Ford Travis in Chapter 8. The aim of this study was an attempt to determine, in the international business environment:

- The more specific effects on international trade or the physical movement of goods across boundaries and foreign direct investment (FDI), covering regional aspects and seeking to distinguish differential impacts on developed and developing countries. Additional attention was paid to reactive and proactive government policies enacted and how they too can equally affect the global economy.
- Time is utilized as a central guiding concept to consider the variegated impacts, and the authors assessed the vicious circle that is resulting in direct investment from the intertwining of comparative advantage, competitive advantage and return on investment factors.
- A critical distinction was drawn between uncertainty and risk, implying that traditional country or political analysis may not provide the necessary tools to deal with this threat for corporate actors.
- In conclusion, terrorism has altered and deteriorated the international

business environment in a 'transitivity' to the spread of vulnerability
through inter-connectability, and requires modified management and
risk assessment.

However, one shortcoming of the macro level is that it tends to be broad
and may include other macro-events, such as economic downturns. Micro-
level analyses in Part III therefore looked at three of the business sectors
most affected by 09/11.

The various events following September 11 dealt serious blows to
tourism, helping to remind us of its great importance not only to the USA,
but also to all countries in the world. Frédéric Dimanche in Chapter 9
examined tourism as one economic sector that has particularly been
affected by 09/11, the more recent terrorist attack in Djerba (Tunisia), Bali
(Indonesia), and the wars in Afghanistan and Iraq. The 'war on terrorism'
resulting from the attacks on the World Trade Center and the Pentagon,
and more specifically the conflict between the USA and Iraq, greatly contribute to a state of uncertainty in several world regions and economic
sectors, and particularly with respect to the economic well-being of
tourism:

- As a whole, travel and tourism has become 'the biggest business in
  the world', worth more than US$4.4 trillion a year, and it is a key eco-
  nomic tool for developing as well as OECD countries. The short-
  term impact of the attacks, combined with a US economic downturn,
  had immediate and disastrous consequences for many companies, as
  travellers suddenly changed their travel patterns and cancelled business and pleasure trips. Somehow, the World Tourism Organization
  recently reassured business observers by confirming that 2002 had
  been a better year than expected (after a 9 per cent decline in international tourist arrivals in September–December 2001) with a 3 per
  cent positive growth in international arrivals.
- Certainly, regional differences appeared: for example, the Americas
  suffered whereas other regions such as Asia and the Pacific compar-
  atively thrived. However, terrorism such as 09/11 sowed the seeds of
  profound transformations and confirmed trends that must be taken
  into consideration by government and tourism officials.
- Dimanche arrived at four main conclusions. Because of its nature,
  tourism is likely to be a major target for future terrorist attacks; the
  terrorism risk is now an integral part of contemporary travel; accepting the terrorism risk and related geopolitical problems is required
  for the tourism industry to manage them effectively; a destination
  that is not safe (or perceived to be safe) cannot successfully take

advantage of tourism's economic benefits; and tourism has become a necessity and is a resilient economic sector.

According to Stefano Gori, the bank sector is part of the very 'nervous system' of the economy. The stability of the financial architecture was seriously tested by the events of 09/11 and its negative spillover on the whole economy, and more specifically on the banking sector, both from an operational and regulatory point of view. Gori stated in Chapter 10 that:

- After the September 11 attack on the Twin Towers and the progressing US military campaign in Central Asia and in Iraq, new tools for risk analysis and a proper international regulatory framework have become a crucial issue for financial institutions, multinationals and the so-called transnational companies. These actors have engaged in a reassessment and repricing of risk due to a downturn in the perceived safety of overseas relations and investment.
- The events have had a deep impact, especially on the insurance industry in the United States, Europe and Japan. This industry absorbed the biggest loss in its history, with the total liability from the attack on the World Trade Center estimated at more than US$40 billion.
- Three interesting trends were scrutinized thoroughly: studying a new regulatory environment (external to the firm), a new approach to risk assessment (internal to a single financial institution), and a by-product of the two, weaker financial privacy for customers, especially 'marginal' customers.
- This chapter also focused on the long-term impact of terrorism, with the example of 09/11, on the banking sector seen from a European perspective. More broadly, the economic scenario since 09/11 has to take into account the new military and geopolitical scenario.

Both business sector studies called for the modification of risk assessment and sustain the argument that a new methodology needs to be established, using a general typology for the analysis of terrorism and international business, and geopolitical scenario planning.

What are the costs of terrorism and disaster, what will be the benefit of a new approach at the micro level, and what guidelines can be developed? Till Guldimann's Chapter 11 proposed post-09/11 new issues of disaster recovery in financial services. He argued that:

- The challenges attributable to the amalgamation of (IT) networks and to terrorism create a vulnerability that necessitates a shift from redundancy to operational resiliency: the design of business to operate right through disruption. Terrorism at the same time uses vulnerability.

- A comparison of 2001 with 1985 reflected that the questions to be answered today are: what do I need to do to keep operations running in the worst-case scenario? The study provided guiding principles for contingency planning, arguing for the importance of data, processing and workgroup availability instead of 'fancy analytics or sophisticated risk quantification'.

After these assessments, Part IV returned to a broader and more long-term analysis of the environment in which international business works, and attempted to make assumptions about the past, the present, and in particular the future. David Weir in Chapter 12 has reviewed the events of September 11, 2001 and the precursor situations in the context of available theories about disasters and crises. His contribution examined the subsequent events in order to form a judgement about how much has been learned in terms of the field of disaster prevention and crisis and recovery management:

- Weir introduced perspectives from two traditions in social science, the study of 'normal accidents' and that of 'man-made disasters' to illuminate in what sense September 11, 2001 represents a significant rupture in previously accepted patterns of behaviour and why it may constitute an opportunity for a transformation of the socio-political landscape leading to new patterns of behaviour.
- He concluded that there is no indication leading to optimism in terms of lessons learned and measures taken which render the geopolitical structures less vulnerable.

International terrorism definitively constitutes a challenge to the international business environment, and it is, as known in the (post-)09/11 era of contemporary history, a phenomenon in transition with globalization. Kai Hirschmann in Chapter 13 underlined this phenomenon and argued that at the same time:

- The vulnerability of society has increased.
- That the terrorist attacks of 09/11 have increased the visibility of previous processes, enhanced by the increased number of actors in the geopolitical arena since the collapse of the East and the overall questioning of national authority. While the classical model of thought suggests that security political relations are secured by competition over influence between powerful nations creating a balance of power,

as of 09/11 we are confronted with new conflict constellations that include private and public groups and that call for the term 'transregional ideological warfare' to be added to the definitions of types of war.

In conclusion, adjustments are needed to meet the challenge of terrorism. They cannot be made with the traditional thinking and reactionary strategies that existed in the pre-09/11 era. They are difficult to quantify, and will be controversial and may be unorthodox. Research will need to counteract any risk of self-fulfilling prophecies in global risk assessment, led by the search for return on investments made.

Through our analyses and reflections we have argued that a 'transitivity' of (1) globalisation, (2) increased systemic vulnerability and complexity, and (3) the transition of terrorism prevails in the international business environment that reflects the crucial realities of the post-September 11 era: the trade-off between security and business has undergone profound changes. Further empirical research will need to deal with the issues of normative theory.

For sustainable competitive advantage, corporations need to learn fast and adapt to this business–security nexus using risk assessment and planning that goes further than traditional, pre-09/11 approaches, through thoughtful planning and the application of empirically verified methods.

NOTES

1. http://www.asisonline.org
2. Amongst others, Shapiro 2003 (see Chapter 5 and 8) calls for an assessment of the effects of terrorism on the economy.
3. For a discussion of the notion of redundancy in corporate assets, it is however useful to see also *Harvard Business Review*, August 2003.
4. US National Strategy For Combating Terrorism, p. 1.

Index